The Queerest Art: Essays on Lesbian and Gay Theater
Edited by Alisa Solomon and Framji Minwalla

Queer Globalizations: Citizenship and the Afterlife of Colonialism
Edited by Arnaldo Cruz-Malavé and Martin F. Manalansan IV

Queer Latinidad: Identity Practices, Discursive Spaces
Juana María Rodríguez

Love the Sin: Sexual Regulation and the Limits of Religious Tolerance
Janet R. Jakobsen and Ann Pellegrini

Boricua Pop: Puerto Ricans and the Latinization of American Culture
Frances Negrón-Muntaner

Manning the Race: Reforming Black Men in the Jim Crow Era
Marlon B. Ross

Why I Hate Abercrombie & Fitch: Essays on Race and Sexuality
Dwight A. McBride

In a Queer Time and Place: Transgender Bodies, Subcultural Lives
Judith Halberstam

God Hates Fags: The Rhetorics of Religious Violence
Michael Cobb

God Hates Fags

The Rhetorics of Religious Violence

MICHAEL COBB

NEW YORK UNIVERSITY PRESS

New York and London

NEW YORK UNIVERSITY PRESS
New York and London
www.nyupress.org

Library of Congress Cataloging-in-Publication Data
Cobb, Michael
God hates fags : the rhetorics of religious violence / Michael Cobb.
p.   cm.
Includes bibliographical references and index.
ISBN-13: 978-0-8147-1668-7 (cloth : alk. paper)
ISBN-10: 0-8147-1668-7 (cloth : alk. paper)
ISBN-13: 978-0-8147-1669-4 (pbk. : alk. paper)
ISBN-10: 0-8147-1669-5 (pbk. : alk. paper)
1. Homosexuality—Religious aspects—Christianity. 2. Rhetoric—
Religious aspects—Christianity. 3. Homosexuality—Political aspects—
United States. 4. Rhetoric—Political aspects—United States.   5. Hate
speech—United States.   I. Title.
BR115.H6C63 2006
306.76'60973—dc22   2005036499

New York University Press books are printed on acid-free paper,
and their binding materials are chosen for strength and durability.

Manufactured in the United States of America
c 10 9 8 7 6 5 4 3 2 1
p 10 9 8 7 6 5 4 3 2

For the students of English 273Y

Contents

Acknowledgments   xi

Introduction: The Last Safe Group to Hate   1

1   The Language of National Security: A Queer Theory of
Religious Language   22

2   James Baldwin and His Queer, Religious Words   53

3   Like a Prayer   79

4   Rights as Wrongs   114

Conclusion: Our Aberrant Future   149

Notes   185
Index   217
About the Author   229

Acknowledgments

In 1992, my hometown of Colorado Springs, which had always been conservative, had suddenly become hateful. This book is my belated attempt to come to grips with that animosity. It could have been written only after a tour of brilliant places and people, who've taught me the value of creative, critical thinking. In Maine, Chicago, Ithaca, Haverford, and Toronto, many dear people have aided me as I thought about and, in Toronto, wrote this book. I'm humbled by their generosity, warmth, attention, and smarts.

I fear the roster of thanks is long. I begin with great teachers: Debra Campbell and Nikky Singh, who taught me religion and feminism; Lauren Berlant, Elizabeth Povinelli, Bill Brown, George Chauncey, Anthony Yu, and Homi Bhabha almost made Chicago a place to stay; Hortense Spillers, Ellis Hanson, Elizabeth DeLoughrey, Jacqueline Goldsby, Mark Seltzer, and Emily Apter made Ithaca the best place to learn.

Now I'm thrilled to be living in Canada. The University of Toronto English Department is an absolute delight, and I simply could list the entire faculty. Brian Corman leads this merry bunch, and our happiness is due in no small part to his direction and vision. Linda Hutcheon is both a stellar colleague and a dear friend. Elizabeth Harvey is so much more than the perfect mentor. My terrific colleagues at the U of T make all the work much more like play, and some deserve special mention: Alan Ackerman, John Baird, Alan Bewell, Ritu Birla, Angela Blake, Elspeth Brown, Corinn Columpar, Jeannine DeLombard, Paul Downes, Andrew Dubois, Uzo Esonwanne, Maureen Fitzgerald, David Galbraith, Daniel Justice, Charlie Keil, Jeremy Lopez, Lynne Magnusson, Jill Matus, Alice Maurice, Naomi Morgenstern, Andrea Most, Nick Mount, Heather Murray, Mary Nyquist, David Rayside, Sara Salih, Paul Stevens, Dan White, and Sarah Wilson.

Colleagues and pals have been more than encouraging over the years. I must thank them by name, even if they don't know how, exactly, they helped: Jennifer Ashton, Samuel Baker, Ian Balfour, Leo Bersani, Amy Bingaman, Rey Chow, Eric Clarke, Jonathan Culler, Ann Cvetkovich, Wai Chee Dimock, David Eng, Diana Fuss, Billy Galperin, Jody Greene, Sara Guyer, Judith Halberstam, Gillian Harkins, Andrew Hebard, Dana Luciano, Dwight McBride, Anna McCarthy, Dorothy Mermin, Doug Mitchell, Rajeswari Mohan, José Muñoz, Tim Murray, Chris Nealon, Andrew Parker, Ann Pellegrini, Jordana Rosenberg, Shirley Samuels, Cannon Schmitt, Bethany Schneider, Dana Seitler, Gus Stadler, Kate Thomas, Amy Villarejo, Rebecca Zorach, and Christina Zwarg.

I need to make some special comments about the writing and production of this book. Audiences at the Queer Matters Conference in London, the MLA, and the ASA all provided fantastic questions and feedback. José Esteban Muñoz was a devoted fan of the project when it was still an idea, and has subsequently become a dear friend. Ann Pellegrini is a most inviting editor and pal, pushing this project into a polished existence. Terrell Scott Herring provided readings of the manuscript on numerous occasions, offering acute advice and always the warmest friendship. Chris Nealon made me understand what this book was arguing and why it was valuable to argue it in the first place. Janet Jakobsen was a superlative reader, whose pages and pages of commentary were a generous gift. Eric Zinner started encouraging me years before I even decided to write this book (when I was a little boy writing another project, a dissertation on race and American literature that barely mentioned the word "queer"). He has been a terrific editor. Everyone should be so lucky to have Emily Park orchestrate the countless details of making a book appear.

Close friends in Toronto and south of Toronto are what make me feel charmed. Toronto is marvelous because of Karen Azoulay, Jeremy Laing, Paul P., Scott Treleaven, Alice Maurice, Mark Rigby, Will Munro, Amish Morrell, Luis Jacob, Joel Gibb, G. B. Jones, and, suddenly, there's Shawn Micallef. Kate Bolick, Rattawut Lapcharoensap, June Glasson, Kate Rubin, Julia Perini, Genevieve Love, Hong-An Tran, Scott Herring, Sara Guyer, Descha Daemgen,

Heather Cadigan, Tina Otto, Jason Walta, Rose-Ellen Lessy, Sonam Singh, Rosten Woo, and Cheryl Beredo are friends who make me long for trips home.

I attempt to find ways to thank Hortense Spillers every time I get some words into print, and each time I can't quite express what I should. I know she is a very patient person, so I hope one of these days, after one of these attempts, she'll know how grateful I am for her superlative mentorship, friendship, and intellect. She, in no uncertain terms, is simply stunning.

A version of Chapter Two appeared in *GLQ* 7:2 (2001). Part of the conclusion appeared in *Social Text* 84–85, Vol. 23, Nos. 3–4 (Fall–Winter 2005). I appreciate Duke University Press's permission to republish those writings. I also thank the Connaught Fund at the University of Toronto for generous research support.

Introduction

The Last Safe Group to Hate

BELIZE: Well I hate America, Louis. I hate this country. It's just big ideas, and stories, and people dying, and people like you.

The white cracker who wrote the national anthem knew what he was doing. He set the word "free" to a note so high nobody can reach it. That was deliberate. Nothing on earth sounds less like freedom to me.

You come with me to room 1013 over at the hospital, I'll show you America. Terminal, crazy and mean.

—From *Angels in America*

Early in 2001, a group of parishioners from Kansas's Westboro Baptist Church, led by Reverend Fred Phelps, descended upon Fort Collins, Colorado. They were protesting Colorado State University's official response to the Pi Kappa Alpha fraternity and the Alpha Chi Omega sorority's 1998 homecoming float. This float had gained notoriety primarily for the not-so-subtle references to the brutal beating of Matthew Shepard, who had just been pummeled and tied to a fence in Laramie, Wyoming. Shepard's assailants had left him to die in a pose that Laramie law enforcement officials and the mountain biker who had discovered his body thought resembled, if not exactly, a scarecrow. The description of Shepard's suggestive and gruesome posture gained quick media appeal, evoking a combination of disturbing, if not sensational, images: lynching, crucifixion, if not *The Wizard of Oz*.[1] Tastelessly, a scarecrow with a variety of written homophobic epithets had decorated the homecoming float, a direct reference to Shepard's beating. It was a particularly cruel display since Shepard was then just a few miles away, dying in a Fort Collins hospital bed. Reaction was fortunately swift, and suspensions and dissolutions of the Greek organizations soon followed.

The lynching and its aftermath flamed numerous queer and other activists into action. In sharp contrast to a crime based in "hate," loving sentiment and outraged concern coursed through the candlelight vigils, the commentaries, the plays, and the made-for-television movies about the tragedy. Yet there was still a very vocal group of people that condoned the brutality—led by Phelps, who had been slandering homosexuals for years. It was nevertheless shocking that he and his church had gone so far as to protest the trials of Shepard's killers. A number of activists were appalled and participated in "angel action": they dressed in angel costumes, with large, seven-foot-high wings, creating a visible barrier so one would not have to see signs such as "Fags Die God Laughs."[2] A wonderful gesture to be sure, but we can't forget that just beyond the love of the angels' barricade were reminders of the violent intolerance of the event—reminders that there are those who did not share in the sympathy and outrage over Shepard's murder.

Over two years later, this disdain for Shepard's homosexuality had not abated, and Westboro Church was still upset about the disciplinary actions against CSU's Greek organizations. "What they did and the way they treated those kids in that frat and that sorority for mocking that homo was outrageous," complained Phelps. "If there's any group that deserves to be mocked for their filthy lifestyle, it's the fags."[3] This kind of inflammatory speech is standard Phelps. He and his followers often give extreme voice to a particularly familiar condemnation of gay, lesbian, bisexual, and trans people. His church's Web site, "Godhatesfags.com," is still on-line at the time of this book's writing. It features the "Perpetual Gospel Memorial to Matthew Shepard," in which an image of Matthew screams electronically and counts the number of days he has been in hell—a biblically just punishment for the "Satanic lifestyle" Matthew lived as a "homosexual."[4] Phelps's church preaches what many Protestants have long thought about queer sexuality: " 'GOD HATES FAGS'—though elliptical—is a profound theological statement, which the world needs to hear more than it needs oxygen, water and bread. The three words, fully expounded, show" that severe punishments are in store when one goes against the strict scriptural and foundational laws of a holy society: "The only lawful sexual connection is the marriage bed. All other sexual activity is whoremongery and adultery, which will damn the soul forever in Hell."

It is important to realize that this expression of God's hate, this expression of rancor toward those participating in unlawful sexual practices, comes not only from the fringe, not only from the CSU students, a disturbed Kansas pastor, or even Matthew Shepard's young and angry murderers. This hatred is mainstream. Rather than dismiss Phelps as simply an extremist, as a number of fundamentalist and evangelical groups strategically do, it is important to relate his church's outrageous hyperbole to the kinds of public, doctrinal, financial, and political gains opposition to "homosexuality" has provided for powerful Christian organizations, not to mention the Republican Party, in the late twentieth and early twenty-first centuries.[5] Certainly Westboro Baptist Church is in the minority when it brandishes placards such as "God Hates America" or "Thank God for 9/11," but the anger it feels toward nearly the entire world emanates from the permissiveness and sinfulness of a nation that does not hate fags enough. The hatred of homosexuals is the members' primary ministry. And there is something about homophobia that arouses a deep religious fervor that extends across the more moderate spectrum of contemporary evangelical groups. For instance, the huge Colorado Springs–based evangelical media giant, Focus on the Family, even though it advocates love for the homosexual sinner who must, with God's grace, be saved from homosexuality's sin,[6] still considers homosexuality the "most difficult issue faced in public policy." It is an "issue" that potentially threatens the most important principle of the group's "practical Outreach" of the Gospel of Jesus Christ: "We believe that the institution of marriage was intended by God to be a permanent, lifelong relationship between a man and a woman, regardless of trials, sickness, financial reverses or emotional stresses that may ensue."[7]

3

Especially now that there are intensified efforts to legalize same-sex marriage and increasing images of queers in the entertainment industry, the religiously reinforced heterosexual family has potent, conservative appeal. The family grounds the conservative traditions that the right holds dearly —traditions it perceives to be viciously under attack by the presence and increasing acceptance of homosexuality. As a policy issue, the publicity around homosexual condemnations proves to be crucial, enabling the so-called religious right to gain, lucratively, a stronghold on conservative constituents of the market-driven United States, longing for "purity," tradition, and financial prosperity. When "homosexuals" are a religious issue, the reproductive heterosexual family is cast as in decline and in need of "traditional values." A resurgence of strong, religious emotion inevitably follows."

Homosexuality, in the early 1990s, became a major topic of policy making—a topic that still helps win elections. Soon after Focus on the Family moved its international headquarters to Colorado Springs in 1991, it supported—along with Pat Robertson's Christian Coalition, the National Legal Foundation, Lou Sheldon's Traditional Values Coalition, Concerned Women for America, Summit Ministries, and the Eagle Forum—Colorado for Family Values' successful grassroots 1992 state referendum known as Amendment 2.[8] The passage of this amendment effectively curtailed the full participation of lesbian, gay, and bisexual (and most likely trans) people in legal claims of discrimination, prohibiting, quite underhandedly, their legal right to assert that they have suffered discrimination. According to the ACLU of Colorado, the amendment "ma[de] it *legal and constitutional* to discriminate against men and women who are—or *who are thought to be* —homosexual or bisexual."[9] The United States Supreme Court agreed, with the majority opinion arguing that such a group could not be targeted. The amendment was ruled unconstitutional in 1996.

The resemblances between the Westboro Baptist Church and Focus on the Family are not hard to detect: for instance, as with Phelps, Focus on the Family helped wage a prominent protest on homosexuality in Colorado, and both organizations garnered huge national and international attention. The reaction to Amendment 2's beating of gay, lesbian, and bisexual rights in Colorado was swift and produced the kind of media attention that ironically aided evangelical groups like Focus on the Family, provoking the homosexual panic and religious relief it needed to promote its particular public and biblical policies.[10] A large-scale boycott of the state was proclaimed, and Colorado soon came to be called, as Wyoming would be after Matthew Shepard's murder, "The Hate State." The *Advocate* ran, in 1993, a glossy, nine-page article hysterically entitled "Colorado Goes Straight to Hell," noting that "the negative publicity" had created battle lines, and "Colorado's gays and lesbians are left to fend for themselves in a poisonous atmosphere."[11] But the religious right was pleased to engage the poison. Although easy to condemn, the religious right operates according to cherished beliefs, believing its work to be motivated by faith and, especially, by a love that refuses to heed its important message. Followers portray themselves as religious victims in a secular world, fighting to bring the light back to humankind. In fact, they claim, as Christians long have throughout the last thousand years or so, to be some of the most persecuted people in a world that devalues their strong religious faith.[12] Conservative fundamentalists are engaged in a form of worship as they battle what they consider to be a corroding and pervasive evil in a world that is less and less holy.

The people of Colorado, led by the state's rapid influx of evangelical Christian organizations in the early 1990s, willed this law, and their righteous and religious leanings legitimized the amendment's discriminatory force.[13] For instance, Kevin Tebedo, executive director of Colorado for Family Values, in a forum produced by the Colorado Springs library system called "Tolerance/Intolerance: Sexual Orientation Issues," summed up the Pikes Peak climate around issues of sexual diversity. He claimed that the country was in a moral crisis that fanned the flames of a religious war—a war that, if homosexuality were to receive political and cultural legitimacy, would be fought and won, and "every knee will bow" in front of the Lord.[14]

Although not everyone bowed in religious defeat and devotion (not yet), Coloradans experienced an intense political and legal atmosphere, leaving quite permanent effects. But it wasn't just Colorado. This "last safe group to hate"—lesbians, gays, bisexuals, queers, trans people—is easily hated anywhere and by anyone. Exactly contemporaneous to Amendment 2, a similar state referendum, Proposition 9, was on the ballet in Oregon, and a number of similar moves on local and statutory public policy were in the works, or on the stark horizon.[15] Moreover, conjoined religious and conservative opposition to lesbian and gay rights would heat up in states as far apart as Hawaii and Vermont, where the questions of civil unions provoked anxieties around conservative notions and definitions of the family, culminating in the Defense of Marriage Act, which has recently been reinforced by the backlash of anti-gay marriage amendments after some strides in same-sex marriage rights were gained in a few liberal-leaning states.

What we specifically learn from situations such as Matthew Shepard's murder and Colorado's passage of Amendment 2 is that a loving God hates that fags might marry, adopt, or live happy lives in their sin; and, somehow, this strong religious rhetoric appeals to a national citizenry that is only partially religious—and even less fundamentally religious. In other words, God hates that fags (and lesbians, bisexuals, trans, other queers) might upset and revolutionize the heterosexual nation. And although Colorado evangelicals are the minority of the state's population, over half of the electorate approved the amendment. Strong religious words about an uncomfortable topic such as queer sexuality not only unite sexually conservative people across economic classes, ethnicities, and races, but are part of a tradition of collective rhetorical expressions about what it means to be an "American." One can simply think of the ways that the terrorist actions of September 11 inspired an entire nation to start singing "God Bless America," to start repeating slogans such as "One Nation under God." These collective utterances do not signal that a terrorist action provoked the conversion of the majority of the United States to a newly found or rediscovered religious faith. What these songs and strong words about God and the blessed nation teach us is that powerful expressions of unity are often religious rhetorics—*not specific religious belief systems or theologies*. The words of God are conveniently and easily used to express the deep sentiments of an anxiously conservative and collective population of people.

Religious language has always been part of the strongest, united descriptions of American communities, with roots that are puritanical, constitutional, and persist today, even as the country has become increasingly respectful, at least nominally, of religious diversity. The expression of the religious intolerance of queers is a kind of hate speech that serves an important role in the rhetoric of American society. Years ago, the influential Puritan historian Perry Miller described a "literary type" of national rhetoric developed by Puritans in the seventeenth century: the fast-day sermon. Otherwise known as "the jeremiad," this kind of religious talk harped on the lapses in religious devotion and practice in a community that had originally been founded as a city upon the hill, as one nation under God. The description of these lapses, and their particular causes, served a variety of purposes that helped reorient and consolidate the community that had been ravaged by religious "declension," or deterioration. According to Miller and critics such as Sacvan Bercovitch, these sermons helped "retur[n] to the exercise of former authority" and did so by naming the spiritual crises at the origins of national decay—and those origins could then be expelled, at least rhetorically. Of course, scapegoats were usually the more provocative elements or members of the community—people who were considered foreign to the traditional values of the group. There were those who did not belong, and they needed to be expelled from the group. Saying as much (even more than doing) became a soothing speech ritual that helped the majority feel connected to the nostalgia of happier, holier times. Miller writes: "Having suffered the intrusion of foreign tyranny and alien ideology, having expelled the invader by an act of will, now resuming the direction of their own affairs, the Court found something infinitely reassuring—what reestablished continuity with the past—in rehearsal of the comfortable array of defects, phrased out of their own experience and accustomed language of their own judgment."[16] "Phrasing out," through this very American literary convention of the jeremiad, was of course not a final

7

act; saying that the intruders, the "decay," were gone did not make it so. But the act of repeating the expulsion (the "rehearsal of the comfortable array of defects"), the act of condemning and lamenting the sins that had appeared in a community that was no longer as religious as it thought it once was, evoked a nostalgia that reconstituted the society as one with nobler origins. Such nostalgia was a comfort that could fuel and strengthen the religious ties of a majority rule that inevitably would become more secular as the colony became colonies, and eventually a nation.

One can repetitively hear the distinguishable features of the jeremiad today, especially in the examples I have already cited. The national, heterosexual family, a religious tradition—if not the core tradition of the nation with civil and legal enfranchisements—is perceived to be under attack by the nontraditional homosexuals. Especially now, as they try to wed, homosexuals threaten the very fabric of the United States because they want to celebrate, enjoy, adopt, and legislate sinful, deviant behaviors. Homosexuals are evidence that the nation has lost its more pristine religiosity. As a result, the traditional family, the conservative predicate of a strong society, needs to be a specific focus made possible by what needs to be "phrased out" of that focus: the decay-ridden homosexual.

What contemporary, anti-homosexual jeremiads signal, among other things, is that gay, lesbian, bisexual, and trans politics must be concerned with the rhetorical force of religion. Religious condemnations, representations, and policies around same-sex sexuality, in large part, compose the parameters of contemporary LGBTQ publicity in a nation that is resolutely not ready to grant full citizenship rights to queer people. The seemingly inherent social conservativism of religious language guards, if not creates, a nation that does not want to have its foundational social organization, *the family,* substantially and systematically changed or challenged. Sure, the aesthetic gains of LGBTQ visibility in the late 1990s and early years of the twenty-first century might suggest that queer sexuality is an acceptable feature of the national entertainment landscape.[17] But the 2004 U.S. presidential reelection of George W. Bush should grimly remind us that there are still very explosive concerns about rights that swirl around the "family": marriage rights, partner rights, and adoptive rights, among other concerns. In fact, that election should reinforce the axiom that a religiously reinforced heterosexual familial unit still remains the political and cultural priority. The perceived attacks on that priority help reinscribe the absolute straightness and religiosity of the U.S. public sphere: there is something necessary and politically valuable in making sure that queers are available to be phrased out of, but not removed from or fully included in, the law, the culture, and the politics of the United States.

Rather than get lost in despair, I want this book to illustrate the unexpected opportunities hatred has occasioned for queers—for quite some time. The conservative uses of the conservative language of religious hate are only part of the story. For hostile language often has a peculiar use-value in oppositional politics. Judith Butler's *Excitable Speech* is a subtle exploration of hate speech, "question[ing] for a moment the presumption that hate speech always works, not to minimize the pain that is suffered as a consequence of hate speech, but to leave open the possibility that its failure is the condition of critical response."[18] I'm provoked by Butler's insights, and in *God Hates Fags* I want to argue that religious condemnations of queers, what often amounts to queer hate speech,[19] does not necessarily only hurt and harm. Rather, I am interested in the fact that queers have long used such hateful expressions as the conditions of their publicity in a U.S. public sphere—a sphere that necessarily always shapes the positions from where anyone, especially queers, can speak. I want to analyze what we might term a "queering" of conservative religious hate speech about queers. Yet rather than produce, as Butler proposes, a "resignification of speech . . . [that] opens new contexts, speaking in ways that have never been legitimated, and hence producing legitimation in new forms,"[20] queers also mine the hostility and politics of the old and very traditional rhetorical forms of national belonging that have always been religiously legitimated by the instances of the strong, conservative language I described above.

Rather than suggest a politics based on another version of the importance of the difference of queers, the American jeremiad should give us pause about formulating identity difference as the antidote to coercive forms of national consensus. The jeremiad should warn us about relying too much on the recognition of difference as the best kind of political action, especially if the nation-state wants, indeed requires, queers to be different. Thus, this book advocates a politics already embedded in the worst words of the nation. Despite the particular rhetorical violence inflicted perniciously on queers by conservative, collective expressions of U.S. belonging, LGBTQ feeling, politics, aesthetics, and ideologies have long understood the kind of power the repetition of religious hate speech offers. While lesbian, bisexual, and gay theologians or spiritually and pastorally minded gay activists and academics dominate much gay-positive thinking about religion,[21] I want to draw our attention, instead, to examples of the virulent rhetoric of the Christian right that accompanies numerous expressions of queerness and queer politics throughout the twentieth and early twenty-first centuries.

Throughout this study, I rely on an analysis of the *rhetoric* of religion, a rhetoric belonging to primarily conservative forms of Christianity in the United States. By focusing methodologically on the rhetoric rather than the belief of certain forms of Christian religion, I remind us of the differences between religious language and religious belief. I do so in order to shed another kind of light on the expressions of religious hatred and intolerance that saturate a variety of important cultural and political objects that constitute, in part, the public sphere of minority sexuality: literature, art, music, media, politics, judicial review, and personal testimonies. The conceptual tools that make this book methodologically possible are interdisciplinary and gathered from literary studies, philosophical inquiries, cultural studies, critical race studies, queer theory, feminist theory, critical legal studies, as well as insights garnered from original archival and historical research of the queers and conservative Christians who share in the intense expressions of the religious hatred of homosexuality. I alternate close readings of objects that are very meaningful for queer people—such as literature, magazines, political pamphlets, gay icons—with the critical legal and political analyses of Supreme Court cases and anti-gay legislation that shape the way such cultural objects can be read, experienced, transformed, and understood. I also pay deep attention to the political strategies, public declarations, Web sites, interviews, and other media made by key religious right organizations that have mounted the most successful regulations and condemnations of homosexuality in the most recent past.

In these pages, I investigate the manner in which religious hate becomes a language through which queers strategically mediate conventional structures of national belonging. Feelings are complicated things, and hate in particular is very messy. So in order to understand religious hate speech, I look to Raymond Williams, and his oft-quoted "structures of feeling" concept. For Williams, structures of feelings are cultural hypotheses rather than explicit facts, the "produced institutions, formations, and experiences" we are so prone to perceive so easily. Williams conceives of a structure of feeling as "a kind of feeling and thinking which is indeed social and material, but each in an embryonic phase before it can become fully articulate and defined exchange."[22] That is, feelings are not fully formed, are not entirely articulate, but still perform a very important service: they can give some kind of shape, however hypothetical or inaccurate, to those things that don't have shape. And hate can be the queer's "embryonic stage." In other words, the hate that marks so much of the way queers are targeted by the religious right and the national jeremiad can nevertheless be made into a structure of feeling that helps queers—who've been forbidden, who've been silenced, and who've been forced not fully to belong to the U.S. citizenry—carve out sustainable, if not yet fully understood or disclosed lives embedded within a politics and culture predicated upon so much violence and hate. The particular form this structure of feeling takes is linguistic. Although religious queer expressions might seem injurious and restricting, these religious *words* are just that: *words*. A language of hatred is not the same thing as the emotion of hatred, and even though the hatred of the right doesn't quite belong to queers, queers, in order to give voice to the complaints and injuries they must endure in the United States, can use the right's hateful words. Religious hate can so often be transformed into inarticulate language of the queer.

What specifically makes this form of emotive language so operative is one important comparison these hateful words can inspire: the comparison between queers and racial minorities. The religious hatred of queers and the nation's shameful history of racism can be made to seem resonant.[23] Expressions of religious homophobia, so we're often told, are much like expressions of racism; a religious slur against a queer is much like a racist slur against a racial minority. The comparison between the experiences of minority sexuality and minority race can certainly be found everywhere: from protest chants, "Marriage is a Civil Right! Gay/Straight! Black/White!" to the highest level of judicial review in the Supreme Court's reversal of Amendment 2 in *Romer v. Evans,* which cites comparisons between Amendment 2 and the infamous segregation ruling in *Plessy v. Ferguson.* Certainly, these are not the easiest or best comparisons to make. There are vast and important differences between sexuality and race that can be obscured by linking the terms. Whole histories of oppressions and nuances of experience can be occluded or forgotten when we start mixing the categories together. We will explore, in greater detail, the particular perils the "like race" analogy threatens. Nevertheless, racial analogies, despite their very real dangers, have had a productive and strategic currency for queers in the sphere of U.S. culture and politics, especially for queers who are also racial minorities. I argue in this book that expressions of religious hate work for queers because the repetition of religious hate speech allows queers to make the race analogy—an analogy associated mostly with the African American experience, which has effectively, rightly or wrongly, become a metonym for all racial minority positions in the United States. The imprecise analogy between queerness and race is made possible by the citation of religious hatred.

Let me be very clear: this book does not attempt to dismantle or denigrate the important analytics that have been ingeniously developed to understand and investigate the awful and wonderful cultures, politics, and histories of race relations in the United States. I have no interest in "doing away" with the concept of race by dislodging it from its most traditional, interpretive frameworks.[24] I understand that the comparison between racial and queer minorities is a dangerous comparison to make. There is much about race and sexuality that cannot be said when we compare the two. Yet, although the racial analogy does not easily fit, does not cleanly identify queers with racial minorities, the analogy flourishes. We must understand why. So rather than critique the fraught comparison, which others, as we will see, have done so well before me, this book pursues the utility of the potent emotional analogies made possible by the language of religious hatred. Because the ferocity of religious intolerance makes queers resemble —that is, be "like" *but not "be" the same* as—"race," an interesting rhetoric of minority protest emerges. This rhetoric has helped gays, lesbians, bisexuals, and trans people, many of whom are also racial minorities, find a way into the *relatively* successful politics of racial minority emotions that have made some small and slow strides since the political transformations of emancipation and civil rights.

Crucially, the comparison between minority sexuality and minority race does not rely on reinforcing the essentialized narratives of race; I have no interest in advancing here an argument that queers are queer because they were "born that way." Instead, the rhetorical connection queers make to race is emotional, sentimental, and charged with a peculiar political force that has developed while the pathology of race relations in the United States has shaded the political and cultural life of the United States. The comparison between queers and people of color is emotional, not genetic. Curiously, this assertion of a "like race" status sidesteps authentic or realistic claims that riddle and often limit much minority-based writing and politics. Queers accomplish as much by using what becomes a prosthetic voice borrowed from sentimental racial protest—a literary and figurative but still very political voice—that need not be overly precise in a hostile public sphere that is always ready to hate, to regulate, and to restrict the freedom of its queers. In the pages that follow, I will describe and develop these racial structures of hateful feeling that have been and will continue to be instrumental for queers as we struggle with religious authority and nationality in the United States. This leads me to a thematic question that will guide this entire book: What, then, does it mean to *feel* like, rather than to *be,* a racial minority?[25]

The book starts with a chapter that introduces a theory of religious rhetoric that provides the foundation upon which I will build the bulk of the book's arguments: a theory of religious language that will lay out the architecture of hate's racial valence. Janet R. Jakobsen and Ann Pellegrini lucidly assert, "To be traditionally American is to be Christian in a certain way. . . . When the president takes his oath of office and makes his inaugural address, there are always references to God, and we all know which God is being invoked (after all every president of the United States has been Christian in some way, and only one has been Catholic)."[26] I can't agree more with this assertion, and I take their first, illustrative example of Christian Americanness, the presidential oath, as a cue for how I want to communicate Christian rhetoric's force in U.S. politics. Put most simply, conservative Christian rhetoric can be one of the most authoritative kinds of political speech that, despite the myriad religious differences in the United States, functions as the lingua franca of the American nationality. This national tongue is a traditional language of authority that all sorts of people, regardless of personal religious orientations and affiliations, can manipulate in order to reconsolidate so-called traditional values. Yet even though all sorts of people can say these religious words, hold and benefit from the values and feel the beliefs these words imply, they are not the people who benefit the most from their utterance. Instead, it is the leader, or leaders, of the United States who stand to gain the most from making some people traditional and others foreign to American traditions, if not to American citizenship. This chapter therefore contends that American religious rhetoric is a sovereign language

—the fundamental language of those who rule in an inequitable manner, enabling some people to count as worthwhile and some as disposable. Sovereign-speak permits some lives to be sanctified by the right kind of national-family value while restricting others from that value. And queers are often those who will be restricted from counting as valuable.

Indeed, this sovereign language of religion helps those who are leading, those who are in power, characterize queers as threats to the national security—a security repetitively figured as the security of the traditional, heterosexual family. Nevertheless, the rhetorics of religious violence are not necessarily and only violent. Violence and language are not the same thing.[27] This chapter explores the manner in which this sovereign Christian rhetoric does necessarily hurt, but also sometimes helps. More specifically, I will show how this sovereign speech has permitted queers access to the "like race" narratives of inequality and social injustice. The evocation of the analogy illustrates the effects of being targeted as people who cannot be fully included in the nation-state. Queers activate the sentimentality of racial civil rights that do not permit, since the Fourteenth Amendment, exclusions based on race. Religious hate speech activates the "like race" analogy, and in some cases operates as the "like race" analogy itself. Angry words, primarily Christian, signal the oppressive forces that inflict feelings of pain, injustice, and loss. These feelings, moreover, are like the feelings of injury, pain, injustice, and loss experienced by those who are discriminated against because of their race, many of whom are also queer. Thus, religious hate speech, in the mouths of queers, signals the queer suffering and pain that are described as the suffering and pain of race, a form of minority complaint and opposition that should not be overlooked or permitted. Religious hate speech gives queers the opportunity to describe their queerness through the feelings of race.

Certainly there are extreme dangers in the analogy—the analogy is not appropriate. This chapter thus also explores the difficulties of this comparison, reminding us how analogous language works in order to still consider why this method of political articulation is so crucial for queers. Indeed, even though critics such as Janet Halley have so smartly critiqued the "like race" strategy, we must continue to ask why this analogy is one of the few options for official recognition of subordinated and oppressed status in the United States. In fact, I wonder if there is really any other way to tell the story of queerness in a politically efficacious manner that would render queers' lives valuable and worthy of constitutional protections.

This attention on the analogous, rhetorical properties of queerness helps us understand that there is enormous political power in figurative, literary language. Thus, the next two chapters feature literary examples of religious hatred that occasion "like race" analogies. I focus on figures and violent rhetorics (rather than historical facts) here because I want to emphasize that we need to move away from strict, ontological considerations of queer representation. Given the adverse dynamics of the American jeremiad, we must stress that the religious rhetoric of violence and the lived reality of queers are not synonymous. We must entertain the possibility that the public articulation of queerness does not mean that one must be truthful or faithful. In fact, there is dire importance in conceptualizing one's public identity as a fiction that can be manipulated for one's political and cultural advantage.

Chapter Two provides us an extended engagement with James Baldwin, who understands the force of "like race" politics perhaps like no other writer. I start with him because he was an important political and literary icon of queer and racial protest throughout the second half of the twentieth century. His example makes salient that the vexed exchanges between religion, queer sexuality, and race are not new. Indeed, in both Baldwin's critical and literary works, queers assume the language of Christianity in order to express their nascent, yet prohibited, queer feelings. Such Christian language, moreover, is traditionally conceptualized as *the* language of normal African American publicity and culture. But it is also a language that nevertheless has its roots in the sovereign powers of white religious morality. Knowing as much, Baldwin frustrates the claims of "real" authentic black experiences that are otherwise communicated through a religious conversion story. Strikingly, John, his central character from *Go Tell It on the Mountain,* repeats the authoritative, sovereign Word of God not because he believes that his queer feelings will be forgiven and forgotten by his conversion (and that he will fully participate in his very heterosexual and natal community), but because the Word comes from the only language that can create connections between him and members of his community, especially his object of desire: Brother Elisha. Although John's own vocalizations of religious sentiments that express both queer sexuality and an irregular racial belonging are supposed to hurt him, such sentiments hurt only *figuratively.* Moreover, John is aided by this fictitious "hurt" of the religious Word; his powerful deployment of religious rhetoric enables John to narrate a story of injury, of his own queerly tortured and minoritized feelings, without saying anything too specific, or too "real," about his experiences as a queer minority. We believe and feel his suffering because we know the supreme harshness and hardness of the Word on its queers. We also are reminded at every point in the novel about the travesty of racial oppression. Yet nothing explicit or identifiable comes to the fore about John's nascent queer desires. I thus argue that John finds safety in the use of a sovereign religious rhetoric that is not therapeutic, confessional, or religious as much as it is strategic.

What Baldwin's novel reveals is a queer politics that is deeply invested in literary representations of religious Word violence, or hate speech. The peculiar collusions and contrasts between race and queer sexuality draw to attention the inadequacy of the comparison, and thus to the incomplete project of minority recognition in the political sphere. Our languages of resistance are severely inadequate in the hostile U.S. public sphere. But the realm of the literary can imagine a politics that moves beyond the contemporary political left that demands, I believe, too much precision and literal confession filtered through these limited languages of protest. The third chapter, "Like a Prayer," thus showcases the powerful function of a literary form of identity testimony, explaining, in part, why queer literature—writing that highlights rhetorical properties and fictitiousness—has long been so important in the constitution of queer culture building and resistance throughout the last hundred years or so. I urge us to look beyond the reading protocol that assigns too much realism to literature (and politics) devoted to the representation of minorities.

This chapter features a variety of examples that deepen the force of Baldwin's example, providing a longer historical lineage for the hate-filled rhetorical strategies more contemporary writers, artists, and political activists employ in the later twentieth century. Examples include Stephen Crane's "An Experiment in Misery," Jean Toomer's *Cane,* and Tennessee Williams's *Suddenly Last Summer.* Each text features misshapen analogies between queers and race, analogies made possible by violent, religious words that can be twisted to block our immediate and realistic understanding of queerness. Such sacred words do not describe with precision or accuracy the minority body. And within the religious racial cover story, there lurks a queer feeling that needs a borrowed language of racial injury and violence to make that feeling felt.

Chapter Four and the Conclusion both argue that the literary, figurative lessons of much of the twentieth century are very necessary political lessons for our contemporary moment. In each, I analyze major developments in queer politics in the 1990s and the 2000s—two decades that have seen the rise of a mainstream queer visibility at the same time as conservative Christian condemnations of homosexuality have intensified. Chapter Four explains how racial sentimentality operates in much judicial review and in political methods of recognition in the fight over queer civil rights. In this discussion, I return to my home state, Colorado. Through an in-depth analysis of the rise and fall of Colorado's Amendment 2, I trace the manner in which Colorado and its persecuted queers were seduced by the fear that queers were seeking the entitlements of race, the entitlements of "special rights." This chapter begins with an overview of Amendment 2's vicious campaign, focusing on how the language of the religious right, despite its intentions, enabled queers to be considered a group of people who had been singled out by hate, thereby permitting queers to suggest that queerness was *like* a racial attribute not because it was a natural condition of the body—not because they were born that way—but rather because the pain and violence inflicted on queers by pernicious laws sponsored by conservative Christians resembled the pain and violence that had been inflicted on racial minorities by other conservative groups. Within Amendment 2, there were clear violations of the Fourteenth Amendment, and the comparison to the history of racial distinctions that perpetuated quasi-slavery status for people within a population that was supposed to be equal made queers legible as a target minority. Amendment 2 was reversed largely because of the explosive political terrain of racial politics and racial analogies. This chapter thus urges that we consider the value of the language of second-class citizenship—a language of hurt and injury that belongs historically to African Americans, but a language that increasingly and dangerously also belongs to queers (as well as other racial categories, not to mention anyone else making a claim of social injustice). Race, however perniciously, operates as *the* fundamental category of difference in the United States—it is the "default font" of difference in the United States.

In the Conclusion, I contend that the religious hatred of queers is still very much a queer political concern, and regardless of the outcome of the same-sex marriage struggle, will be so for quite some time. For all the talk about the increasing tolerance and visibility of gays, lesbians, bisexuals, trans people, and queers in the world of entertainment, there is a genuine reluctance to give queers their full status as national citizens in terms of marriage, adoption, probate, employment, and civil rights. In order to navigate the increasing visibility of queers, especially since the outright disdain for LGBTQ persons was not successful in the 1990s, I point to a more oblique but very effective way the religious right can continue to hate fags (and other queers): the tenacious invocation of homosexuality's association with pedophilia and incest.

The Catholic Church sex scandals, in particular, have helped politicians and media fortify this association. As the media buzz on about the scandals, conservatives again and again will usually mark the limits of liberal tolerance and inclusion by casting the homosexual as an incestuous, pedophilic predator. With such a shady hobgoblin lurking about, anyone, not just Catholics, is free to speak about queers with great outrage. I must emphasize that I am not pursuing a line of inquiry in which pedophilia is viewed as a valued part of queer sexuality. Instead, I want to explore to what lengths those who are in charge will go to insure queers will not fully belong to America. Among the figures I discuss are a pedophile priest, Father Geoghan, who was murdered for being a homosexual; Rick Santorum, one of the most powerful U.S. senators who wondered if we would have to accept incest and pedophilia as rights if we were to accept private, consensual homosexual behavior; and David Sedaris, who autobiographically highlights how queer men are always considered potential sexual assaulters of children.

Of course, because outraged religious language operates in the ways I have been arguing, queer writers, theorists, and activists such as Dorothy Allison, Alice Walker, and Judith Butler, among others, have found ways to use this sex panic, exploiting the ferocity and sympathy of the debate to articulate the queer's minor, racial plight. The feeling of injustice, of politics that refuses to become enlightened and truly tolerant of queers, saturates these writers' works. But rather than pose incest and pedophilia as the apocalyptic outcome of a society that tolerates, rather than hates, its queers, these female authors use the associations of pedophilia and incest to characterize the structure of the traditional American family as already disastrous, especially when it is a structure that asserts to be the best of national institutions, but is an institution that is actually and viciously built upon exclusivity and hate.

But there is no simple reversal here, no simple volley of incest and pedophilia accusations from left to right. Instead, we are brought back to racial, sentimental politics in order to understand that the rhetorical violence spoken by the sovereigns among us have been spoken before, spoken perhaps in a meaner voice. And with all the hate and upsetting emotion one might feel about the current violence and the bleak future, there are still moments of survival, of complicated lives full not only of hate, but also love, success, pleasure, pain, and all sorts of experiences that escape the political radar, or even the sovereign's awful grasp. Like others have done before us, we can choose to be rhetorical, fictitious, and analogical when called to account for ourselves. We do not have to admit to who we are, whom we love, whom we hate, or whom we fuck. Instead, we can lie, or tell a story, or do anything to make coping and survival, and not just realistic, precise minority recognition the only object of the politics game. We can manipulate some of the few narratives of resistance available, thereby disturbing us into a feeling that might move us, however undetected, into a better political future, even if that future is still aberrant.

Certainly, it is not easy to hate. And it is even harder to think of hate as a useful and strategic emotion. But hate is everywhere around queers, especially when religious morality and conservative forms of national belonging often constitute the nation at the expense of same-sex sexuality. By aligning such hatred with the shame of racism, queer political protest forces an analogy that deliberately does not fit. We must consider the use-value of the explicit use of hate speech. And after all has been said, we are left with the violence of religious rhetorics' racial analogies that have helped, and will continue to help, shape and direct the political, religious, aesthetic, and intellectual achievements and coping strategies of queers who understand and embrace that God might not give sanctuary to his queers through his love but through his hate.

1　The Language of National Security

A Queer Theory of Religious Language

The word "safety" brings us to the real meaning of the word "religious" as we use it.

—JAMES BALDWIN[1]

Fighting Words

The conservative, Christian speech against queers patrols American citizens. It achieves its force, in part, because religious language is thought to be a secure form of language. Its semantic security reveals something unique about religious rhetoric, at least in the United States: there's something about Western religious language—mostly white Anglo Protestant Christian religious language—that makes one feel its importance for reasons well beyond the actual content the language communicates. According to the National Association of Evangelicals, the number 1 statement of faith is, "We believe the Bible to be inspired, the only infallible, authoritative Word of God."[2] One cannot challenge the feeling of this rhetoric's absolute authority, which makes the "Word of God" seem full of important meaning that cannot be challenged. We really have no choice.

Kenneth Burke's crucial study of religious rhetoric, primarily Christian, argues that religious language is an "entitled" kind of language—a language that can lay claim to all sorts of meanings. "Imagine the ideal title of a book," suggests Burke. "An ideal title would 'sum up' all the particulars of the book. It would in a way 'imply' these particulars."[3] The Word of God acts as if it is a title, summing up whatever might be suggested by the title, mainly the contents of a book. Certain forms of religious rhetoric function as titles that are entitled to be very generic but still imply all the particulars that are not there—the religious word announces a story that one won't necessarily hear. But by virtue of the title, we believe there is much behind the title; titles logically must have important words behind them. In fact, the Word of God's force comes from its abbreviated utterance—it is strong because it can mean so much, but a "so much" that one might not even need to hear the rest of the story in order to be convinced by what the title suggests. We can consider religious rhetoric to be an abstract language that, because it is abstract, can guarantee—can be and carry the title on—almost any assertion one might have.

Although fundamentalists and evangelicals purport never to be "reading too much" into scripture, we should be suspicious. The Bible is a massive and textually unstable document, which must be translated, implied, refined, interpreted, and applied in very ingenious ways all the time. But one cannot emphasize the rhetorical complexity; the Word of God is trumpeted to be simple and true. So in order to characterize the infallibility of the message, certain textual gestures are needed. The blessed assurance of God's Word must be made to seem intact. Just think of the simple, quick citation of highly decontextualized passages from sacred scripture that will often underwrite the important meaning of the assertion we are supposed to believe. Westboro Baptist Church's "Godhatesfags.com" Web site, for example, illustrates what must be emphasized to assure the authoritative, inerrant "nature" of God's Word. In an effort to explicate their Web site's name, they post the following list:

1. the absolute sovereignty of "**GOD**" in all matters whatsoever (e.g., Jeremiah 32:17, Isaiah 45:7, Amos 3:6, Proverbs 16:4, Matthew 19:26, Romans 9:11–24, Romans 11:33–36, etc.),
2. the doctrine of reprobation or God's "**HATE**" involving eternal retri-

bution or the everlasting punishment of most of mankind in Hell forever (e.g., Leviticus 20:13, 23, Psalm 5:5, Psalm 11:5, Malachi 1:1–3, Romans 9:11–13, Matthew 7:13, 23, John 12:39–40, 1 Peter 2:8, Jude 4, Revelation 13:8, 20:15, 21:27, etc.), and

3. the certainty that all impenitent sodomites (under the elegant metaphor of "FAGS" as the contraction of faggots, fueling the fires of God's wrath) will inevitably go to Hell (e.g., Romans 1:18–32, 1 Corinthians 6:9–11, 1 Timothy 1:8–11, Jude 7, etc.).[4]

We should ignore, only for a moment, that number 2 does not make "HATE" plural so the outline of the three very important theological Words could correspond with the grammar of the slogan "God Hates Fags." It is more useful to see how this kind of passage is characteristic of much of the evangelical and fundamentalist applications of God's authority to the practical problems posed by the secular world. Amid a flurry and excess of quotations that carry important, sacred weight in the Web site's citations, we are left with the implication that there is much force, much "sovereign" authority, behind God's condemnation of "fags," an "elegant metaphor." In fact, there is so much authority that biblical citation (which, as the persistent "etceteras" insinuate, could go on forever) takes the place of explanation and coherent detail of the particular position of religious hatred of queers. Just nodding to the Bible's words, in fact just citing the location of sacred words from the Bible, will guarantee the strong, religious truth of any assertion one might have. God hates fags . . . it's in the Bible; I know where.

Milder versions of evangelical sentiment embellish the citations of the Bible but retain the quoting fervor. Stanton Jones, former chair of the Psychology Department at Wheaton College in Illinois, in a piece called "The Loving Opposition," writes: "When I confront the issue of homosexuality, I do not immediately think of the theology of human sexuality, of Christian sexual ethics, or of matters of church order. To think about homosexuality is to think about people." But Jones can't really think about the people too much. The individuals Jones evokes urge him quickly to remember the authoritative Word of God they are violating: "I think of Tom, who begged me to help him regain his Christian faith and stop both his compulsive pursuit of anonymous sexual encounters and his seduction of teenage boys."[5] And after a quick list of similarly unlikely friends, we are soon treated to over a page of "explanations" from the Bible (Leviticus 18:22, 20:13, Deuteronomy 23:18, Genesis 19, Romans 1, 1 Corinthians 6:9, Timothy 1:10). We are told that in order to love the opposition (homosexuals) we must first take into account that "Leviticus, Romans, 1 Corinthians, and 1 Timothy are binding."[6] We don't have detailed, textual exegeses of these passages; often we just have the titles of passages or the biblical books that suggest strong laws, strong condemnations about homosexuality's sinfulness. People, in this analysis, immediately disappear into manageable and managing religious words, and from that disappearance we can elaborate a faithful and useful doctrinal opposition, based on the fundamental and, ironically enough, "high view of Scripture."[7] Of course, we don't really get that great of a high, panoramic view—Leviticus is just a bold reference that footnotes the fact that no matter how much one might love the sinner, the sin's outlaw qualities cannot be overlooked.

Scriptural rants such as these are what we might call political sermons about authority. Strong, entitled words situate sinners as those who must be opposed, who are violating strict prohibitions that are in place to insure the prosperity of a healthy, holy society. This form of religious justification, to be sure, is jeremiad speech. In fact, the American jeremiad, which was always much more than a religious gesture, was called the political sermon, with designs on creating social cohesion through linguistic acts of religious devotion. Bercovitch, years ago, noted:

> The ritual of the jeremiad bespeaks an ideological consensus—in moral, religious, economic, social, and intellectual matters—unmatched in any other modern culture. And the power of consensus is nowhere more evident than in the symbolic meaning that the jeremiads infused

into the term America. Only in the United States has nationalism carried with it the Christian meaning of the sacred.[8]

And it carried that meaning well beyond the theocratic beginning of the
United States, with its puritanical errand, not to mention its colonial economics. That meaning is still embedded in the rhetorics with which we create or say "America." Something about this rhetorical consensus form of
unity—which is an ambiguous, if not contradictory, form modeled by the
jeremiad—links nationalism to the Christian conception of the sacred. But
this link endures for reasons that are less about sacred devotion and more
about being able unify the many into the one. A diverse nationality must
have some universal goals. And, in particular, one goal would be the fulfillment of the promise of great, future piousness. We could be that city on
the hill, that great, world beacon provided that actions today are cleaned
up, made more pure, and directed toward holier, more sacred aims.[9] The
muscular strength of the Christian Word promises this possibility, this
unity, this "one nation under God." Indeed, endless citations of Leviticus's
condemnations of homosexuality, which by its sovereign citation sounds
so strong and certain, guarantees strength in religious meaning where now
there is vulnerability. We are secure in the Word because, as the circular
logic has it, the meaning of that Word, so we're told, is secure. And if we
are secure in the Word, we might also be secure in the World.

When we think of the Christian jeremiad about queers as an important
language of the state—a language that need not be specific because it is
entitled to ultimate and forceful meaning—we begin to see the rhetoric's
designs on sacred consensus building. We thus can make a difficult but necessary conceptual shift: instead of dismissing this rhetoric as "just" the
beliefs of those who have deeply felt religious convictions, we must track
the value of this language in the production of national consensus. Certainly religious believers do feel deeply and gain a great deal from those
convictions. They also care and love deeply all sorts of people, even those
who are the targets of their perhaps unwanted attention. My objective is

not to belittle the importance of those beliefs, nor to devalue the faith systems that give meaning, emotion, community, and history to those who share faith.

By focusing on the generic rhetoric of Christian religion, and how that rhetoric has been implicated in American nationality, I hope to point to why this language is so complicit in some of the worst forms of social coercion and injustice. I intend to demonstrate that religious rhetoric is not simply about religious belief and practice, but rather also about nation and state building. When I speak of the religious word, I am not simply talking about a moral language about those who are sinful, nor about a language that designates who among us might be redeemed. I am not simply evoking the connotations of the Hebrew Bible's vengeful language. Nor am I simply referring to the redemptive language of sin and salvation everywhere in the New Testament. Although the religious words I will cite are derived from conservative brands of Protestant Christianity, and although there will be examples that are Catholic, Jewish, and Mormon words that will be left out,[10] these different genres of religious language, important in most contexts, will not make that much of a difference in the theory of religious language I am advancing. In fact, in the chapters that follow, I will say very little about the theology, history, philosophy, or ethics of particular Western religious traditions. Religious rhetoric is used so generically (especially in a nominally secular nation of many religious faiths) that a specific kind of religious word will not figure prominently. Instead, I am asking us to move beyond the divides between typical conceptions of the sacred and the profane, or the way these realms are always cleanly divided and pitted against each other. I want to consider religious language in another way— one that will not be sufficient for other studies of religion in America, but which will help us understand the violent force of religious rhetoric that targets queers in the United States. The jeremiad speak that most directly concerns this study is a language of authority that is essential for the nation-state, as well as what that nation-state needs in order to keep people in line —legally, aesthetically, culturally, politically, morally, and emotionally.

Married Gay Terrorists

I am investigating a language of national security, if you will, with questions that go well beyond whether or not queers will be permitted to marry. In fact, a point I must emphasize is that the Christian rhetoric swarming around the queer is a vague but enormously powerful language of "absolute" sovereignty. And this kind of talk is directed at the undesirable queer, who often functions as the rhetorical enemy of the state. For example, let's quickly look at two statements of sovereign faith, articulated just a decade or so apart. In 2004, the successful conservative Christian Family Research Council, which defends "family, faith, and freedom" as the Judeo-Christian principles of a strong and solid culture, lists some core principles that queers, we are told, jeopardize. For all the focus on the family I already cited, this list should be familiar, but note the explicitly authoritative tenor of these statements:

God exists and is sovereign over all creation. He created human beings in His image. Human life is, therefore, sacred and the right to life is the most fundamental of political rights.

Life and love are inextricably linked and find their natural expression in the institutions of marriage and the family.

Government has a duty to promote and protect marriage and family in law and public policy.

The American system of law and justice was founded on the Judeo-Christian ethic.

American democracy depends upon a vibrant civil society composed of families, churches, schools, and voluntary associations.[11]

The Family Research Council (FRC) has substantial clout in the GOP (it was started during the Reagan years, with many prominent members of the

Republican Party). Its statements of faith are also quite typical of many mainstream religious-right organizations' guiding principles, offering concise explanations about why many conservatives are still very opposed to the legal enfranchisement of queers in those institutions cast as most at risk: primarily families, churches, and schools. The religious ethic of the American system of law and justice, which relies on good, virtuous families drenched in the correct kind of faith, cannot be violated by substantial policy and legal gains made by queers. The strong words don't really need much explanation—they are so authoritatively stated, they are so clear in the rightness of conviction.

Now, with these statements in mind, consider one 1993 speech, delivered during the height of Colorado's Amendment 2 controversy (which had erupted near the end of the presidency of George Bush, Sr.). Audiences at the First Congregational Church in Colorado Springs heard Colorado for Family Values founder Kevin Tebedo argue:

> I submit to you today, to every one of you, this issue with Amendment 2 is not about homosexuality. And it's really not about sex. It's about authority. It's about whose authority takes precedence in the society in which we live. Is it the authority of man, or is it the authority of God? . . . Now the authority of man would dictate that homosexuality is perfectly okay, that there is nothing wrong with it. The authority of God says no, that there is plenty wrong with homosexuality. And so I say to you today that Amendment 2 is about authority; it's about whose authority gets to make the decision.[12]

We are not really worried about queers here or homosexuality per se. Instead, we are worried about power and control and who will assure that sovereignty, rule, power, and tradition reign in anything that tries to break the foundation, the law, upon which all God's will rules—the traditional family. Note that although "man's authority" is subordinate to God's, this morality play is hardly about God's will. We are told to be concerned with how God's Word will continue to underwrite "man's" word and his straight and traditional claims of authority. Absolute authority. Tebedo was invoking a jeremiadic speech, which articulated a desire for God's authority to be brought into fuller authority through American law. Then American law could proclaim homosexuality as wrong and ban it from our proper, civil society. This desire uncovers the not-so-secret heart of sermons against queers: my natal country needs its queers, and needs them, me, terribly.

I believe we should think of religious language as a language of authority, as an instrument of sovereignty, because the current fight over queer rights has much to tell us about where contemporary politics seems to be disastrously and rapturously heading. Moreover, much of the force of this form of religious rhetoric comes from its ability to describe and situate queers as both external and internal to the nation. The Christian language of the jeremiad helps make queers America's inside-outsiders, whose status as such helps not only win presidential elections, but something much more pernicious. Religious language, that is, serves the United States as it continues to evolve into a coercive, extralegal empire that needs enemies inside and outside its borders.

I might sound paranoid, but it does not seem coincidental that, in 2005, two major political issues that traversed both foreign and domestic arenas included the War on Terror and the battle for queer civil rights. Certainly the accidents of timing had something to do with these issues' simultaneous emergence, but both of these issues have strong religious connotations, and both strike at the heart of what enables the consolidation of power in a mass-democratic society. The link between the two, which is sort of outlandish, is not far-fetched. Thomas Frank, in *What's the Matter with Kansas?* offers this witty line: "Like a French Revolution in reverse—one in which the sans-culottes pour down the streets demanding more power for the aristocracy—the backlash [against liberal politics and values] pushes the spectrum of the acceptable to the right, to the right, farther to the right."[13] Throughout his book, Frank presents an irrational, topsy-turvy conservative world, in which people vote against their best interests and demand more

30

power for the few. They cut off their noses to spite their faces because Republicans have helped engineer a great "derangement" in order to distract people with moral American-values conflicts when they should really be able to see that their interests are not being protected. Cultural issues such as the concern over queer civil rights have aided greatly in the national derangement.

On March 11, 2005, Princeton economics professor and *New York Times* writer Paul Krugman was promoting his book, *The Great Unraveling: Losing Our Way in the New Century,* on Jon Stewart's *The Daily Show.* During his segment, he and Jon Stewart were commenting on that week's series of unfortunate events: the Bush administration's push to privatize Social Security and the passage of a new bill transforming bankruptcy laws—a bill, deeply wanted by credit card companies, that kept some crucial bankruptcy protections in place for the wealthiest of citizens but made those in the direst of economic circumstances more vulnerable. While Krugman and Stewart shook their heads in disbelief, Krugman offered a flip but still very accurate analysis. On both issues, he asserted that such special-interest-driven legislative priorities were made possible, in part, by acts of cultural distraction that would prohibit voters from detecting and being outraged about the brazenness of the conservative agendas that were not benefiting the majority of the U.S. population. Krugman, half-seriously, explained that voters had reelected and now support Bush because he was supposed to protect them from "The Married Gay Terrorists." He later repeated the joke, suggesting that most would not connect the dots between the interests of credit card companies and personal, crippling debt because they would be blaming, instead, "The Married Gay Terrorists."

In a quick turn-of-phrase, Krugman economically called attention to both the queer and the terrorist panics that threaten the minds of Americans who now crave security, even at the expense of civil liberties and the loss of economic safeguards and opportunities. He melded the culture war of queer rights with the War on Terror in order to suggest that the moral panics about the American way of life, the spread of democracy (or

31

capitalism) built upon the right kind of faith, the right kind of government, and most stringently, the right kind of families are what drive the
"average" American voter to the polls. By linking the two issues, Krugman
emphasized the ridiculousness of the political climate not to mock his
imaginary "average" voter, but in order to argue that the subterfuges of the
Bush administration (and all the conservatives who support that administration) have been made possible because people are more afraid of America's enemies—the queers, the terrorists who might be anyone or anywhere
—than the unbridled corporate interests that are driving policy and the
accumulation of power as the United States fortifies its empire. Whether he
meant it or not, Krugman, in one phrase, although not explicitly, enabled
the same-sex marriage issue to imply the religious morality that opposes it,
only to then permit the religious ban on marriage to be connected to what
Americans are not: terrorists. Krugman forced us to think about the political effects of the unhappy marriage between religious rhetoric and national
rhetoric at a moment when the United States nervously pursues its supreme sovereignty, its supreme love of democracy, all over the world.

I must insist that the days of the political sovereign are not over, especially as we are engaged in a very holy war at home and abroad. Yes, the
forces of political and cultural power have dispersed, with multiple opportunities for the regulation of people and their lives that exceed the direct
influence of any one government or head of state.[14] But Judith Butler and
numerous others have been, lately, invoking concepts of sovereignty because there is a nagging sense that proliferating centers of power still have
some definable zones of intensity, zones that still need to be thought of as
having features of sovereignty. Not sovereignty as the capacity for self-
determination and self-rule, but rather sovereignty as the power, often
wielded outside of proper legal venues, to determine who should live and
who should die—perhaps the ultimate exercise of power.[15] Susan Buck-
Morss calls these zones of wild, extralegal power "war zones," "for it is the
real possibility of war and the threat of the common enemy that constitute
the state not merely as a legal entity but a sovereign entity, the legitimate

embodiment of the collective, with the power to wage war in its name. As sovereign of the collective, it has sovereignty over the collective, with the right to order to their deaths the very citizens in whose name it rules."[16] I hope that the political climate of the late twentieth and early twenty-first centuries adequately illustrates these characterizations, and one need only think about post-9/11 security measures, the U.S. Patriot Act, and the Bush Doctrine of preemptive force in Iraq and elsewhere to see just how common these enemies of the state are becoming. Our task is to see how religious rhetoric aids in the production of enemies, not to mention the production of war zones that confirm the sovereign's power.

Giorgio Agamben helps here because he articulates the dynamics of modern forms of sovereignty by invoking a religious concept and a religious language, not unlike the American jeremiad, not unlike Kevin Tebedo's conception of God's authority. Following on the heels of Hobbes, Schmitt, Arendt, and Foucault, Agamben focuses his analysis of sovereignty by introducing readers to an instructive figure—an ancient religious figure he locates at the origin of Western political paradigms: the *homo sacer*, or the sacred man. This "enigmatic" figure, this religious designation, produces some conundrums that illuminate some of the conundrums queers currently pose to our own systems of government. "An obscure figure of archaic Roman law, in which human life is included in the juridical order [*ordinamento*] solely in the form of its exclusion (that is, of its capacity to be killed)," writes Agamben. This figure "offer[s] the key by which not only the sacred texts of sovereignty but also the very codes of political power will unveil their mysteries."[17] "Sacred Man" is neither religious nor secular but belongs to "a zone prior to the distinction between the sacred and profane, the religious and juridical."[18] In ancient texts, the *homo sacer* is a sacred being that is nevertheless banned from the profane world. It is at once an object of religious fascination, and an object that is reviled by the community; it is blessed and cursed simultaneously. More miraculously, however, this figure must be banned from the community, "phrased out," if you will, even though its presence is still very much a part of the community (the excluded are always embedded within the group). Moreover, this banned being might even be killed, but unlike other ritual sacrifices—well documented in various theories of religion such as those of Emile Durkheim, Sigmund Freud, and René Girard[19]—the murder of this sacred figure does not count as sacrifice. "[S]o *homo sacer* belongs to God in the form of unsacrificeability and is included in the community in the form of being able to be killed. *Life that cannot be sacrificed and yet may be killed is sacred life.*"[20]

This figure challenges our notions of what sacrifice might mean. The easiest way to think about sacrifice, then, would be to think about sacrifice as a term for something that has enough value that its explicit loss would count as loss.[21] Its loss would mean something significant. But if one no longer can detect the value of the loss, the sacrifice does not count, and then the loss has slipped below the legal and political radar. Such slipping, however, does not mean that the killing—which might be figurative or awfully literal—does not have extreme political or legal consequences. As the jeremiad tells us, someone must be imagined as not-belonging, as not figured as a loss, to the United States in order for the nation to be directed in its sovereign purpose, especially a sovereignty authorized not by humans, but by God (or his awful proxies).

The figure of the sacred man belongs to the wild war zone so necessary for mass democratic governments:[22] it represents that which, through its exclusion, constitutes the nation in violent, paralegal ways, giving power to the sovereign, specifically the power of the sovereign to determine who lives and who dies. The state of exception, the state of those who are made exceptional to the state by not officially belonging, produces the possibility of the sovereign's power. And those who are made sacred in this strange, peculiar, extralegal manner—in a realm not quite religious and not quite secular (as we conventionally understand those terms)—are also those who serve as the evidence of the wild, warlike power necessary for the United States' existence and coercive development. For our purposes I want to stress that the queer, who is denied some important kind of legal status, who is reviled and banned from full citizenship, currently functions as a homo sacer of the United States. Queers have become quasi-enemies of the state, and as such, can quite easily be detained, indefinitely, in a status, determined by sovereign power, that renders their lives available for slaughter, but slaughters or deaths that will not become sacrificially symbolic, either through legal forms of distributing justice and revenge or through a kind of martyrdom one is often accustomed to thinking about when questions of religious sacrifice are at hand. We understand the power of the sovereign by its ability to decide not only on our qualities of lives, but also on whether or not our lives will be protected or discarded.

Here is where contemporary politics, according to Agamben, has taken one of its nastiest turns: the political field ceases to be a fight for the good or just life (for, say, universal health coverage, education, welfare, distributive wealth guarantees), and instead politics becomes a fight just for the basic condition of life. The fight for life becomes the only political imperative allowed, which, not-so-oddly enough, helps consolidate the power of the sovereign who has control over whether or not one has a right to life. All kinds of lives are thus stripped down to their most basic fact—life—in order to divest those lives from their immediate cultural and political significance, enabling any life to be made sacrosanct by its very insignificant disposability.

In the current political climate, all sorts of people are turned just into the bare fact of their lives—the fact that they have only biological life. They become what Agamben calls "bare life." With a menacing tone, Agamben offers the following analysis, which is really a warning:

> If it is true that the figure proposed by our age is that of an unsacrificeable life that has nevertheless become capable of being killed to an unprecedented degree, then the bare life of *homo sacer* concerns us in a special way. Sacredness is a line of flight still present in contemporary politics, a line that is as such moving into zones increasingly vast and dark, to a point ultimately coinciding with the biological life itself of

citizens. If today there is no longer any one clear figure of the sacred man, it is perhaps because we are all virtually *homines sacri*.[23]

We all are in danger of becoming sacred in this manner—we are all in danger of no longer counting as sacrifices, but as that which can be killed nonetheless. We are all capable of not counting as something valuable in the official legal and political realms that nominally guard us from harm. And queers in particular have much with which to be concerned.

In this light, the 2004 elections have aided, in some degree, this process of fighting for life—for instance, the queers' right to live happily ever after. It is a fight that exacerbates this march toward everyone becoming sacred in Agamben's sense of the concept. These issues are not wedge issues, but stripping issues, stripping people down to a politics concerned only with bare life, with who will slip into the sovereign ban, or who will be phrased out of the nation, right out into its terrible Red core. But it is from this core, and from the language that got queers to this core, that I want to articulate how queers can get back their lives, how they can become those who can be killed; but their murders would nevertheless count as a sacrifice. That is, I want to tell you about a form of political resistance to the power of the sovereign that is at once religious and literary, that gives queers currency, or at least safety, in a political and legal sphere that would otherwise prefer to strip queers of citizenship, of human status, into disposable, bare lives. I want to tell you a story about queer martyrdom, as it were, which, curiously enough, stalls the evolving process of political sacralization.

Racial Sacrifice

In response to these life-canceling political dramas, queers have narrated their pain, their threatening losses, as not their own deserved failures, but the abusive failures of a nation that was full of the promise of equality, of revolutionary words about freedom and justice, only to come dreadfully short in making good on that promise. We understand the queer's dilemma because of the heartbreaking losses that are organized and instructed by the protest politics that hums the jeremiad to the different key of the excluded. It has long been noted that gay and lesbian politics have relied on, as Michael Warner asserts, "the buried model . . . [of] racial and ethnic politics."[24] The racial model, in particular, persists, and it gives the queers a surprising form in which they can become described as political sacrifices. Race, among other things, has the capacity to give people a language of sacrifice—at least in the current political and legal system in the United States. The words of race bring sacrifice, which we could consider the assertion of political, social, and cultural values, back to the awful sovereign word drama being played out in the banning of the queer from full enfranchisement. Racial rhetorics have the capacity to make the deaths or loss of the queer matter, which would thus enable queers to count as lives that should count as lives worth living.

When Matthew Shepard was murdered, his death, which could have escaped notice, was figured as the death of a sacred martyr—a status that made him not disposable, but essential. He was a religious sacrifice, and thus not a *homo sacer*: "The notion that Matt had been strung up in something akin to a crucifixion became the starting point for the reporting and reaction to come."[25] This image provided the basis for much of the outrage over the brutal slaying and minoritization of the queer who has no acceptable place in a world that wishes that body beaten or diseased on its way to death. Indeed, in Dennis Shepard's address to the jury during the sentencing of one of Matthew Shepard's assailants, he figured his son as a poster boy for hate crimes legislation and queer tolerance issues worldwide: "Matt became a symbol—some say a martyr, putting a boy-next-door face on hate crimes. That's fine with me. Matt would be thrilled if his death would help others." It did, but in a very complicated manner that relied on Matt's connection to a sentimental race history that had long preceded his lynching.

Dennis Shepard's statements to the court were, in part, his response to the hostile, traditional values of American heterosexuality that have long circumscribed queers. He focused on the loss of his son to impress upon the

reader, or the court, some sense of the despair and violence that must sub-
tend the effective articulation of why queers need protection:

> By the end of the beating, his body was just trying to survive. You [one
> of Shepard's murderers] left him out there by himself, but he wasn't
> alone. There were his lifelong friends with him—friends that he had
> grown up with. You're probably wondering who these friends were.
> First, he had the beautiful night sky with the same stars and moon that
> we used to look at through a telescope. Then, he had the daylight and
> the sun to shine on him one more time—one more cool, wonderful
> autumn day in Wyoming. His last day alive in Wyoming. His last day
> alive in the state that he always proudly called home. And through it
> all he was breathing in for the last time the smell of Wyoming sage-
> brush and the scent of pine trees from the snowy range. He heard the
> wind—the ever-present Wyoming wind—for the last time. He had one
> more friend with him. One he grew to know through his time in Sun-
> day school and as an acolyte at St. Mark's in Casper as well as through
> his visits to St. Matthew's in Laramie. He had God.

The rhetoric of this last sentence, given the protests from fundamental/
evangelical and Catholic sources over Matthew Shepard's lifestyle, is a
forceful appeal for his tragic value. How could people hurt those who had
God? How could some violence, which was approved by some forceful religious voices in the United States, be acceptable? The implication is that this
violence represents a variety of values (whether they are religious or not)
that are irrational and not part of a decent society. This should not be the
form of religious feeling one finds in America's heartland.

The familial injury brought on by Shepard's death certainly provoked
deliberate manipulations of the heart. And these manipulations flutter
between hate and love, especially when the tragedy of Shepard's slaying, an
instance of hate, has its conclusion in a gift of love: Shepard's family urged
that the killers be shown compassion, that they not be put to death. When

Dennis Shepard spoke to the jury he pulled on our heartstrings. The transcript reads like a page from the nineteenth century:

> How do I talk about the loss that I feel every time I think about Matt? How can I describe the empty pit in my heart and mind when I think about all the problems that were put in Matt's way that he overcame? No one can understand the sense of pride and accomplishment that I felt every time he reached the mountaintop of another obstacle. No one, including myself, will ever know the frustration and agony that others put him through because he was different. How many people could be given the problems that Matt was presented with and still succeed as he did? How many would continue to smile—at least on the outside—while crying on the inside to keep other people from feeling bad?[26]

At the heart of this statement we are taught, in the best kind of sentimental way, how to feel, or how we can't possibly feel, about extreme loss. And later we are told how to motivate that loss into a political acknowledgment that something must be done to ameliorate this social injustice. Acts of hate must be transformed into acts of love. Shepard, perhaps unwittingly, followed narrative conventions that fall under a rubric of sentimentality that literary critic Shirley Samuels quickly describes as "a set of rules for how to feel 'right,' privileging compassion in calibrating and adjusting the sensations of the reader [or viewer or listener] in finely tuned and predictable responses to what is viewed or read."[27] This kind of political instruction has roots well before the twentieth and early twenty-first centuries, and the extraordinarily influential and best-selling sentimental novel of Harriet Beecher Stowe, *Uncle Tom's Cabin*, is a key text to have in our minds as we think about sentimentality's political influence.[28]

Crucial to sentimental appeals are not merely the manner in which private feelings should be made public through the painful evocations of loss and cruelty, but also that such sentiments are often inextricably linked to the anti-slavery cause, which, along with women's suffrage, inaugurated the long project of drawing political attention to the ways that the U.S. citizenry is not as abstractly equal as the founding, religiously inflected principles of the country proclaim. Emotional dissent still informs the ways that oppressed members of the nation narrate their exclusions, their painful losses, and inspire the country to feel right, to feel "religious," about what must be done about equality.

When addressing the Court, Dennis Shepard associates his son's murder with race crimes: "You screwed up, Mr. McKinney [the murderer]. You made the world realize that a person's lifestyle is not a reason for discrimination, intolerance, persecution, and violence. This is not the 1920s, 30s, and 40s of Nazi Germany. My son died because of your ignorance and intolerance." Dennis Shepard does not stop there. He pushes Shepard's minoritization beyond the concerns for Nazi racial purity into an immediately violent racial context the Court and the U.S. public sphere could quickly grasp: he mentions that Matthew and he had "discussed the horrible death of James Byrd, Jr., in Jasper, Texas," which brought his son's lynching into stronger relation to race. Matthew Shepard had God, he had some history with religion, but he also had a claim on a history of racial violence.

Queers, and their advocates, have often used racial sentimentality to frame their demand for justice and equality. Just read a passage on the implications of Colorado's Amendment 2 published by GLAAD/Denver, which conceptualizes LGBTQ rights as part of a longer lineage of civil rights:

> The American experience with slavery and decades of official racial segregation fueled the modern-day civil rights movement, which began in the late 1940s. This movement focused on eradicating racial discrimination and legal barriers preventing people of color from exercising their fundamental rights. The 1964 and 1968 Civil Rights Acts are major achievements of the civil rights movement.
>
> The desire for freedom and equality is alive in other movements

working to remove discriminatory barriers: the women's rights move-ment of the 1970s (which added "sex" to the 1964 Civil Rights Act); the disability rights movement of the 1980s (which produced the 1991 Americans with Disabilities Act); and the current lesbian and gay rights movement.[29]

Race unifies this lineage of civil rights acts and demands. It gives legibility, if not a strong emotion of political dissent, to those who are struggling with issues of equality.

So it makes sense that the religious right in Colorado would deliberately attempt to keep queers from trying to fit into this history of injustice. In Amendment 2's campaign, which we will return to extensively in Chapter Four, conservative Christians claimed that queers were asking to be let into the "special rights" they assigned to suspect class minorities such as African Americans. But what are these "special rights"? As a May 1993 pamphlet circulated by the ACLU of Denver explains, " 'Special rights' is a made-up phrase. It does not appear in the amendment and has no specific legal meaning. It is a scare-tactic campaign slogan that was used very success-fully by Colorado for Family Values. 'Special rights' is an emotionally loaded catch-all phrase that Colorado for Family Values uses to group to-gether 'minority status,' 'quota preferences,' 'protected status' and 'claims of discrimination.' "[30] The term is emotionally loaded in part because it sug-gests the kinds of sentimentalities that were, at least in part, effective in producing protests and politics that ended slavery, influenced the small and not-yet fully achieved gains of civil rights, and made the national citi-zenship acknowledge, however grudgingly, its diversity.

This kind of politics inspired change primarily through the assertion that official and unofficial slave status could no longer be tolerated, at least at the level of the federal government. With the advent of anti-slavery and effective protest politics, those who were systematically excluded from the citizenry could rephrase their exclusion as a basis of a strong, affective cri-tique of conservative forces. By referencing the controversial and often unjustly maligned results of civil rights legislation and a national public culture that, at least superficially, could no longer focus its exclusionary impulses on African American minorities, the creators of Amendment 2 suggested that quotas, hiring preferences, and other issues surrounding minority status might also soon belong to lesbians and gays. This prediction upset the majority of Colorado voters in 1992. A not so subtle implication of the vote for no "special rights" is that the nation structurally needs its own enemy inside-outsiders, its members of the community on whom the social ills and impurities of the nation could, through jeremiadic echoes, be rhetorically pinned. The country might lose yet another of its impure second-class citizens who could symbolically be blamed for the dissolution of the nation's or family's optimism. The particularly effective vilification and moral outrage over homosexuality would be harder to produce in public, especially in statutory and national legislation and judicial review.

For all this concern over special rights and the religious war of words that ensued, the racialization of the queer was the ironic twist. The religious right in Colorado got exactly what it did not want: lesbians, bisexuals, and gays were reinforced in their claims of minority status because they had been targeted as a class of citizens who were effectively stripped of not only "special rights," but of all claims of discrimination. Indeed, as I mentioned in the Introduction, the Supreme Court's majority rejection of Amendment 2 relied on the Fourteenth Amendment and produced the occasion for making the nation begin to understand that queers could be recognized, martyred, as if they were part of a racial minority in the United States, as if they were a population that could no longer be disposable.

Not or Like Race

There are enormous flaws in pursuing this "like race" strategy: there are differences, for instance, between the life experiences that are impacted by race and those impacted by sexuailty; there are differences of opinion in the origins and histories and experiences of race and queer sexuality; and there are justifiable anxieties about even getting close to an argument about biological determinism when explaining the various challenges of homosexuality, thereby opening the discussion of "cures," defective genes, and physiological excuses for the reduction of citizenship rights. But most pressing are the kinds of issues that Janet Halley, Janet Jakobsen, and Ann Pellegrini describe in their critiques of the comparison. The "like race" argument "has been taken up by conservative opponents of affirmative action,"[31] and the precedents are dangerous for legal review. Halley instructs:

> When gay rights advocates began to invoke the "immutable characteristic" simile, they were working from a set of scattered, sketchy rationales occurring at happenstance in race and sex discrimination cases. By translating these "immutable characteristic" references into an "indicia of suspectness" checklist, and implying that its items were not merely sufficient but necessary conditions for heightened judicial protection, they invited judges to "harden up" the law in this area. Which is just what judges did: federal district courts increasingly stipulated for immutability not as a mere factor but as a prerequisite for heightened scrutiny, even as they persistently concluded that sexual orientation was not an immutable characteristic. . . . Gay advocates making the immutability argument then bear some responsibility for a legitimation of universalizing understandings of race and a delegitimation of—indeed, a constriction of the social space for—minoritizing ones.[32]

The cautions that Halley advocates certainly make salient the real dangers of the "like race" simile. Once the "universal understandings of race" so easily become immutable characteristics, so many dangerous implications follow—in particular, as Halley quickly notes, there is then a "hidden assumption that racial discrimination would be morally acceptable if blacks could change the color of their skin."[33]

Halley provides one example of one of the major pitfalls of comparing queers to racial minorities. Part of the frustration and danger comes from the practice of analogizing itself. Although the uneasy relationship between analogy and politics is hardly a new topic, it is one that needs to be revisited when one argues for the use-value of the "like race" analogy. We have the traditional definition of analogy, which is often lost in analogy's political translations, in which an analogy can be traditionally thought of as a relationship drawn between four terms—A is to B as C is to D. For our purposes, we could say that queers experience homophobia in a way that African Americans experience racism. That would not mean that queers are the same as African Americans, but rather that queers have a relationship to hatred and political coercion that resembles (but is not the same as) the hatred and political coercion experienced by African Americans.

Through the analogy, we then begin to grasp some of the quality of hatred endured by both groups, but there is a danger. Like most political talk, comparisons between relations, especially in politically charged activities based on identity complaints, can get stripped down to questions of similarities, or even similitude. There is power in analogies because analogies, through explicit connections, help identify, explain, or articulate various people or groups or contingencies. As Miranda Joseph explains, "analogics" aid in "making the other known."[34] It is this kind of powerful and potentially dangerous word work that has produced some necessary critiques and concerns, mainly because the analogy between one group or another might obscure the distinct differences and claims between one group (for example, queers) and another group (those who experience racism—who might also be queers who are racialized), however intertwined those groups or categories might often be. Most distressingly, the relationships between them cease to illuminate the relations and instead fix or "naturalize," often unevenly and perniciously, the categories that are being articulated by the comparison. Janet Jakobsen delineates the pitfalls between making equivalent different categories in too simple or too quick a fashion; she rightly worries about what gets lost in the comparison, about what happens to the distinct category when its historical specificity is elided, forgotten, or undercut. Jakobsen nevertheless understands that there is no easy way to do away with analogies, and so she describes the linguistic structure that make analogies work, especially when the comparison between the one term is reliant on a more understood or fixed second term. The properties of one term, through metaphoric operations, can be transferred into another term. When queers, then, argue that they are "like race," the less legible category, queer, relies on assumptions about the more known category, race, which has more value and legibility as a concept in the history of the United States. Race can then cease to be an inchoate category, and all sorts of commonsensical, if not racist, notions adhere to the category, producing, too often, a disastrous effect: "Advocates of gay and lesbian rights—even as they invoke the [like race] analogy—can ignore, marginalize, and exploit the struggles of African Americans, thus reenacting the racism of mainstream American political life."[35] This is an incredibly useful corrective, especially when Jakobsen argues that the terms cannot be interchanged, that they are not an easy equivalence, and that they are dangerous. Moreover, Jakobsen urges us to pay attention to how analogies work, often in unexpected ways: "The mechanism by which [the transfers between one term's properties to another] occurs is not simple, because the transfers depend on a fundamental category error. Analogizing queers to Jews [for instance] violates the categories that might otherwise separate them. This category is a space of constraint or of possibility."[36]

I couldn't agree with her more, and I want to pursue both the constraints and the possibilities. I want to pursue the fundamental, categorical mistakes made in the queers-are-like-race analogy, and how that error is becoming increasingly necessary in queer, if not all, politics. Years ago, Butler made me believe that it "is possible to argue that whereas no transparent or full revelation is afforded by 'lesbian' and 'gay,' there remains a political imperative to use these necessary errors or category mistakes, as it were (what Gayatri Spivak might call 'catachrestic' operations: to use a proper name improperly), to rally and represent an oppressed political constituency."[37] Indeed, the name of power, like all names, writes Spivak, "is a misfit."[38] J. Hillis Miller, in a slightly different conception of catachresis, illuminates Spivak's definition for our purposes here: catachresis is the use "of terms borrowed from another realm to name what has no literal language of its own."[39] So I wonder: Can we extend this logic and wonder if it is also an imperative that we use the mistakes of race to articulate the mistakes of "lesbian," "gay," and whatever inadequate sign-vehicle we might choose to name ourselves? Which is to say, might it be in our best interests to produce a whole layer of mistakes, obscuring the transparencies, in a hostile public sphere that always hates, even when it tolerates, the queer? And can we use a form of religious hate speech as the catachrestic language that will imprecisely align (not make identical) queers with racial minority status without naturalizing either queers or racial minorities?

We can at least assume that racial analogies of queer sexuality are deliberate mistakes if what we're looking for are precise, coherent, or respectful names that emphasize distinct differences between kinds of identity—racial or sexual. This imprecise analogizing, which we'll discover in the next chapters, is a substitute for explicit testimonials and definitions of minority sexuality. They are fraught and perilous, these analogies, but they are abundant, not to mention effective in urgent political and legal debates such as the holy culture war waged in Colorado. We can certainly consider the religious rhetoric responsible for these mistakes as providing a form of exquisite and necessary mistake making, and we can understand that rhetoric often is, as Aristotle long ago taught us, "stylish," with great attention paid to the ways the words are delivered and presented.[40] If we think about the "like race" analogy as a stylish form of language, we can think about how it works as a metaphor that will not "succeed" in fully communicating.

I'm convinced that the queer use of religious hate speech is often a literary or metaphorical usage that helps arrest the ordinary forms of communication, representation, and protest that compose, at first and at "face" value, contemporary U.S. rhetoric about national membership. The very serious politics of minority complaint are indeed necessary business, with brutal histories of inequalities and unbudging hostile ideas about difference in the United States that remind us that we really have not changed too much in our hostility to the particulars of U.S. citizenry. But when we are not too aware of the techniques of rhetorical entrance into the limited narratives of national belonging, and the even more limited narrative of national not-belonging, one important vector of political power is woefully neglected by those who are most hurt and restricted by the names given to them before they even begin to speak. By learning to be mistaken, to be figurative, to be literary and stylized in one's answers to the nation about who one is, the minority begins to be tentative, strategic, and is perhaps able to circumvent certain toxic rhetorical patterns such as the American jeremiad. It is perfectly acceptable to lie about oneself when the nation goes looking for its internal enemies—the ones whom God needs to condemn.

But we need not stop there and think of the "like race" analogy as simply a mistake. There's more to it, this interruption. The race analogy gives us not only figuration, but something more: figurative opposition. Histories of slavery and civil rights and the speedy way race so menacingly marks race—through quick and often erroneous readings of physiological marks such as skin color—as an undeniable fact of the body. Race is often considered a form of biology that is so loaded with what Hortense Spillers calls "mythical prepossession that there is no easy way for the agents buried beneath [it] to come clean."[41] Racial differences make so much knee-jerk sense because the differences are so readily apparent; the histories "capturing" such difference are so awful, so inhumane, that one can hardly believe that a nation founded on basic principles of equality could so spectacularly[42] dehumanize and subjugate whole segments of the population on such physical grounds. But believe it, we do.

Spillers, however, recognizes the terror of always capturing racial minority status in too much realness, in an unmediated reality, an "unmediated thereness," that cannot imagine to "encompass change, both willed and induced."[43] By relying on the set notions about what blackness—or any racial position that is problematically and synecdochally represented in the

United States by African Americans—might be, one cannot move beyond a very realist-obsessed notion of "race," always reliant on or held captive or "captivated" by dominant ideas about race created by those in control from the very beginning. Spillers concisely worries that a simple category of "otherness" produces the possibility that the "captive body translates into a potential for pornotroping and embodies sheer physical powerlessness that slides into a more general 'powerlessness,' resonating through various centers of human and social meaning."[44] The sense that the racial body is ever really "real," or accurate, or even a tenable distinction is a fraught sense, one which should be resisted. "While there is never a doubt that 'Black' and 'Wasp' are sign-vehicles that signify real political constituencies and concrete cultural allegiances," writes Spillers, "it is also true that there is enough overlap between these intersubjectivities—for good or ill—on the cultural and social plane that a strict division between them is messed up everywhere *but on paper*."[45] Thus, in a moving cry that has not been sufficiently heard in critical race circles and politics, Spillers urges us to move beyond a rethreaded "identity politics":[46] "[B]lack writers [and I think she'd also say 'any writers'], whatever their location and by whatever projects and allegiances they are compelled, must retool the language[s] that they inherit. The work of logological refashioning not only involves the dissipation of the poisons of cliché and its uncritical modalities but it also takes a stab at the pulsating infestations that course through the grammars of 'race,' on 'blackness' in particular."[47] What Spillers suggests here, I feel, is that the *words* of race, and indeed the words of any minority protest, need to be refashioned, need to played with, in order for the poisonous grammar of easy and coercive racial (and perhaps other) distinctions to be challenged. Race cannot only be real, it also has to be rhetorical, and as such it can be transformed, made literary, if not strategic for realms that go beyond literary analysis or theoretical speculations.

This logological project, informed by the philosophies of Kenneth Burke, is more than simple wordplay—it is necessary political work. Spillers believes that those who are in an oppositional relation to a dominant, sovereign politics and culture might be strategically considered as belonging to "black culture."[48] The power of being on the outside of dominant culture—the power of being the scapegoated and sacrificed "other"—is often a persuasive "negativity" that can keep the political critique of dominant culture vibrant and central. According to this provocative formulation, anyone, regardless of biological race, can be "black" as long as she or he is in a productive opposition to dominance. Spillers argues:

> Ellison harnessed "blackness" to a symbolic program of philosophical "disobedience" (a systematic skepticism and refusal) that would make the former available to *anyone,* or more pointedly, *any* posture, that was willing to take on the formidable task of *thinking* as a willful act of imagination and invention. In other words, *Invisible Man* made "blackness" a *process,* a *strategy,* of culture critique, rather than a condition of physiognomy and/or the embodiment of the *auto-bios-graphe.*[49]

Black cultural critique, that is, marshals the energy of opposition to dominance quite effectively, and Spillers's own context of her own African American position in culture serves as a model of a culture and politics of resistance that is available to all sorts of bodies, and must be so.

Of course we know that blackness is not the only possible minority position—there are many others that deserve this kind of explosive and interesting work that pervades American culture and politics. But something about the historical divisions between black and white, and the tragic histories of slavery and segregation, as well as emancipation and civil rights, has enormous *formal* influence on how protest about abuses of authority often occurs in the United States.

Queers who evoke the hatred of fundamentalists understand that issues of sovereign authority, more than of "sexuality," are at hand, so they also draw on "blackness" to produce an important kind of opposition to dominant culture. They do so mistakenly, catachrestically, in order to engage the adversity of American culture and politics without having to speak deeply or specifically about the lurid specificities of their own identifications as sexual minorities. By speaking a religious language of hate, they can speak in an authoritative register of religious language that evokes feelings and sentiments of blackness and its complaints. Queers take on the hate of religious words in order to render their experience "as if" their experiences were the experiences of a racial minority, thereby inspiring a *feeling* (rather than the *being*) of valuable minority status that can hide behind other strategic representations of racial minorities who have fought for their civil rights, including freedom, desegregation, and access to institutions of power, prosperity, feeling, culture, art, and politics. It is not a theft but a strategic assertion of a somewhat, if very qualified, "successful" strategy of minority protest, which seems to be one of the few opportunities for minority legibility in a nation that likes its queer minorities to serve as a rhetorical opportunity for national purification and cleansing.

Although this practice is not necessarily a noble or heroic moment of courage and not geared toward imagining the better possibilities of democratic feeling through the pursuit of more inclusive policies, it understands the limited repertoire of oppositional choices available for those who must respond to the attacks and rhetorical manipulations of those who are automatically valued by U.S. national politics and culture—by those on top. It understands, however unaware, that a national jeremiad is always in sovereign play, and instead of detailing and conforming personal expressions into national purification narratives by listing or confessing of "the array of defects" queers are made to offer to the heterosexual nation, queers deliberately "lie" about their status like a wounded, national racial minority. They do so in order to register that they are lives that can be sacrificed—that count as something—and thus should not be lives that are destroyed.[50] I do not want to say that there are no painful and very real stories of abject queerness, trauma, and pain that need to be told and are indeed told in other moments of queer resistance. I am not disputing that sometimes this strategy does a disservice to the very real claims of injury made by members of racial minority groups who have no choice but to be affiliated with disenfranchised members of the nation.

What I want to highlight, rather than immediately admonish or reject without deeper critical scrutiny, is the relatively long history of the uses of strategic minoritization reflected in queer political tactics—especially when those queers already "belong" to racially distinct and disenfranchised groups. What I want to offer is a deeper analysis of the hateful Word of evangelical and fundamental America, which is once again center stage in U.S. conservative, right-wing politics. This hateful Word helps render a particular form of queer minority status that inspires, through its analogous connections to racial difference, a minority feeling that still seems to be the only way to move a very slow and coercive political system into political recognitions of a national otherness that should not be destroyed and not mourned. I want to argue for the strategic usefulness of this emotional, racial analogy—which is a mistake, or lie—before we critique its impurities. Perhaps a more polite way to describe these deceitful acts would be to emphasize the "literary" qualities of this politics, and to argue for the strategic deployment of rhetorical, racial analogies which stress that representational politics are not necessarily truthful statements. Personal testimonies might not be personal at all.[51] Full-frontal queer disclosure should not always be part of a political, public culture that would prefer its minorities to be literally available for all sorts of political, personal, emotional, economic, and ideological abuses.

Although it is extraordinarily useful to resist the political and cultural landscape of the United States, and although it is useful and necessary to be utopian and wishful in one's revolutionary thinking,[52] we still have basic, market-driven conditions of political, aesthetic, cultural, and ideological possibility, or impossibility, that do not offer all that much, especially in the realm of resistance and protest. Wendy Brown worries about the limits of resistance inscribed in "contemporary politicized identities" that rely on "logics of pain," which iterate the very dynamics the identities attempt to critique. It is "freedom's relationship to identity—its promise to address a social injury or marking that is itself constitutive of identity—that yields the paradox in which the first imaginings of freedom are always constrained by and potentially even require the very structure of oppression that freedom emerges to oppose."[53] Although it seems as if Brown and I would be worlds apart on how to negotiate with the dynamics of political action, we are close on one point: there are methods we can use that might take us away from a purely faithful or realistic identity politics. Brown wonders, "What if we sought to supplant the language of 'I am'—with its defensive closure on identity, its insistence on the fixity of position, its equation of social with moral positioning—with the language of 'I want this for us'?"[54] She wonders about desire, about making the identity complaint a demand of desire—a desire to be something better or a desire for something more. Although I am less optimistic about desire, I appreciate her willingness to go beyond the "closure on identity." Rather than desire, I suggest we explore another kind of feeling. So in conversation with her, I want us to entertain that there is, at least, an indirect power in *not* confessing that "I *am* a queer" but rather deliberately lying, "I *feel* like a racial minority." This kind of erroneous feeling occasions so many opportunities for useful, political evasions while certain, basic citizenship rights are still stringently foreclosed from queer persons. The most controversial point I want to make and explain throughout this book is that the queer's repetition of strong, authoritative religious hate speech, the "Word," produces, beyond a literal understanding of the queer religious hate speech, a quality of queer feeling that is rendered more akin to racial minority status than illustrative of queer practices, affects, desires, or sensations of being minor. I want to demonstrate that the queer evocations of conservative, Christian hate speech—the lingua franca of state sovereign power and control in the United States—enables queers to lie about who they are, choosing instead an emotional, literary association to racial minority status to be the feeling, rather than being, that will move their, our, politics along.

2 James Baldwin and His Queer, Religious Words

James Baldwin understood that the sovereign power of religious words could still be a powerful form of minority complaint. I focus on the example of Baldwin because his writing is iconic for both race and queer politics.[1] We should consider how, as a writer, he was immersed in the complicated relations between queerness, blackness, and religious rhetoric, but he told us a story that is different from what people often tell us about African American religious responses to a racist American culture. Baldwin's use of religious rhetoric was not merely a "conjuring" or "signifying"[2] use of religious rhetoric; nor did his rhetoric exactly belong to the black church tradition that Theophus Smith describes as "conjurational performances at the level of social history [that] employ biblical figures with a curative intention . . . and for the purposes of reenvisioning and transforming lived experience and social reality through mimetic or imitative operations,"[3] serving what might be thought of as a therapeutic role, enabling black culture to produce a thriving community in an otherwise hostile and racist world. Baldwin understood that there was more than therapy going on in these rhetorical performances. He knew that the black church tradition was not free of homophobia and hate; he knew that even the most excellent examples of black conjuring could still express a hatred that hurts and renders violence on its own constituents.[4]

Nevertheless, Baldwin did not shy away from the hatred that often subtends the religious expression of the black church that dominated his earliest childhood experiences. In fact, for Baldwin, religion was sometimes a *figure* of hatred. "To destroy a nigger, a kike, a dyke, or a faggot, by one's own act alone," writes Baldwin, "is to have committed a communion and, above all, to have made a public confession more personal, more total, and more devastating than any act of love: whereas the orgasm of the mob is drenched in the blood of the lamb."[5] This religious communion stands in for the violence of the American public expression, but Baldwin did not back away from that religious violence. Instead, he often used religious language as a form of provocative hate speech that was crucial for articulating the experience of queerness. For a primary example, let's begin with John Grimes, the queer protagonist from *Go Tell It on the Mountain,* who experiences a conversion experience to Christianity that is rendered in violent terms. The narration describes his conversion as a "power that had struck John, in the head or in the heart; and in a moment, wholly filling him with the anguish that he could never had imagined, that he surely could not endure, that even now he could not believe."[6] What is literally striking about the acceptance of John's religious conversion and evocation ("everyone had always said that John would be a preacher when he grew up, just like his father")[7] is that something so normal for this novel's black religious community is so painful for John, who had wanted a "another life"[8]—one that is not religious, one that does not tell him that his queer desires are sinful and damned. He wanted a life where he is not hated for his sinful sexuality.[9] And yet curiously, for all of the evangelical Christian hate, John does convert.

Yet through such a conversion, I will demonstrate, John finds safety in a use of religious rhetoric that is not therapeutic as much as it is strategic. He learns how to inflect, queerly, the normal, religious rhetoric of Baldwin's world, showcasing the particular ways hostile, religious words can equip queers with a language that possesses "normal" or sovereign authority. The queer's use of the heterosexually dominant language, however, does not signal that the queer has assimilated the norms of the black church, nor is it even an example of the appropriation of a white religious language for black use. But rather John uses the closest language of authority at hand— the language of state power that drenched his black church. This hate speech, this language of sovereign authority and normalcy, for John also serves as a particularly capacious register that could include, indeed hide, him and his queer feelings.

Baldwin, throughout his novels, often uses the dominant language of religion that surrounds his characters to produce the possibility of what Lauren Berlant and Michael Warner would call "counterintimacies,"[10] or zones of revolutionary relations, emotions, cultures, and connections. In their suggestive essay, "Sex in Public," Berlant and Warner locate queer counterintimacies and queer "counterpublics" in the less official and slightly romanticized locations, the worlds of "entrances, exits, unsystem- atized lines of acquaintance, projected horizons, typifying examples, alter- nate routes, blockages, incommensurate geographies."[11] Counterpublics are points of important if not illicit contact and identity-making that are not necessarily authorized. Yet queer counterpublics, it must be stated, are also found in things other than the "dirty-talk"[12] of the world-making and hazy spaces that Berlant and Warner pose against an official heterosexual nor- mal. Queerness, for instance, can also be found in the sanitized versions of national religious rhetoric, in the normative words of a religious lexicon that, by many definitions, quickly offers the possibility of a life that cannot be explicitly articulated at the present tense of its experience. Sometimes, that is, the form of the "normal," and the assumption of identities that are quickly recognizable and socially understood, that *seem* normal, expresses a desire not merely for heterosexual enfranchisement and authority, but perhaps something else. Perhaps the "normal" is the desire for legibility, a desire for community, and a desire for another route into social resistance and minority complaint that need not be so "counter" public in order to be innovative and queer.[13] Berlant elsewhere acknowledges that "the wish for normalcy everywhere heard these days, voiced by minoritized subjects, often expresses a wish not to have to push so hard in order to have a 'life.' "[14] Certainly, the decision to pursue routes *through* rather than *against* more socially recognizable structures and institutions of intimacy does not always imply that one has uncritically submitted to, or is even protected by, the state or even the church.[15] Perhaps this decision is not so much about ease as it is about protection, about insuring that one's life is still valuable enough not to destroy.

Baldwin's peculiar exploitation of religious rhetoric helps describe the contours of a more counterintuitive institutional resistance that uses the normalizing, sovereign authority of religion to make quite vibrant what is not supposed to be part of such normalcy: the queer. What I will suggest in the following pages is that Baldwin's queer evocation of conservative, Christian language—conservative because it's still quite homophobic—produces a different picture of just how normal the normal is in the dominant public sphere.[16] I will argue that the queer, through a rhetoric that is both religious and racial, exploits the figurations of religious hate that produces normative narratives of belonging. He takes on all of this rhetoric's painful and injurious effects in order to have the privileges of hateful publicity without having to reveal anything specific or "really" painful about minority sexuality. Religious words thus provide queers with a strategic language of hatred that produces the sensations of racial sentimentality that articulate the valuable feeling of queer sexuality that has no language of its own.

The language of race hatred, as I have so far suggested, is also a language of minority access into a compromised political recognition. Yet the position of minority injury, of painful pasts with violent histories such as slavery, desegregation, and racial civil rights, is a frequently told story that can be manipulated in all sorts of unforeseen ways for a variety of reasons. As Baldwin's description of the American nation-state articulates—with a deep sense of the typical forms of nationality implied by the American jeremiad —the contemporary public sphere thrives on hate, especially when that hate targets minorities' bodies.[17] Probably as a consequence, it has now become almost obligatory to focus on the violent effects of discrimination and hatred on the body to narrate a history of historical injustice, abuse, and amnesia. As I alluded to in the previous chapter, Wendy Brown helps us understand that minority resistance is often articulated through injury that gives the minority a strong voice and claim through that violence.[18] Indeed, words about hurt bodies have saturated much critical work that is influenced by theorists like Michel Foucault, who incites this interest when he writes:

The body is the inscribed surface of events (traced by language and dissolved by ideas), the locus of the dissociated Self (adopting the illusion of substantial unity), and a volume in perpetual disintegration. Genealogy, as an analysis of descent, is thus situated within the articulation of the body and history. Its task is to expose a body totally imprinted by history and the process of history's destruction of the body.[19]

Certainly contemporary criticism has taken this cue, corporealizing history that Foucault describes as the manifestation of "the stigmata of past experience."[20] Baldwin's John conceptualizes the past in terms of the injured bodies of his ancestors: "They were despised and rejected, the wretched and the spat upon, the earth's offscouring; and he was in their company, and they would swallow up his soul. The stripes they had endured would scar his back, their punishment would be his."[21] Such impulses, rendering historical events through metaphors about the body, preferably a body that is wounded, also correspond with what counts as public expression, according to Mark Seltzer in his revision of public sphere theory. Seltzer argues that the contemporary public is a "sociality that gathers, and public that meets, in the spectacle of the untoward accident and in an identification with the world insofar as it is a hostile place—the pathological public sphere."[22] This publicity, situated around the torn open body of the minority, constitutes what he calls the pathological public—a public sphere increasingly needy for injury, pain, and corporeal markings that make its figuration of historical hatred coherent. That is, the national public sphere—what we could call the "normal"—is understood to be both painful and violent. Significantly, Baldwin understood this kind of dominant and "normal" figuration of minority history, and complicated it through his critique of the way religion most often serves to render the specificity of African American historical experience. Let me explain.

At first reading, Baldwin indeed appears to follow a typical pattern of African American letters that, as Eric Sundquist argues, relies on how "black" religion operates as the "core expression of African American culture," serving as "a foundation for modern African American culture as an extension of slave culture."[23] So much has already been written on the connections between African American and religious experience that I have no need to rehearse that scholarship here.[24] What we must note, however, is that religious language is quickly connected to specific historical or theological aspects of the African American church. And even when critics usefully foreground the linguistic dimensions of the rhetoric of the black church, they do so to elaborate an abstract, historical foundation and origin that explains religious language's relevance for a contemporary moment that might be otherwise considered secular.[25] Undeniably, John's religiously marked flesh leads him back to where "history" often, however effectively or ineffectively, seems to lead us: to an image of an "origin," the image of John's ripped open and scarred ancestors, that lends shape, if not causal coherence, to what happens in the present.[26] As Sundquist indicates, so much African American criticism, in an attempt to "right" the historical amnesia of official, national culture,[27] elaborates "histories," often taking shape through imaginative reconstructions of the African American past. One result of such historical recovery, however, is the conflation of religion with African American history, leading, I feel, to a persistent reduction of the more flexible figuration of a *language* of religious blackness Baldwin creates through his writings.

In a late essay, Baldwin, however, articulates his persistent reliance on a religious idiom that puts into tension, without abandoning, the sociological centrality of the black church. For he shifts the focus away from a typical conception of African American history when he speaks religiously: "*Every good-bye ain't gone*: Human history reverberates with violent upheaval, uprooting, arrival and departure, hello and good-bye. Yet, I am not certain that anyone ever leaves home."[28] Sure, Baldwin recognized that a debt must be paid to the past, but instead of lauding or even elaborating such a past through the quick figure of the black church, he chose to describe the most characteristic expression of black culture as an *expression,* as a *phrase.* And this phrase is severed from the church's past and applied to his present context—a context outside of the historical events of his own participation in a religious faith community. I am convinced that Baldwin's reliance on religion is entirely lexical, and the force he attributes to the specific properties of religious rhetoric has very little to do with African American history as it is conventionally conceived. For, indeed, throughout his entire career, Baldwin isolated the rhetorical strength of religious words, and figures of speech such as "keep the faith" and "revelation" have little to do with conveying coherent religious doctrine or encouraging a strict religious belief system that only references a historical phenomenon. Significantly, he let religious rhetoric model more than a history of African American belonging. Moreover, in order to stray from the familiar narratives about what makes blackness blackness,[29] and in order for Baldwin to move beyond historical fact and a mimetic representation of the African American lifeworld, he frustrated the connection to a past through religious words that do not draw into relation, so cleanly, rhetorical figures of speech with racially distinct and injured bodies. In other words, he troubled history, with its claim on realism, by an innovative use of religious rhetoric.

Baldwin knew something back then that is now sometimes forgotten: Christian forms of religion do not uncomplicatedly belong to African Americans, especially for African Americans who, like John, do not necessarily want the history provided by the black church. In his famous attack on the protest fiction that dominated the African American literary scene of his early career, Baldwin critiqued Harriet Beecher Stowe's portrayal of black characters. He disliked the way she "would cover their intimidating nakedness, robe them in white, the garments of salvation; only thus could she be delivered from ever-present sin, only thus could she bury, as St. Paul demanded, 'the carnal man, the man of the flesh.' "[30] Stowe solidified, according to Baldwin, the link he then troubles in *Go Tell It on the Mountain*: "black equates with evil and white with grace."[31] By dramatizing this connection in the struggles of John, Baldwin highlighted the negative qualities of religion's relationship with the representation of black characters that a strictly historical reading misses. Baldwin did not want to articulate, uncritically, the relation that makes black evil, without investigating other possible meanings that blackness could have, even within such a pernicious, religious language. So as he fixated on the sinful qualities of blackness, Baldwin questioned the more ambivalent relationship that African American characters have with the religious descriptors that too conveniently become the signs of a coherent African American history with a coherent community—a primary obsession of African American literary and cultural work. As he moved away from the protest tradition of African American literature, part of his written labor and innovation, then, was the creation of a piece of writing that does not "bury" the "carnal man, the man of the flesh," with a white, religious-historical garment that confirms the flesh's negative (and black) carnal qualities. He wanted the flesh to assert something more than a version of historical and literary captivity, the extension to slave culture that continues to hurt, imaginatively, the ancestors' descendants.

Within his critique of African American historical and originary obsession, Baldwin assigned to the queer a very critical role. The carnal man of the flesh has, in Baldwin's imaginary, queer flesh, and this flesh is deemed, by the hate expressed by religious belief, quintessentially sinful and related to a history of enslavement. Queerness quickly signals such sin because Baldwin understood just how toxic sovereign Christian rhetoric, *even* in its black church form, is for the queer body. For instance, Baldwin's most obliquely black novel,[32] *Giovanni's Room,* pushes the private love plot out of a small, private space into the open, but devastating, public sphere that makes the protagonist's "love" deadly. David's spurned lover, Giovanni, whom the narrator David could not let himself love and support, is executed. David imagines Giovanni's final moments as follows.

Mary blessed mother of God

He [Giovanni] kisses the cross and clings to it. The priest gently lifts the cross away. Then they lift Giovanni. The journey begins. They move off, toward another door. He moans. He wants to spit, but his mouth is dry. He cannot ask that they let him pause for a moment to urinate— all that, in a moment, will take care of itself. He knows that beyond the door which comes so deliberately closer, the knife is waiting. The door is the gateway he has sought so long out of this dirty world, this dirty body.[33]

The Christian words echoing throughout the passage frame the inevitable and sought-after death of the novel's queer outlaw, Giovanni. Here, the movement toward a violent death is figured as inevitable, a necessary next step, now that the queer affect has been made public by a series of misfortunate events in the novel. David's interior monologue (the primary mode of the novel's narration) responds to his imaginings of Giovanni's final moments: "And I look at my body, which is under sentence of death. It is lean, hard, and cold, the incarnation of a mystery. And I do not know what moves in this body, what this body is searching. It is trapped in my mirror as it is trapped in time and it hurries toward revelation."[34] The contemplation of Giovanni's body loops back into the contemplation of his own. And while David is confused by his desires, the narration of David's mediated voice ranges from oblique Christian reference ("the incarnation of a mystery") to quite explicit allusion ("hurries toward revelation"). The severity of the situation, as well as the severity of David's first real moments of open regret are punctuated and punctured by the religious rhetoric in David's thoughts. He concludes:

> I long to crack that mirror and be free. I look at my sex, my troubling sex, and wonder how it can be redeemed, how I can save it from the knife. The journey to corruption is, always, already, half over. Yet the key to my salvation, which cannot save my body, is hidden in my flesh.
>
> . . .
>
> I move at last from the mirror and being to cover that nakedness which I must hold sacred, though it be never so vile, which must be scoured perpetually with the salt of my life. I must believe, I must believe that the heavy grace of God, which has brought me to this place, is all that can carry me out of it.[35]

Until this point, religious language has been conspicuously absent from much of the text. Both characters can hardly be described as devoted to any religion. But because there's no explicit mention of David's desire for Giovanni, we can conclude that the appearance of religious words helps render not religion but queer desire. The "key" to "salvation" is "hidden" in David's flesh—it is a nakedness that David must hold sacred. Moreover, this religious body is not cracked open by this key. Instead of revealing explicitly this nakedness, religious language helps express, while still concealing, the "hidden" qualities lurking within queer flesh.

Religious language thus functions to represent, however negatively and obliquely, the socially painful minority qualities of same-sex sexuality that have been unfairly attacked by the forces of hatred and intolerance. And as

I've been pleading throughout this book, before we dismiss this less-direct form of representation, we must explore its usefulness. Nancy Armstrong, in a discussion of Toni Morrison's *Beloved,* succinctly asserts: "What matters is one's ability to constitute a self within the material givens of the moment, no matter how hostile are those givens to the very existence of such a self."[36] People crave representation, regardless how lethal such representations, at the level representation, may seem to the imagined integrity of a private body. With such logic, sometimes there is no such thing as bad publicity. Or, more accurately, sometimes bad publicity can serve other kinds of positive, descriptive functions that are harder to detect, and thus harder to condemn. I would not be inclined to argue that religious words are the only available "material givens," but rather that religious discourse responds well to the abusive calls of a hateful public not because it offers a spiritual therapy for the queer, but rather because it offers a powerful and strong racial voice that does not adequately describe the more personal, sexual affect occurring within the queer's body.

These religious representations, moreover, are not representations that directly refer to the history of the literal body; unlike Foucault, the queer political subjectivity articulated by the religious representation does not luridly describe the corporeal. Through religious language, the Baldwinian queer *figuratively* responds to the pathological public sphere's demand for a recognizable, jeremiadic "array of defects." It does as much by making the queer minority's voice an authoritative, racial voice—one that circulates in a pathological, if not sacrificial, register. The religiously represented queer assumes the persona of racial injury in order to gain publicity in a pathological sphere, in order to have the representations and uses of public representation. The rhetorical assumption of injury gives a value that makes the queer not disposable. These uses of religious words are not the same heterosexual statutory and narrative enfanchisements Berlant and Warner assign to official, "normal" public culture.[37] Instead, religious language is a strong language that simultaneously hides *and* articulates the queer within the more "normal" and recognizable narratives of racial violence, pleasure, and survival that people understand as constituting the public, however intimate or pathological that public might be.[38]

Despite the pain of being normal or going public, membership in a normative story does have its privileges.[39] Near the end of *Go Tell It on the Mountain*, John comes through his conversion experience with the desire and the "struggle to speak the authoritative word"[40] of his father's religion. As this quotation suggests, religious words, indeed, have a unique and strong position in John's community, as well as the history of critical discourse. Jonathan Culler correctly suggests, "Religious discourse and religious belief seem to occupy a special privileged place; as though it went without saying that any sort of challenge or critique were improper, in bad taste."[41] This resistance to critical engagement with religious rhetoric has much to do with a huge volume of religious studies scholarship constantly elaborating the dichotomized relationship between "the sacred and the profane,"[42] scholarship that has an interest in maintaining a privileged category of the "sacred." The sacredness of the religious rhetoric is coded as both a limit of language, the expression of what cannot be expressed, as well as the literal indication that something exists outside of language, and by extension, human culture.

Baldwin's own critics rely on a similar separation between religious and critical discourses.[43] David Leeming, Baldwin's biographer and former secretary, comments that the reception of *Go Tell It on the Mountain* indicated a fundamental misunderstanding of Baldwin's work: "Some reviewers saw it as a work that was concerned primarily with ethics and religion."[44] People refused (and still refuse) to engage his religious discourse critically, and thus read the "religious" as a "belief system" that Baldwin must eventually abandon in favor of his more "secular" writing concerns (race relations, homosexuality, nation-formation, literary invention). For example, Sondra A. O'Neale concludes her essay on the force of religion in Baldwin by explaining something he said to Nikki Giovanni: " 'Well, it depends on what you mean by God . . . I've claimed Him as my father and I'll give Him a great time until it's over because God is our responsibility.' Although that is not belief, his religious rhetoric at least indicates that his search for God, his primal father, is not abandoned."[45] Here, O'Neale struggles, like many of Baldwin's critics, to situate Baldwin's arguments in relation to an under-articulated "belief" context. It seems as if we can never be rid of the sacred/profane discussion, and other critical engagements are left out of the picture. Because Baldwin does not appeal to "belief," or to a discussion of how religious belief works, O'Neale dismisses the religious in his work. For O'Neale, Baldwin must then be talking about the importance of fathers. And critics who want to use Baldwin to understand religious belief, ritual, and doctrine wrestle with the manner in which he evacuates religious language from its historical specificity. Baldwin, although called a preacher by some,[46] is neither a theologian nor a historian. One learns very little about the religious traditions and "belief" Baldwin references throughout all of his work. But this peculiar employment of religious rhetoric does not devalue its place or importance in his work. And religion has a peculiar role to serve.

In all texts with religion as a feature, religious rhetoric, despite its sacred aspirations, still appears in quite worldly cultural artifacts—words. We thus have some profane problems with which to contend. I outlined my theory of religious rhetoric in the first chapter, but I want to deepen that theory through the close scrutiny of Baldwin in order to flesh out the significance of religion's rhetorical authority. I want to know why it is a language that is so fruitful for the kinds of embedded oppositional politics I see operating in queer, "like race" uses of religious hate speech. I return to Burke, who writes: "In general, there was a tendency to assume a simple historical development from the 'sacred' to the 'profane,' from the 'spiritual' to the 'secular.' But logology systematically admonishes us against so simple a dialectic."[47] By the term "logology," Burke means an in-depth study not about theology per se, but about people's relationships to words that indicate religious experience. "We are to be concerned not directly with religion," explains Burke, "but rather with the terminology of religion; not directly to man's relationship to God, but rather with his relationship to the *word* God.

Thus the book [Burke's study] is about something so essentially rhetorical as religious nomenclature."[48] Through his approach to religious rhetoric, Burke redirects critical attention away from the sacred/profane dialectic and into a more demanding taxonomy of how religious words work.

As I argued in the first chapter, Burke exploits the hierarchy, indeed, the "strength," of religious nomenclature. Through a series of analytic analogies, Burke addresses the privileged rhetorical force and power that religious words are thought to have. Confronting the "sacred" not as a category beyond experience but as a category that *claims* to be beyond experience, Burke investigates just how sacred rhetoric achieves the sensations of its "superior" position in (or beyond) discourse. He concludes that the feelings of sacredness in religious rhetoric come from their linguistic characterization as the supreme title of experience. Burke explains his "fourth analogy," which I only partially quoted from in the previous chapter:

> Imagine the ideal title of a book. An ideal title would "sum up" all the particulars of the book. It would in a way "imply" these particulars. Yet the particulars would have all the materiality. Similarly, with a movement towards a title of titles (the unifying principle that is to be found in a sentence, considered as a "title" for the situation it refers to): such a movement is towards a kind of *emptying,* it is a *via negativa*. . . . The stress in the fourth analogy is not upon this negative element, but upon a search for the title of titles, an over-all term (which turns out to have this negative principle as an essential part of its character) . . . the fourth [analogy] concerns the nature of language as a process of entitlement. Such a secular summarizing term would be technically a "god-term," in the sense that its role was analogous to the over-all entitling role played by the theologian's word for the godhead.[49]

There is something semantically thrilling about using words that refer to the "sacred" or the "god-term." Of course, the continental formations of logocentric philosophy enter into this description, and one can read the paragraph recalling Derrida.[50] Yet, as I have said, Burke is so important because he dubs religious rhetoric as a search for the "title of titles," the ultimate entitlement. Whether or not religious words can actually guarantee such authority is not as important *as recognizing the desire that some words have for such ultimate authorizations.* Religious language that seeks this kind of entitlement, that wants to be authoritative and powerful while still claiming to reference some kind of experience, is a language that craves and is thought to provide definitive speech. In other words, according to Burke, religious language (among other things) attempts to be a language of powerful, unquestionable speech. As I argued, it is the language of the sovereign. Religious language is a form of speech that *thinks* it can order other kinds of speech, and it therefore parades as the most public and authoritative (read normal) mode of talking. I hope, here, we can recall Agamben's *homo sacer,* for it is this figure that is neither sacred nor profane, but a powerful figure that enables sovereign authority to thrive. Religious language is an entitlement tool that enables the sovereign to assert control not only over meaning, but also those who need meaning to count as valuable and thus not disposable—for instance, the queer.

But Burke does not stop there. By fixating on multiple analogies in order to theorize the force of religious language, he gives us directions for why the sovereign power of the entitled titles is not comprehensive, and perhaps why Baldwin would then fixate on a religious rhetoric that can make the injury of race communicate the value of queerness. There's a concealing function within this powerful religious rhetoric, which helps explain why religious language's "like" racial properties are so operative for Baldwin. In Burke's fifth analogy, the anxiety of a religious sentence's "history" in discourse is most directly addressed. Burke writes:

> Here [in an Augustine quote] the succession of words in a sentence
> would be analogous to the "temporal." But the *meaning* of the sen-
> tence is an *essence,* a kind of fixed significance or definition that is not
> confined to any of the sentence's parts, but rather pervades or inspirits

the sentence as a whole. Such meaning, I would say, is analogous to "eternity." In contrast with the flux of the sentence, where each sylla-ble arises, exists for a moment, and then "dies" to make room for the next stage of the continuing process, the meaning is "non-temporal," though embodied (made incarnate) in a temporal series. The meaning in its unity of simplicity "just is."[51]

The flux of a religious sentence, the movement in time of particular words, is not unsettling when the "essence" of an "eternal" sentiment inspiriting the sentence is thought to be freed from the possible historical derivations that the temporal words might produce. I do *not* intend to assert that there really is an essence lurking within religious words, that there is something radically ahistorical and essential in a religious sentence. Burke is much more critical when he explores the *connotations* of a lan-guage that wants to be sacred, that functions *as if* it were sacred and essen-tial. The words, certainly, are important because they manifest the hope for sustained intention and meaning within the fleeting existence of a sen-tence in time—a sentence at the mercy of a language that exists within a disintegrating history. But the sentence as a whole retains its importance because the words are thought to matter less than their fixed significance, or "essence." Religious words thus create an aura of underspecified whole-ness that, somehow, points to a significant "essence." As the earlier analogy helps articulate, the authorizing words of the religious make its words seem entitled to this aura, despite the potentially negative movement into words that might contradict the essence, or intention, of the sentence. The reli-gious sentence will then always mean an enduring something, but a some-thing not necessarily specified in and stringently bound to its language. This "essential" sensation, combined with Burke's earlier analogy of entitle-ment, helps us understand that the religious sentence will thus mean a something that cannot be characterized, but that which can be guaranteed in its validity and ability to mean ultimately without a reliance on specificity. The religious sentence produces value, then, regardless. For instance, it does not matter specifically what the word "Amen" describes; instead, it is a strong speech act, enabling the religious thought, experience, or emotion to have a definitive weight.

Certainly, there are similarities between Burke and Baldwin. In "Every Good-bye Ain't Gone," Baldwin repeats the story of Ezekiel's wheel, a story of a theophany that represents that which cannot be, by virtue of religious doctrine, visibly rendered: the image of God. Baldwin writes:

> *Circumstances*: a rather heavy word, when you consider it, connecting for me, by means of Ezekiel's *wheel in the middle of a wheel*, with the iron, inescapable truth of revolutions—we black folk say what goes around, comes around. Circumstances, furthermore, are complicated, simplified, and, ultimately, defined by the person's reaction to these circumstances—for no one, no matter how it may seem, simply *endures* his circumstances. If we are what our circumstances make us, we are, also, what we make of our circumstances. This is, perhaps, the key to history, since *we* are history, and since the tension of which I am speaking is so silent and so private, with effects so unforeseeable, and so public.[52]

All people are circulating, circularly, in publicity, and this publicity forces everyone to take on the burdens and pleasures of representation. Importantly, these publicized histories are also "heavy words," words made understandably heavy with the religious allusion and word "Ezekiel." These histories cannot escape the "truth of revolutions," they cannot escape the manner in which the repetition of historical circumstance suggests the "truth" of God, of Ezekiel's wheel, that goes around regardless of what happens in the human's circumstantial world. The significance of history, of people, then, accrues value not because it is history, but because the unspecified history reflects a religious meaning that will mean something *ultimately*.

For Baldwin, religious language, then, serves to lend definitive, strong, and valuable characterizations to people circulating within circumstantial history—"heavy," definitive codings that characterize rather than describe historical circumstances. In other words, the religious register provides a mode of talking that *seems* powerful and valuable without needing to communicate anything specific. Religious words thus parade as meaningful expressions that are not contained by their historical, lexical transformations, or even its specific referents. There is another story lurking behind the abusive words: an unstated "essence" that we have faith exists. Religious words then do not describe historical situations and people directly. Instead, religious rhetoric suggests something powerful that need not specify from where that power comes.

It is extralegal speech, and it belongs to the sovereign, kind of. But because it is a language that is so nonspecific, with a power that has no essential source, it can be quickly spoken by others, but still retain the sovereign power to assert what is valuable. So in Baldwin, religious words work as an excellent dialect that gives voice to the queers who might not be able to specify exactly what they are trying to say: they make heavy and meaningful their queer desires, but the words acquire that meaning not from a specific narration of actual, historical sex acts, but from the authorizing, normal authority that already disregards any of the particular histories a queer might want to articulate. Put another way, religious language's sovereign power is a powerful illusion that perhaps anyone can access. And more specifically, the language of religious hate is open to anyone who can then manipulate that authoritative register in unforeseen ways. By taking on the strong, valuable words of hate, queers, that is, can begin to speak grandly, with great outrage, not about specific, historical injustices they endure, but rather something that won't be specified. This rhetorical gesture, perhaps, might be more important than telling the "real" historical story of queer difference that can never compete with the guaranteed force and meaning of the sovereign's word—the force and meaning that comes, in part, from its hatred of queers.

In weariness and painfulness in watchings often, in hunger and thirst, in fastings often, in cold and nakedness. / He began to shout[53]

But accessing strong, authoritative speech to conceal the queer minority's complaint is not nearly enough. One still needs to disturb the public, which is a public, as I suggested in the first part of this chapter, made legible by the language of hate and pain. In her essay, "Wounded Attachments," Brown asks, "what are the logics of pain in the subject formation processes of late modern politics?"[54] Although she rightly notes that modern, painful identities often "redraw the very configurations and effects of power they seek to vanquish,"[55] this effect cannot be the *only* effect of one's nominal investment in an identity in pain. Yes, there are indeed very real and very pressing painful concerns that must be addressed in oppositional politics. But something more emancipatory might also be possible as one takes on the quick and strong publicity offered by a martyred condition that acts *as if* it is something painful. One's injured claim might not be as comprehensive, accurate, or perhaps as truthful as one might represent.

When Baldwin's John, for instance, falls to the floor to convert, the descriptions conspicuously are not realistic but fantastical: the descriptions of the pain of religious conversion are imagined—they are in John's head. Despite the numerous images of physically injured bodies brought on by religious conversions, these violent images do no "real" harm to his body. The physical violence provoked by hate is *entirely* imaginary. If the logics of pain in hateful political subject formation are also the logics of normal publicity, being public, as a despised minority, requires the assertion of an experience of injury. The images of corporeal harm brought on by religious words, however, does not describe John's hurt shape as much as it serves to point to what does not have an adequate language—a reference that defies conventional narratives of belonging. Specifically, the queerness of Baldwin's characters is oblique and underdescribed by the wounds of religious words created by his forced religious conversion. Queerness, I want to argue, is the strong, authoritative, but hidden story that the religious words

71

imply. And it is a sentimental story that is told subtextually, or even emotively, through the strong representations of racialized bodies in pain.[56] Hence, queerness becomes the ambiguous "it" of religion, of *Go Tell* It *on the Mountain,* that must be told, however indirectly and violently through a more recognizable drama of pain and violence: the drama of race.

But I must explain more slowly. When John experiences the power and force of conversion, he lies on the ground feeling the "agony" of religious conversion, and he questions, *"Is this It?"*[57] John's body is splayed out on the normal, pathological public of the floor of his church, where he is the center of everything. He cannot find the adequate voice to describe the transformations that are painfully occurring within "his soul."[58] "Soul," however, is not accurate. The "it," the queerness of John's experience, more specifically dwells inside his body. It is important to note that Baldwin was obsessed with what becomes a queer, biblical passage about Noah and his son Ham. John is twisting on the "threshing floor":

> Yes, he had sinned: one morning, alone, in the dirty bathroom, in the square, dirt-gray cupboard room that was filled with the stink of his [step]father. Sometimes, leaning over the cracked, "tattle-gray" bathtub, he scrubbed his father's back; and looked, as the accursed son of Noah had looked, on his [step]father's hideous nakedness. It was a secret, like sin, and slimy, like the serpent, and heavy, like the rod. . . . Then the ironic voice, terrified, it seemed of no depth, no darkness, demanded of John, scornfully, if he believed that he was cursed. All niggers had been cursed, the ironic voice reminded him, all niggers had come from this most undutiful of Noah's sons.[59]

Even though the tale has a specific exegetical history of interpretation, Baldwin uses this story as pathological shorthand for the birth of blackness. The scriptural narrative of Ham, who "saw"[60] a naked and drunk Noah, is, *for John,* the interpretation of how the mark and curse of Canaan (Ham's son) was originated. This passage, which famously has given racist ideologies a powerful scriptural justification, becomes a narrative explanation for why the sin of seeing, and desiring to see, the "nakedness," the "troubling sex," of John's stepfather is a reenactment of a same-sex sexual action that resulted in "All niggers [being] cursed." This story is a story of the inaugural queer sex act of Genesis that marks Ham's children as an inferior race.

Lee Edelman makes explicit the connections between homophobia and white racism that echo in this biblical verse. He argues:

> Made to articulate the "racial" dynamic of a masculinist culture, homo-phobia allows a certain figural logic to the pseudo-algebraic "proof" that asserts: where it is a "given" that white racism equals castration and "given" that homosexuality equals castration, then it is proper to conclude that white racism equals (or expresses through displacement) homosexuality and, by the same token, in a reversal of devastating import for lesbians and gay men of color, homosexuality equals white racism.[61]

Edelman's assertion that racism and homophobia are intimately linked is exemplified by the manner in which John interprets the Ham and Noah story: those who are not cursed by racism are those who did not see Noah's nakedness. White people are *not* descendants of Ham, so they never had a family member "look" at Noah's naked body; they never had a queer rela-tive, and so they are not subject to the mark of Canaan (blackness). But the queer Ham *did* "look" at Noah, he did engage in a queer sex act, and be-queathed the mark and curse of "blackness" to his ancestors. So, for John, not only do "homosexual acts" equal justified white racism, they actually create the "punishment" of blackness itself. Queerness and blackness are closely aligned in Baldwin's eyes—and with that connection he upsets tra-ditional, religious history about the blackness by founding the race through queer sexuality. He turns the history of the black race into a perplexing, religious and queer "It."

John is therefore encouraged to avoid the darkness of Ham's act and sons and, instead, achieve a "better" state of existence through his adoption of a religious morality that overtly denigrates and orders the "nakedness" of his desires and his body. The double bind of being black and queer pushes John farther away from a sinless, uncursed white Israel. To return to the promised land, if one who is bound by black queerness actually can, is to strive for a heterosexual "whiteness," which is another figuration of a toxic history of African American belonging that makes the black body religiously sinful in its queerness. From this perspective, John, through the narrative voice, ponders what God has to offer:

> "Salvation is real," a voice said to him, "God is real. Death may come soon or late, why do you hesitate? Now is the time to seek and serve the Lord." Salvation was real for all these others, and it might be real for him. He had only to reach out and God would touch him; he had only to cry and God would hear. All these others, now, who cried so far beyond him with such joy, had once been in their sins, as he was now —and they had cried and God had heard them, and delivered them out of all their troubles. And what God had done for others, He could also do for him.[62]

Reality and community are thus normative narratives of painful pasts that can be made better through the optimistic and strong, religious belief. There are grave difficulties resulting from "once be[ing] in [one's] sins," but the image of God offers a way out: if only John were to "reach out," to let "God touch him," God would deliver him like all of the others—"Salvation was real for all the others." Canaan's curse, John's reenactment of the origin of that curse, and the isolation that both the sin and the curse require, would all be eradicated if John were to cry out to God. This is the promise that "only the hand of God could deliver"[63]—a promise that suggests that Ham's queer sin could be overcome (that John's black body could be overcome), and that a better, more equal existence eventually would be achieved if only John were to become a Christian. Conversion is the way in which John could strive for the publicity of white straightness, free of queerness, that is also the story of the way African Americans can make themselves known in white, heterosexual sphere. According to this logic, this conversion, however, must kill the queer affect, the generating qualities of blackness and injury in a public sphere.[64]

Significantly, in John's conversion experience, the intention to replace queer affect with a new, more socially and spiritually acceptable heterosexuality that is tragic because of its racial injuries is not successful. The promise of conversion fails and John remains not only queer, but his queer feelings are given a religious voice. He mines the hostile rhetoric of the church to articulate the troubling affect of his "sex." Baldwin later describes the conversion experience with a humming:

> [it] was a sound of rage and weeping which filled the grave, rage and weeping from time set free, but bound now in eternity; rage that had no language, weeping with no voice—which spoke now, to John's startled soul, of boundless melancholy, of the bitterest patience, and the longest night; of the deepest water, the strongest chains, the most cruel lash; of humility most wretched, the dungeon absolute, of love's bed defiled, and birth dishonored, and most bloody, unspeakable, sudden death. Yes, the darkness hummed with murder: the body in the water, the body in the fire, the body on the tree.[65]

Instead of conversion turning to rebirth, conversion aurally turns toward a death that scatters the dead body all over the landscape: the water, the fire, and the tree. Eventually, the humming, the inarticulate sound, does stop, and John learns to speak his father's authoritative text. He learns to speak the black, religious lament for white normalcy and legitimacy— the religious lament for sovereignty's value and protection. But here's the rub: John is still full of inarticulate queer feelings that can only be forcefully voiced through his newly acquired rhetorical position: "He wanted to stop and turn to Elisha, and tell him . . . something for which he found no words. 'Elisha—' he began, and looked into Elisha's face. Then: 'You pray for me? Please pray for me?' "[66]

What this story provides is the characterization of the "religious" as a helpful publicity that can only be effective if it characterizes itself (not its queer bodies) as a potent and toxic publicity—as a racial injury that needs the white garments of salvation. But this characterization is simply that: a characterization. John can use the racial language of his community to suggest a queerness that is still very much present, but hidden behind the black/white garment.

Although there is an admitted desire to be forthright about who "one is," the pathological, racist, and religious public sphere that so controls and organizes Baldwin's time, as it does our own, is not changing fast enough. In Baldwin's schema, queer bodies, through a racial, religious nomenclature, are given a public voice in pathological representation without having to have that voice lead back, in the form of actual physical violence, to the physical body. Queers are given a larger, abstract name, "saved," that is valued by the nation but does not accurately represent the queer and, instead, makes that "racial" (and queer) body work or function within a larger community: "He moved among the saints, he . . . was one of their company now . . . he scarcely knew how he moved, for his hands were new, and his feet were new, and he moved in a new and Heaven-bright air."[67] When queers assume the safety of religious expression, although at the level of representation it might seem like violence, religious words actually endorse the queers' ability to be public. In other words, religious rhetoric is not the queer's own specific voice—it's the racial voice that the public already can hear. The rhetoric, the renaming offered by Jesus, not the historically ravaged queer body, gets to do the talking—thereby enabling intimate forms of communication that are racially legible and yet not queerly intelligible. As a consequence, suddenly, John is able to assert, " 'I'm going to pray God,' said John—and his voice shook, whether with joy or grief he could not say—'to keep me, and make me strong . . . to stand . . . to stand against the enemy . . . and against everything and everybody . . . that wants to cut down my soul.'"[68] John, despite the way his body shakes his authoritative voice, has the ability now to stand up against the world, to address the world, and to remind people that he was "saved," and that he can now move with the aid of prosthetic voice that the violent conversion into religious words has offered. Although John has not confessed his desire, he expresses powerful emotions, which is still an important political gesture.

Indeed, John has found an authoritative name that does not erase him into the difficult whiteness that is supposed to be offered by the conversion. His religious language does not negate the fact that he is, indeed, still queer and thus black. He now has the language that hides and speaks his own difficult circumstances:

> And the Holy Ghost was speaking—seeming to say, as John spelled out the so abruptly present and gigantic legend adorning the cross: *Jesus Saves.* He stared at this, an awful bitterness in his heart, wanting to curse—and the Spirit spoke, and spoke in him. Yes: there was Elisha, speaking from the floor, and his father, silent, at his back. In his heart there was a sudden yearning tenderness for holy Elisha; desire, sharp and awful as a reflecting knife, to usurp the body of Elisha, and lie where Elisha lay; to speak in tongues, as Elisha spoke, and with that authority, to confound his father.[69]

John, through religion, finds the speaking authority, a holy tongue of Elisha, if not the holy tongue of the sovereign, as he is wrenched out of his cursed heart. This authority, which seems so violent in its images, approximates the "sudden yearning and tenderness" he has no ability to communicate explicitly. This hate's authority has some love and tenderness—queer feelings that have no voice. But we should not be utterly dismayed by the silence: this authority provides a crucial distance from and perspective on the conditions of his life that offer only racial damnation—the life world of his father and the saints. And this distance is what creates a sentimental punch that forces us to see that there are differences between words and bodies. Such a figural distance, reinforcing the distinctions between the figurative and the literal, reminds us that there can be fields of resistance even within the most normative and violent of words. There can be another kind of racial "essence" indirectly referred to by a "normal," sovereign religious expression—the tragedy of queerness that craves a name, however antagonistic that name is supposed to be. Such queer inflections remind us that although public, rhetorical expressions might viciously excite and express racial injury, there might be another, more literal and sentimental story of a child whose self, whose skin, might be hidden from a hateful and pathological congregation by something like a pulpit.

3 Like a Prayer

God Almighty no

James Baldwin was not the first writer of queer and African American experience to use the rhetorical race feelings made possible by religious hate speech. So in this chapter, I want to give Baldwin a history. I start with Jean Toomer and his *Cane,* published in 1923. Throughout the last section of Toomer's book—and with much of *Cane*—the prevalence of a specific kind of religious language is striking. Rather than detail a kind of Christian belief, the religious rhetoric emphasizes the deep conflicts the central character, Kabnis, experiences as a displaced African American teacher in a racially hostile South. He laments: "God Almighty, dear God, dear Jesus, do not torture me with beauty. Take it away. Give me an ugly world. Ha, ugly. Stinking like unwashed niggers."[1] Kabnis's voice writhes much like his body, and his blasphemies follow an inconsistent logic: "God, he doesnt exist, but nevertheless He is ugly. Hence, what comes from Him is ugly" (83). Kabnis, through God-talk, is wrestling with some voice from within. Siobhan Somerville has helped us see this text as a queer and race narrative, which I find so helpful. But we can augment that reading by explaining why the hideous, religious words help express a sexuality that is made most salient by a race narrative.[2] We might as well change, as Kabnis will soon, his wish for an ugly "world" to the wish for an ugly "word," for Kabnis offers a series of ferocious, unappealing expletives to make the gorgeous southern landscape resemble, be like, "unwashed niggers." As in Baldwin, the connotations of dirt and race are here emphasized by the evocation of an outraged religious language (Kabnis often starts sentences with an emphatic "Jesus" or "God"), and this "dirty" language gives us an idea of the even harder to describe queer desires. In a long, late speech, Kabnis offers a drunken theory about the difficulty of expressing what lurks within his African American body:

> KABNIS: Cant keep a good man down. Those words I was tellin y about, they wont fit int th mold that's branded on m soul. Rhyme, y see? Poet, too. Bad rhyme. Bad poet. Somethin else youve learned tnight. Lewis dont know it all, an I'm atellin y. Ugh. The form thats burned int my soul is some twisted awful think that crept in from a dream, a godam nightmare, an wont stay still unless I feed it. An it lives on words. Not beautiful words. God Almighty no. Misshapen, split-gut, tortured, twisted words. (110)

So much is unnamable inside of him, but it needs to be fed, and it is fed on words that come from an ugly, hateful lexicon.

The kind of "literature" that Kabnis must produce in order to speak about "the form that's burned int" this black folk's soul is a twisted, incomplete, bad rhyme, and it's quite ugly. But this kind of ugly language is necessary because, as Kabnis quickly qualifies, "This whole damn bloated purple country feeds it cause its goin down t hell in a holy avalanche of words" (110). It seems that Kabnis understands America's pathological rhetoric; he seems to understand, however unaware he may be, the deformed jeremiad that sees unholiness everywhere. He combats it with his own take on the holy avalanche—a take that twists a race and a sexual narrative into an imprecise, hateful, and bad form of expression. There are no easy words; there are only arduous and treacherous ones, which have the power to access the limited narratives of belonging—the limited narratives of authority and sovereignty—that are available for those who must find a way to make a public, minority complaint. What I want to suggest is that the Kabnis story tells us that we need bad words, bad poems, when making public statements about dangerous sexual desires. And although Toomer is a literary figure, and not the most traditional icon of queer writing, the struggles around public expression that bewilder Kabnis still have a special, if not accidental, insight into a longer history of lesbian, gay, bisexual, and trans resistance and liberation. It is a troubled history that relies on the figurative, the rhetorical, or what we might simply call the "literary" to articulate, torturously, queer feelings. Often this literary vocabulary comes straight from an angry God. And, although literary, it is not eloquent.

We are confronted by nominal choices that precede, influence, and project any designs we might have on political and cultural transformation.[3] But often, we use the wrong names to make a claim on representation. Even though "queer" is a useful word—one on which I rely—it still fails to capture the sheer expansiveness of queers' experiences, especially if I am saying that word in order to achieve certain political and legal effects. Identities somehow connected to one's sexual orientations are most likely as diverse as the potential desires that anyone might have. Nevertheless, there must be translations of those desires into an identity that can go public.

These routes into legible political identities, however, are fraught because queers are forced to have a strained relationship to the language of political respectability or value. We are not permitted easy access into proper, political language for numerous fallacious reasons: for example, one Illinois judge in 1897 described homosexual sodomy as that which is "not fit to be named among Christians."[4] But whether or not "sodomy"[5] or any kind of queer practice or affect "fits," the consistent not-naming, the silence that, even as a small group of New York AIDS activists in 1987 proclaimed, equals death, homosexuality has never been completely silent.[6]

Before Gay Pride, queers had to take linguistic or rhetorical detours or indirect routes into public expression.[7] One of the earlier, and now most iconic, pre-Stonewall gay activist groups, the Mattachine Society, created at nearly the same time as James Baldwin's publication of *Go Tell It on the Mountain*, pursued various nominating strategies intending to inspire political change. The need for group coherence required a form of naming that was capable of confronting, however indirectly, that period's culture of persecution, danger, and repulsion—not to mention the McCarthy un-American "witch hunts" that focused on communists and homosexuals, among others. This group of men and women, many of whom were both homosexuals and communists, were faced with some difficult decisions about what unified this sexual minority:

> Throughout the winter of 1951 the five men [who headed the Mattachine Society] met frequently to share their histories, focusing especially on their gay experiences. They exchanged stories of coming out, of discovering cruising places and bars, of the years of loneliness. Trying to find patterns in their individual experiences, they posed questions: How did one become a homosexual? Was homosexuality an adopted trait, or was it innate? Were homosexuals sick? Did the five exhibit the psychopathology that supposedly characterized the homosexual personality? If not, why were some homosexuals so disturbed? Were there special cultural traits that developed in a gay life? Were homosexuals merely a conglomeration of individuals sharing only a sexual orientation, or did they perhaps have in common something more that made it feasible for them to work together?[8]

The Mattachine Society, as well as other groups such as the Daughters of Bilitis, were certainly galvanized by the hugely popular, best-selling Kinsey reports on sexuality published in the late 1940s and early 1950s. But the sharing of stories and the profuse questions that still elusively pursue the ways one even begins to imagine what makes sexual orientation into an identity and a community deserving of social equality could not be just a statistical and scientific account. There had to be a way to translate the larger-than-assumed numbers of homosexuals into representations that could be uttered and that would make strategic sense.

It was the legacies of coalitional associations between other oppressed groups that helped the Mattachine founders to determine what unifies sexual minorities. Will Roscoe explains:

> The Lesbian/Gay movement has often been portrayed by historians as arriving on the coattails of the Black civil rights and women's movements. That is, these movements developed the goals, principles, and strategies of identity-based politics, and Lesbians and Gays borrowed them in the 1970s. But the origins of the Mattachine . . . require a correction to this view. In the 1940s, the concept of "ethnicity" as a cultural-political identity not subject to assimilation was no less controversial when applied to Black Americans than to homosexuals. There is nothing "natural" about viewing Black Americans, Chicanos, women, and other groups as having a culture, history, or art, although we take such views for granted today. That we do so reflects in no small measure the enduring legacy of the 1930s Popular Front.[9]

Michael Denning explains the Popular Front as "the insurgent social movement forged from the labor militancy of the fledgling CIO [Congress of Industrial Organizations], the anti-fascist solidarity with Spain, Ethiopia, China, and the refugees from Hitler, and the political struggles on the left-wing of the New Deal." Through these movements, a radical sense of coalitional and leftist politics gained an increased importance in U.S. politics and culture: "Born out of the social upheavals of 1934 and coinciding with the Communist Party's period of greatest influence in U.S. society," explains Denning, "the Popular Front became a radical historical bloc uniting industrial unionists, Communists, independent socialists, community activists, and émigré anti-fascists around laborist social democracy, anti-fascism, and anti-lynching."[10] And according to Roscoe's suggestion, these coalitional movements gave many minority groups fundamental and transferable understandings that one's "ethnic" history and culture of oppression need not be assimilated, and that those ethnic understandings can galvanize political and social movements.

Such insights were crucial: "Out of their discussions," writes D'Emilio, "an analysis gradually emerged of homosexuals as an oppressed cultural minority."[11] Homosexuals faced "ethnic exclusions," and they "were [victimized] by a 'language and culture that does not admit the existence of the Homosexual Minority.'"[12] This conception of homosexual minority politics was not necessarily a "born that way" argument such as the one Donald Cory makes in *The Homosexual in America*. Instead, the Mattachine deliberately applied the "cultural understandings" of racial and ethnic status[13] in order to argue not for comprehensive and singular understandings of the homosexual minority, but, as one founder of the society, Harry Hay, urged at the group's first discussion in 1950, the "basic and protected right to enter into the front ranks of self-respecting citizenship, recognized and honored as socially contributive individuals."[14]

It is extremely relevant that many of these political movements had also been so influenced by a leftist charged literary landscape that had been developing in the United States at least since the late nineteenth century, and which took perhaps its most "effective" form, according to Denning, in the 1930s "mobilization around civil liberties and the struggles against lynching and labor repression."[15] It is no accident that the "Cultural Front," which Denning's study of its aesthetic and cultural dimensions describes, joined with the protest power of literary and other cultural artists and critics (such as John Dos Passos, Malcolm Cowley, Langston Hughes, Edmund Wilson, Kenneth Burke), who saw explicit political connections between activism and their own writing practices. These artists ushered in a "new generation of plebeian artists and intellectuals who had grown up in the immigrant and black working-class neighborhoods of the modernist metropolis."[16]

A political literature of protest, either through anti-slavery and early feminist movements of the mid-to-late nineteenth century, or through the genres of realism and naturalism that gained momentum during industrialization, urbanization, and the great migration of the late nineteenth and early twentieth-century United States, did produce some wonderful gains. But such a focus also did some harm that persists to this very day, but harm that can be undone by the very insights groups such as the Mattachine undermine by their cultural rather than biological understandings of racial and ethnic oppression. Let me explain. The Popular, or Cultural, Front of the 1930s pursued a specific genre of political activism—literary activism—that had been flamed by the social, cultural, and political arrangements of a modernizing and decidedly unequal United States. This literature sought out harsh versions of "realism," difficult and quasi-accurate portrayals of the dire and unjust circumstances in the United States. William Stott describes the character and history of the Cultural Front's literary moment as obsessed less with literary achievement and more about social documentation: "I believe—though I never again put this belief so boldly—that the primary expression of thirties America was not fiction but fiction's opposite. This genre of actuality I call by the name given it then: documentary. And I see of its essence as the communication of not imagined things, but of real things only."[17] We can extend Stott's conclusions to a larger history of American letters, one obsessed primarily with realism rather than imagination. Although modernist experiments with language and form obviously made their mark, critic Lionel Trilling was shrewd when he wrote about the dominance of American realist writing, which required us to be extremely critical, to be always in a state of protest. He believed that "there is only one way to accept America and that is in hate; one must be close to one's land, passionately close in some way or other, and the only way to be close to America is to hate it; it is the only way to love America."[18]

Such an overwhelming sentiment about hating America is often heard in criticism about a literature devoted to exposing the "truths" of American culture—the protests about or from the marginalized, the minority.

Although there are certainly exceptions and although such a statement is overly stated, there is also a common assumption that the "subaltern," or the oppressed, must always wield this hateful critique that is close to "land." The literature of American minority is thought not to be too fanciful or interested in crafting aesthetically invested works of art. As a result, the atrocious "realness" of one's minority status is presumed, even at the expense of noting that the deliberate manipulation of the minority's words might not be so invested in an "actual" or "real" "hate." In a discussion of Chinese writing, Rey Chow persuasively has advanced an argument that certainly can be applied to our own discussion:

> No matter how nonmimetic, experimental, subversive, or avant-garde such diasporic writing might try to be, it is invariably classified, marketed, and received in the West as Chinese, in a presupposed correspondence to that reality called China. As in the case of representations by all minorities in the West, a kind of paternalistic, if not downright racist, attitude persists as a method of categorizing minority discourse: Minorities are allowed the right to speak only on the implicit assumption that they will speak in the documentary mode, "reflecting" the group from which they come.[19]

Chow is echoing a common lament about the reception of minority writing. There is an assumption that letters about or by racial and ethnic minorities in the United States and elsewhere are assigned too much truth-value, even when there might be something more figurative or rhetorical in the expression. But there must be more than realism for minorities. There must be something more than documentaries about the minority condition in the United States that still persuade us that social justice must be done.

I am convinced that the legacy of the Mattachine, through its "like race" strategies of group articulation, has helped queers escape some of the realistic traps of other protest politics and literatures. It is with this cultural and literary historical backdrop that could often trap those expressing minority life in too much realism that I want to frame the various queer literary maneuvers that produce not actual or even realistic political coalitions but rather political names for queerness that maintain that distance between the literal and the figurative. By building upon my last chapter's readings of Baldwin, I want us to understand that the rhetorical addition of queerness to the race story evacuates much of the realism from the assertion of minority difference. Such an evacuation might remind us that "race" might simply be, among other things, a "cover" story, a figurative and strategic narrative capable of hiding the other salacious, if not inarticulate, stories that can't be easily pronounced using the conservative, religious idiom of traditional, national belonging. When the blackness of Baldwin's John is also like his queerness—when something that is supposed to be so antithetical and paradoxical is made almost equivalent—our ordinary and knee-jerk understandings of the categories of both "queer" and "race" are interrupted. I hope we are then encouraged to read deeply into the words that swirl around Baldwin. I hope we are encouraged to think deeply about the words he chooses in order to make himself connected to those who are not ready or willing to accept the complexity of his racial and queer difference. One can grasp that Baldwin's and Toomer's craft reveals that the religious Word, the community's "normal" sovereign lexicon, is not merely as literal as fundamentalists believe. It can be wrenched away and thrown deliberately into the imaginative, rhetorical landscape of fiction. For it is "literature," where queers, as Eve Kosofsky Sedgwick so elegantly describes, can read for important news about themselves, and do, sometimes reluctantly, through the "arduous defile through textual interpretation."[20] In other words, the "literary" has historically and enormously powerful functions; figurative, self-conscious language, as we are seeing throughout my archive, has proven instrumental in the ways that queers have conceptualized their own political challenges to the religious and national fundamentalism that necessarily despises them.[21]

Although perhaps overlooked, the incorporation of literary strategies in queer representation and politics, furthermore, is hardly a new or contro-versial tactic. Literature by or obliquely about minority sexuality has long been cited, used, enjoyed, made iconic, and referred to by many pro-queer activists for some time. The trials of Oscar Wilde, flamed by his literary achievements; the obscenity controversies over the publication of Radclyffe Hall's *Well of Loneliness*; writers from the Harlem Renaissance; and Virginia Woolf's *Orlando* and Walt Whitman's poetry, for instance, all frequently appear in the early writings and apologies for homosexuality. It makes sense, then, that the activist "homophile" magazine that was started by early members of the Mattachine Society, *One Magazine,* was named after a Thomas Carlyle quotation, and featured issues such as July 1954's "The Mystery of Walt Whitman." In that number, close readings of Whitman's poetry and biographical details were employed by the magazine's writers to debate both Whitman's homosexuality and whether or not "Whitman's disavowal [of his explicit sexual leanings was] a resort to the public masks almost all homosexuals must use?"[22] The publication and reception of "queer" literature had and continues to have an important contribution to make to LGBTQ politics. Perhaps resorting to a "public mask" was and is not so much a disavowal as a literary form of willing concealment—a lin-guistic prophylaxis in a pathological and intimate public sphere. Months before *One's* special issue on Whitman, the magazine, in a piece called " 'Thorn in the Spirit': The Homosexual on the Horns of a Christian Dilemma," contains very literary and somewhat incoherent speculations about religion and homosexuality. It named same-sex sexuality and eroti-cism a "dark secret" called "the thorn" in the flesh.[23] In lieu of easy names or accurate facts, we find "a holy avalanche of words" that is mistaken, wrong, hurtful, and twisted. But it floods the emotions and impresses rather than documents the feeling of racial injury queers claim in order to be intelligible as misfits who could be considered valuable in the U.S. nation-state. This rhetorical, religious play gives queers a "like race" model of literary articulation, which is a powerful queer protest, if not queer coping mechanism, that emerges as a hideous mistake. "And it lives on words. Not beautiful words. God Almighty no. Misshapen, split-gut, tortured, twisted words" (110).

Make Me Feel Real

Curiously, we find these "misshapen" words in some unlikely protest literatures—literatures that predate Baldwin and Toomer. Take, for a strange example, the naturalist and realist writing of Stephen Crane, who, during the time of Oscar Wilde, experienced and wrote about the late nineteenth century challenges of post-Reconstruction U.S. industrialization and urbanization. Often he wrote provocatively about the socially excluded parts of his America. In one short story in particular, "An Experiment in Misery," Crane presents us with a socially minded youth who goes "slumming" in the lower parts of New York City—the Bowery—in order to figure out how a "tramp" "feels."[24] According to George Chauncey, the Bowery was a spectacle for homosexual activity, "the center of the city's best known sites of homosexual rendezvous at the turn of the century." Chauncey also reminds us perhaps why Crane's youth, who is writing from an eye on documenting and reforming, travels to the lower regions of Manhattan: "As the anti-vice crusaders who sought to reform the model order of turn-of-the-century American cities discovered," Chauncey argues, "gay male society was a highly visible part of the urban sexual underworld and was much more fully and publicly integrated into working-class than middle class culture."[25] Typical of the closely related genres of American naturalism and realism, the story features a youth who travels to document and "see" the slums—to witness the kinds of subculture, sexual and otherwise, he might find in this center of "commercialized vice."[26] And what he found was a center full of curious men. Many have taken Sedgwick's long influential cue to read "the 'homosocial' back into the orbit of 'desire,' of the potentially erotic," enabling us then "to hypothesize the potential unbrokenness of a continuum between homosocial and homosexual."[27] Crane's more "homoerotic" than "homosexual" writing can then also be considered queer. But more than being an example of queer literature, Crane's story illuminates the way a queer writing could find expression in the kind of literary protest work that was executed at this point in U.S. history.

There was much cultural reporting that inspired people to think, or at least wonder, about those who were increasingly disenfranchised by the industrialization and urbanization of an America that had moved swiftly away from its theocratic roots in the Plymouth Colony. The realist and naturalist penchant to survey and account for the degraded American populations, moreover, became an eroticized operation of the eye. As Mark Seltzer argues, in realist and naturalist fiction of the late nineteenth and early twentieth centuries, this powerful desire to "see" is also a desire to touch, "a complex and tense interaction between vision and embodiment, between the visual and the corporeal."[28] We might say that as the youth wants to see, he learns to touch and thus be "touched" by the experiment. The senses can be confused when one wants to document something so homoerotic. At key moments in the story, his desire for understanding and surveillance obscures his ability to see. For instance, while spending a night in an all-male, cheap lodging house, a place described as dark and full of "unholy odours," we have the confusions of the youth's sensual point of view:

> And all through the room could be seen the tawny hues of naked flesh, limbs thrust into the darkness, projecting beyond the cots; upreared knees, arms hanging long and thin over the cot edges. For the most part they were statuesque, carven, dead. With the curious lockers standing all about like tombstones, there was a strange effect of a graveyard where bodies were merely flung. (160)

The ability to see clearly gives way to morbid imaginations of imprecise bodies that are positioned in an incoherent, "flung," manner. So this young reporter resorts to a more intuitive project of articulation. He soon hears a disturbing sound in the air of this room:

the sound in its high piercing beginnings, that dwindled to final melancholy moans, expressed a red and grim tragedy of unfathomable possibilities of man's dreams. But to the youth these were not merely the
shrieks of a vision-pierced man: they were an utterance of the meaning
of the room and its occupants. It was to him the protest of the wretch
who feels the touch of the imperturbable granite wheels, and who then
cries with an impersonal eloquence, with a strength not from him, giving voice to the wail of a whole section, a class, a people. This, weaving
into the young man's brain, and mingling with his views of the vast
and somber shadows that, like mighty black fingers, curled around the
naked bodies, made the young man so that he did not sleep, but lay
carving the biographies for these men from his meager experience. At
the times the fellow in the corner howled in a writhing agony of his
imaginations. (160–161)

Numerous features of this passage must be noted. First of all, clarity of
vision is obscured by the dark, which lends the youth another kind of perspective from which he can interpret the noises and sights of the space as a
particular kind, style, of protest. This protest's eloquence, moreover, is described as "impersonal," belonging not to one individual, but to an entire
group or class. Immediately, a personal expression or confessional mode of
anguish and hardship is thwarted. Instead, we start to "see" the naked men
as synecdoches for the "wretched," but the wretched at rest, recreating in
the darker spaces of the night, removed from the travails of the day. Significantly, we don't have realism, or even naturalism, here. Instead something
else appears—romance.

Romance is a literary concept that might include what we conventionally know as a "romance" between two partners, but more significantly
denotes escape, transgression, possibility, lack of clarity, darkness, mystery,
etc. In the context of the Crane story, we have the writing of men's bodies
cast in a romantic genre, a form of departure from the restrictions of reality
or realism. Bill Brown tells us that "the recreational [in Crane and other

American realist and naturalist work] becomes a chronotope [a name for richly layered time-space figures] that by excluding those 'actualities . . . so terribly insisted upon . . . in America,' as Hawthorne phrased it, permits the American novel to explore the romantic possibilities within the parameter of realism."[29] Through the homoerotics of the bodies recreating, we have a romance that violates the genre of actuality and reporting with the elusive and dark feelings of the wretch, feelings that overwhelm the youth. The carving of the unspecified "biographies" out of these naked men's bodies is described as a homo-eroticized recreation that is analogized to race: "like mighty black fingers, curled around the naked bodies."

With something like romance on the brain, Ralph Ellison, who wrote an introduction for a later edition of Stephen Crane's most famous novel, *The Red Badge of Courage*, advocated another theory about how "race" operates as a symbol in society and culture. I mentioned Spillers's reading of Ellison earlier in the book. But let me focus directly on Ellison's version of the uses of "blackness." Ellison—years before Toni Morrison popularized (but did not cite) his ideas about the dark Africanist presence in American literature —was keenly aware of the manner in which "the Negro" had an enormous impact on American literature and culture since the so-called Enlightenment. "And while the Negro and the color black were associated with the concept of evil and ugliness far back in the Christian era," writes Ellison, "the Negro's emergence as a symbol for value came, I believe, with Rationalism and the rise of the romantic individual in the eighteenth century."[30] He understood that the value of blackness[31] is not singularly a value of no-value, but rather value that came from its status as an "evil" symbol that could be more than evil: "The romantic was in revolt against the old moral authority, and if he suffered a sense of guilt, his passion for personal freedom was such that he was willing to accept evil (a tragic attitude) even to identifying himself with the 'noble slave'—who symbolized the *darker*, unknown potential side of his personality, that underground side, turgid with possibility, which might, if given a chance, toss a fistful of mud into the sky to create a 'shining star.' "[32] In other words, there is revolutionary, if not fraught, value in the "black" even if that blackness had always been religiously associated with sin and evil—Baldwin's *Go Tell It on the Mountain* certainly suggests as much. Yet this complicated dynamic adhering within the "negative" of blackness is lost, according to Ellison, in the twentieth century in part because the twentieth century loses its struggle with the enlightened concepts of "democracy" and "freedom."[33] For Ellison, something about the political achievements of modern America had flattened the otherwise round symbol of blackness, rendering blackness as an evil that could not imply the "nobility" or revolutionary appeal of earlier, rational moments. In other words, during the twentieth century, "the Negro" loses his ability to be rhetorically vital, to be manipulated in peculiar ways. "The Negro" fails to be thought of as emancipatory words, and instead the symbol of "the Negro" is caught in its "evil and ugliness," or, I would add, its obsessive realism that does not permit romantic oppositions to be suggestive and inexplicit. Perhaps influenced by Ellison's notions about what blackness can accomplish when it is not flattened into an anti-supple realism, Henry Louis Gates, Jr., argues, "Black literature is a verbal arts like other verbal arts. 'Blackness' is not a material object, an absolute, or an event, but a trope; it does not have an essence as such but is defined by a network of relations that form a particular unity."[34]

I am convinced that when writers such as Baldwin, Toomer, and Crane resort to the religious and racial cover story to speak of sexuality, they are engaged in a play of analogization between race and sexuality ("like" race) that reflects Ellison's claims about revolutionary appeal of the black figure. They permit the black designation also to speak, indirectly, of the "potential" and "muddy" quality of queerness that can also become a "shining star," if not a religious star. Ellison quite simply reminds us that "blackness" can function as a trope. Further, something about the religious language he and others—such as Crane in his story of a lost youth—employ paves way for the possibility of "romance," or "sexuality," or that which is unspeakable and defined, but still a feeling that is very much there, in the dark. And in the shadows by the bed, "black fingers" with a horrible weight are daring to "speak" a religious tongue. And these fingers so fruitfully become confused tongues. Let me explain.

In his introduction to *The Red Badge of Courage,* Ellison describes Crane in terms often assigned to Baldwin: "Crane was concerned very early with private emotions publicly displayed as an act of purification and self-definition; an excellent beginning for a writer interested in ordeals of the private individual struggling to define himself against the claims of society. Crane, who might well have become a minister, turned from religion but transferred its forms to his art."[35] It's no wonder that twisted or transformed religious rhetorics help Crane display those private emotions. At the end of "An Experiment in Misery," the slumming youth articulates his own private ordeals against a social backdrop that fails to account for the private emotions that cannot be easily explained. Instead, the voice of the narrative sums up the youth's "unholy" experience of sight, sound, and touch with a religious image of the Tower of Babel—the Ur-religious image of the confusions of language. The youth sits in the City Hall Park and watches the people, "the people of the street hurrying hither and thither made a blend of black figures changing yet frieze-like" (165). He then watches the New York skyline. The passage reads:

> And in the background a multitude of buildings, pitiless hues and sternly high, were to him emblematic of a nation forcing its regal head into the clouds, throwing no downward glances; in the sublimity of its aspirations ignoring the wretches who may flounder at its feet. The roar of the city in his ear was to him the confusion of strange tongues, babbling heedlessly; it was the clink of coin, the voice of the city's hopes which were to him no hopes. (165)

The youth is unable to report, cleanly, what he has seen, quite possibly because the clarity of his vision is obscured by the sexuality and romance of the experiment, and what he has felt and feels now has no easy or ordinary form of communication. Instead, sounds and voices are confused, and the proud edifices of the city—the towerlike structures of modernity and progress—speak not hope but babble. This babble and these strange tongues produce the kinds of confusion exemplified by the biblical story of the Tower of Babel, which is told, according to the New Revised Standard Version commentary of the Hebrew Testament, "to portray divine judgment upon the continuing sin of humanity."[36] But the darkness of the fingers, the darkness of the city's sins, cannot be made assertive or strong enough to emblematize the "nation forcing its regal head into the clouds." Instead, the subordination, represented by confused tongues, must exist in wretched and hopeless figures at the bottom of the towers, at the bottom of the social ladder, and indeed at the bottom of otherwise clear and unified expressions. We can read the "wretched" as located in the lower, less-articulate parts of the urban and literary landscape, without easy recognition or, more importantly, easy articulation. But that does not mean that there is only silence. There is all kinds of confused talk, religiously marked as "inferior," generating sympathy and sentimentality that might inspire a romantic, revolutionary sense that we should do more than sit down in our despair.

Crane is writing, or babbling, about what we could call queer figures through religiously inflected figures in black during a time of great interest in those who are "flounder[ing] at the feet" of those in higher social positions. One of the closest historical associations we have with an "Experiment in Misery" is Jacob Riis's *How the Other Half Lives,* an illustrated reporting of late nineteenth-century immigrant and tenement living, including whole chapters devoted to the kinds of cheap lodging houses found in Crane's text. Riis, a police reporter who became a social reformer, published his own lived "experiment in misery," in the form of a study, eventually replete with illustrations, musings, and eventually photographs of New York's Lower East Side. This work is drenched in a highly sentimental and morally indignant tone that sought, with varying degrees of success, to transform the living conditions of New York's most oppressed inhabitants.

Because he was a reform-minded writer, Riis peppered religious language and allusion throughout his prose. But crucially, such rhetoric is not about advocating specific religious beliefs. Instead, his language lends weight to the severity of social ills he sees among so much misery. The book was written in response to the "moral firmness" of Alfred T. White's advocacy of well-built apartments. Upon hearing White's social reform agendas, Riis "wanted to jump in [his] seat at that time and shout Amen."[37] Religious phrases have a rhetorical enthusiasm that conveys the extreme seriousness and sentiment of the public work Riis and others did, and indeed, his very popular project struck a moral chord, like many social reformers—such as Ida B. Wells-Barnett[38]—and "seared the conscience of prominent New Yorkers," reaching the targeted audience of reform—those who could perhaps make some sort of difference.[39] The text caught the eyes of religious-minded social crusaders such as Dr. Charles H. Parkhurst, and Riis received numerous invitations to speak on the social ills of the United States—social ills that were then frequently filtered through a religious voice often characteristic of many moments of national lament.

The first chapter of *How the Other Half Lives* is boldly and religiously titled, "The Genesis of the Tenement," and starts with a biblical allusion that is racialized and sexualized: "The first tenement New York knew bore the mark of Cain from its birth, though a generation passed before the writing was deciphered."[40] Riis encourages our own decodings of the mark as he interprets the tenements. We've read Baldwin's own take on racial marks, the mark of Canaan, which is often confused with the mark of Cain —both marks are often "deciphered," exegetically, as theological rationale for racial division and hierarchy that is founded in a nonnormative, homosexual desire. And Seltzer, in his reading of Riis (and another Crane story), tells us that the racial and other "hyperembodied bodies" that one desires to see are so quickly sexualized: "this eroticizing power" makes the "(social) other half," in terms of the "(sexual) lower half."[41] At Riis's historical moment after the so-called successes of anti-slavery activism, this mark sufficiently remarks on the severity of social injustice infesting these tenements.

National heterosexuality, as is to be expected during most social reform moments, rears its ugly head. The youths Riis documents without families are considered criminals.[42] He quotes the 1860s testimony of the secretary of the Prison Association of New York: "By far the largest part—eighty per cent. At least—of crimes against property and against the person are perpetrated by individuals who have either lost connection with home life, or never had any, or whose *homes had ceased to be sufficiently separate, decent, and desirable to afford what are regarded as ordinary influences of home and family*" (1, emphasis in the original). Riis quarantines those who are disassociated from home: "The boundary line of the Other Half lies through the tenements" (1). The boundary of the Other Half, the Lower Half, is the precise line Crane's youth crosses, and it's a line that ushers him, like Riis, into a world of dark and unholy spaces, with homeless people searching for stability and hearth, but instead only finding dark fingers, prostitution, substance abuse, different races, and ethnicities.

Riis also importantly casts the boundary of the Other, Lower Half in specifically racial terms at a crucial moment in his text. In the same language of lines, and just a few years before W. E. B. Du Bois's famous declaration about the twentieth century, Riis writes: "The color line must be drawn through the tenements to give the picture its proper shading" (115). The word "proper" and all the frequent plays on the language of color throughout the narrative (e.g. "shading," "that his [the white landlord] does not quite make as black a mark as it did") suggest that all the unholy social decay of the text will be put into appropriate highlight, finding the language that will impress upon, that will leave "dark" enough "pencil marks" about the most severe moments of injustice that crowds this social world. Quite aware of the power of the late-nineteenth century's familiarity with the sentimental anti-slavery plea, Riis, amid even-then disturbing generalizations of "the negro," made significant nods to the genre when describing the ways that African Americans are the "lowest level" of this Other, Lower Half: "Of such slavery [the even worse housing conditions of Black Americans], different only in degree from the other kind that held him as a chattel, to be sold or bartered at the will of his master" (115).

Such resonant moments when the perils of social injustice can be made most salient by references to the tragedies, if not the religious tragedies, of slavery are indeed frequent in both Riis's and Crane's literature and reporting (in more or less fictional testimonies of documentary experience). The tragedies of the Other, Lower Half, doubly marked by the concern over race, feed emotional, overwhelmed aesthetics. We're then left with the kinds of religious images of the confusion of tongues we find at the end of Crane's story. The protest aesthetic becomes a prosthetic romantic aesthetic that leaves us with the artifice of images of the hopeless wretches, with a sinful sense of the nation that cannot make good on its religious promise. It is a fallen culture, and the youth falls into a dark and unholy space where he "confessed himself an outcast, and his eyes from the lowered rim of his hat began to glance guiltily, wearing the criminal expression that comes with certain convictions" (165). The youth is lost to a kind of outcast criminality we've seen—he is the jeremiad scapegoat; he is the dark and seedy outsider who is left only with "criminal expressions" he must wear when addressing or acknowledging the national pride that attempts to reach, through its towers, "God." Yet this outcast position, this heedless babble, functions not as a defeat but as a precondition for the articulation of wretchedness, weakness, or alterity, conjuring up the kinds of sentiments that will move people into exploring what might be behind the babble, what sins have occurred that must be rectified. Who has been left out of the national religious promise? Who confuses our national language about nation, self, and citizenship? Whose value might we have neglected? Would their loss count as a sacrifice?

As I mentioned already, sentimentality has a racial force that is hard to deny. Kenneth Warren argues that the legacy of *Uncle Tom's Cabin* was something that could not be denied at century's end. He perhaps sheds light on the combination of images we often circulated through a sentimental kind of documentary "experiment":

For writers such as [Henry] James, [William Dean Howells], and [George Washington] Cable who believed, albeit in different ways, that fiction could count heavily in the quest for social betterment, Stowe was an inspiration and a problem. The success of her novel confirmed the belief that fiction could achieve social and political ends yet her success seemed to accommodate a deplorable aesthetic. Her characters were often sentimentalized, her plot often creaky, and her attention to craft apparently nonexistent. In light of these perceived failings, the definition of the realistic novel as an instrument for altering social relations could not include an embrace of a sentimental aesthetic. In fact, some of the central tenets of that aesthetic—a dedication to duty, the valorization of sacrifice and renunciation, and appeals to the heart rather than the head—were often held up for critique and ridicule within realistic fiction.[43]

Despite their refusal of the "deplorable" emotional aesthetic's "failings," realist and naturalist modes of narration persistently appeal to the heart rather than the head. Warren tells us that the realist text must contend with *Uncle Tom's Cabin* and sentimentality in general, even if the two kinds of writing often seem opposed. He seems to suggest that they are related genres even if they are thought not to fit together.

Protest and sentimentality, realism and romance, and all sorts of tangled categories of fiction and politics make the work of describing how the Other and Lower Half lives exceedingly difficult. We should not dodge such difficulty. I think we should keep our critical glare on the manner in which the highly "deplorable" feeling aesthetic persists throughout the late nineteenth and twentieth centuries, with numerous writers relying on the articulation of race relations as a point of comparison that will articulate queer relations. With black fingers come a deplorable aesthetic, bad poems, and bad rhymes. And within that awful aesthetic, we have a babbling that produces an emotional force that impresses an intense feeling of wrong.

Theological Terror, Theological Babble

For the sake of a more "appropriate" and less oblique instance of queer work, I turn now to *another* literary example, a bit more contemporary and explicit with its homosexual content: Tennessee Williams's *Suddenly Last Summer.* In the play, the matriarch, Mrs. Venable, laments the loss of her child, Sebastian, a poet, to the perils of dangerous sexuality that she had long known about, but a sexuality that she had had the ability to control, participate in, and describe to others. Her official statement about their time together is one of profound beauty and high art. "My son, Sebastian, and I constructed our days, each day, we would—carve out each day of our lives like a piece of sculpture.—Yes, we left behind us a trail of days like a gallery of sculpture! But last summer—."[44] Sure, she was able to make their days "like art," by which she means that she obscures and makes beautiful their shared adventures. The untold, the silent story is perhaps less appealing: Mrs. Venable, an attractive woman, would be the bait that would attract men for the predatory impulses of her son's homosexuality. Men would flock to her, but be enjoyed by her poet. But suddenly last summer, she not only lost her son, but also her control over the public narrative about her son's sexuality. And because this high "art" is more flattering than the truth, Mrs. Venable is at a loss when certain details about last summer come to light, details offered by her niece, who replaced an aged Mrs. Venable as Sebastian's lure on the annual summer trip: "With her tongue for a hatchet, she's gone about smashing our legend" (26). So, not surprisingly, Mrs. Venable wants the truth about Sebastian's deviant sexuality to remain concealed, or contained, which is why she wants a doctor to lobotomize Catherine.

It might be a mistake to look to Tennessee Williams as an example of the kinds of queer protest literature I have been describing. He is not what one might call the most optimistic of queer playwrights. But the mistake is important. The queer figure in Williams's plays provokes a kind of sentimentality we have been pursuing in this book: the queer activates the sensations and concerns over the kinds of losses homosexuality might exact on the childlike men Williams offers in plays such as *A Streetcar Named Desire* and definitely *Suddenly Last Summer.* Certainly, *Suddenly Last Summer's* critiques of medicine, especially psychoanalysis, refer to Williams's own personal distress over cruel operations such as lobotomies; and this critique is a further hesitation over the ways that medicine and criminality combined to produce an oppressive force in the queer lifeworld, demonizing and offering the possibility of relief over the drama of homosexuality. Yet beyond its well-known themes over the clash between medical "science" and sexuality, *Suddenly Last Summer* features the confusion, if not the deliberate silencing, of queer tongues that cannot say queer names, but can cite, in bad, babbling literary language (bad rhymes, bad poems) the drama of God in order to align themselves with the race protest the United States needs in order to understand and make legible the oppression of its citizens.

It is not surprising, then, that Mrs. Venable characterizes Catherine's confessions about what happened to Sebastian, why he was killed, as "babble," as nonsense that must be stopped, and even if, as the doctor cautions, he "can't guarantee that a lobotomy would stop her—*babbling!*" (30, emphasis in the original). Mrs. Venable would at least want Catherine's words not to be believed, not to be trusted. She was the final witness, so she must be discredited. Something must be lost, then, in Catherine's translation of the event.

But Catherine is the victim who will appear on stage, not Sebastian. In many ways, she is no longer his decoy but his replacement. And rapidly we understand that her struggles with expression, with putting up with oppressive forces that would prefer her silence, are standing in for the silenced queer's struggles of articulacy. And, as we should anticipate by now, the persistent recourse to the description of the religious confusion of tongues, to babbling, is the rhetorical tactic Williams chose to represent the sentimental tragedy of homosexuality in an unjust and cruel society.

In the tradition of translation theory, "Babel" is an image that has a hold on the critical imagination. From George Steiner's *After Babel* to

Jacques Derrida's "Des Tours de Babel," one can understand the complexity of translation across languages, groups, and constituencies by thinking about the biblical story, which instructs us about confusion.[45] Derrida, in particular, reminds us perhaps why we rely on the name, "Babel," today:

> The "tower of Babel" does not merely figure the irreducible multiplicity of tongues; it exhibits an incompletion, the impossibility of finishing, of totalizing, of saturating, of completing something on the order of edification, architectural construction, system and architectonics. What the multiplicity of idioms actually limits is not only a "true" translation, a transparent and adequate interexpression, it is also a structural order, a coherence of construct.[46]

Babel's inability to translate is about more than losing something in translation. Babel signals that coherency, legibility, order, completion, among other "totalizing" operations (say, something like realist, racial distinctions) are often failed undertakings, for there is, as Babel marks, "an internal limit to formalization."[47]

Williams creates a babbling drama that pushes queer language to this very "limit," and he makes information about a queer life into Babel-like confusion and incoherency. He relies on a Tower of Babel as well as a series of religious and literary allusions that obliquely characterize the sentimental story in racial terms. The religious story he uses is a hateful, vengeful one, propped up by what Williams included in a late draft of the play:[48] Herman Melville's 1854 travel sketches for *Putnam's Magazine,* "The Encantadas." These sketches feature a collection of images about the "enchanted" Galapagos Islands, particularly the scenes of sea turtles and a slave struggle—a struggle reminiscent of Melville's more well-known *Benito Cereno,* which includes similar conflicts over cannibalism and race.[49] According to Mrs. Venable, Sebastian read her an excerpt from the sketches, lauding the Encantadas' beauty. They were so moved, they felt the need to travel to these islands to witness the beauty firsthand. What they did see, however, was "something that Melville *hadn't* written about" (15; emphasis in the original), something Sebastian seems to have wanted to witness: the seasonal occurrence when newly hatched sea turtles would fall prey to "flesh-eating" birds.

Not accidentally, both the beach, because of the turtles, and the sky, because of the birds, were transformed into the "color of caviar," black. And by now, I hope we can understand the ways that color—with its narrative, romantic possibilities—is so connected with racial distinctions that can be invoked to improperly name the feelings and sensations of queerness in public. For the turtles, the flight from the beach back to the sea is one that results in acts of cannibalism that are rendered in a typically black hue: Mrs. Venable and her son are at a view to a kill, where the sea turtles rush "to escape the flesh-eating birds that made the sky almost as black as the beach" (16). A black vision of birds that were "diving down on the hatched sea-turtles, turning them over to expose their soft undersides, tearing the undersides open and rending and eating their flesh" (16). Mrs. Venable, "a reasonably loyal member of the Protestant Episcopal Church" (19), further qualifies this sight as an image of God, which Sebastian was looking for: "God shows a savage face to people and shouts some fierce things at them, it's all we see or hear of Him. Isn't it all we ever really see and hear of Him, now?" (20).

Over a decade earlier, in 1946, Williams wrote a story, "Desire and the Black Masseur," which can help us understand *Suddenly Last Summer*'s racialization of God's fierceness, his hatred, as one way to talk about queerness. It is the story of Anthony Burns, a small thirty-year-old white man with a face and a body that had "the unformed look of a child," which he "moved like a child in the presence of critical elders."[50] In fact, "in every move of his body and every inflection of speech and cast of expression there was a timid apology going out to the world for the little space that he had been somehow elected to occupy in it" (205–206). He is by all accounts a weak and uninterested character; the curious and aggressive fact about him, however, is his desire for being overwhelmed, for being taken over. In a figurative language of cannibalism, which soon becomes quite literal, we learn that Anthony, despite his nervousness, loves to be "swallowed up." He loves to be absorbed by experiences such as watching a film.

But we are also told that these consuming experiences are a relief from his sense of guilt through a particular feeling that fills him up: "This one [compensation] is found in atonement, the surrender of his self to violent treatment by others with the idea of thereby clearing one's self of his guilt" (206). It is quite easy, given typical narratives about race, to read guilt in this story as "white guilt." But I would caution us against such a quick read. The explicit content of the story makes the narrative more of a queer story, and we soon discover that his desire for absorption gives way to a desire for a sadomasochistic relationship he swiftly develops with a black masseur in a Turkish bath house. We have a very explicit account of the relationship:

> Burns tried vainly to move but the luxurious tiredness made him unable to. The Negro laughed and gripped the small of his waist and flopped him over as easily as he might have turned a pillow. Then he began to belabor his shoulders and buttocks with blows that increased in violence, and as the violence and the pain increased, the little man grew more and more fiercely hot with his first true satisfaction, until all at once a knot came loose in his loins and released a warm flow. (209)

This is, indeed, a complicated relationship, one that defies easy explanation or description. Of course, the language that is used to mediate the intimate, violent sex between white and black is the language of religion and the vague concept of "atonement" that provides the explanation for why Burns falls into this toxic and deadly sex play.

Near the end of the story, after the masseur has been fired for beating up his client, the two men still visit one another. For a week, during Lent, they stay in "the town's Negro section," repeating their erotic routines. I hope the soundtrack is by now too familiar:

Across from the room where Burns and the Negro were staying there was a church whose open windows spilled out the morning exhortations of a preacher. Each afternoon the fiery poem of death on the cross was repeated. The preacher was not fully conscious of what he wanted nor were the listeners, groaning and writhing before him. All of them were involved in massive atonement. (210)

Religious words, religious shouts, promise something like atonement, but immediately give the narrative a sense of intensity, which will punctuate the sexual acts being perpetrated in a room nearby. While the black congregation and the preacher are wailing, the black masseur beats Burns to death, and then begins to eat, slowly, Burns in his entirety. We don't hear the moans or screams of the couple. We only get very basic but graphic descriptions of the final encounter and last supper from the narrative voice. We have no strong and public utterances about the sex that occurs between the masseur and his lover; the only words are intimate communications, that can barely be heard: "Burns . . . whispering something," which is as vague as anything he explicitly says. " 'You know what to do now?' The victim asked him. The black giant nodded" (211). Kill and then eat.

But in public, we do hear the words of the black congregation. As a kind of prosthetic voice, we have the "not fully conscious" religious words that are uncertain about specifically what the speakers of the words want. Why are any of the characters seeking atonement? We hear: " 'Suffer, suffer, suffer?!' the preacher shouted. Our Lord was nailed on the cross for the sins of the world! They led him above the town to the place of the skull, they moistened his lips with vinegar on a sponge, they drove five nails through his body, and He was The Rose of the World as He bled on the cross!" (211). The strong, furious rhetoric refuses to be more specific than a familiar story of Christ's sacrificial atonement for the world's sins. And this story, these words, inspire the congregation to launch into an incoherent frenzy, much like typical, evangelical "speaking in tongues" ceremonies indicating the grip of the spirit on the various churchgoers. The service is so powerful that the congregation "could not remain in the building but tumbled out on the street in a crazed procession with clothes torn open" (211).

It is the unspecific punctuation on the complicated sex acts that interest me greatly. These unspecific acts bring us into a realm of feeling and protest that is both terribly sentimental and related to the "race problem" of the United States. In a passage that is reminiscent of "An Experiment in Misery," the story concludes. The black masseur waits for his next victim inside a "milky white door," and his sex is translated by the narration into what the story had been hinting at by revolving around a drama of black and white strangers. The story becomes a large question about race relations, which is also a story about queer relations: "And meantime, slowly, with barely a thought of so doing, the earth's whole population twisted and writhed beneath the manipulation of the night's black fingers and the white ones of day with skeletons splintered and flesh reduced to pulp, as out of this unlikely problem, the answer, perfection, was slowly evolved through torture" (212). Within this perhaps terrible "answer," the small, queer, boylike man is consumed, is "eaten" by blackness, by black fingers, with the drama of race being announced by religious lips, with religious shouts, with the somewhat incoherent, unconscious babbling of a black congregation.

Suddenly Last Summer operates with similar suggestive figures of Christian religious language, cannibalism, and blackness (such as the black consumption of turtles). According to his mother's euphemistic account of his summer, Sebastian's sexual pursuits were actually searches for "God" (19), for an image of God. What Sebastian does discover, however, is the distressing scene of the turtles, forcing him to exclaim, "Well, now I've seen Him!" (19). His mother translates the "Him" into God, implying that God is as destructive as the beach carnage. The doctor protests this explanation, because that image, that "equation" (19), is the kind of spectacle that is better "equated with a good deal of—experience, existence!—but not with God!" (19). The equation, the equivalence of that particular image is much too hideous to bare, especially if God were to be figured as that which brings us such carnivorous and upsetting events. Not missing a beat, Sebastian's mother demonstrates the flexibility of the meaning of Sebastian's, the poet's, image of God, which produces a more harmful vision of what one might encounter with God in a search for "poetry," a "search" that Mrs. Venable uses as the cover story for what their summers were really about. As I quoted above, Mrs. Venable explains, "He [Sebastian] meant that God shows a savage face to people and shouts fierce things at them, it's all we see or hear of Him. Isn't it all we ever really see and hear of Him, now?—nobody seems to know why" (20). This quest to see, to seek out the fierce, awful things shouted by God is the name for the travels she shares with her son, to the detriment of her marriage; their religious travels throughout the world, from India, China, and beyond lead all the way to the Hotel Cairo and the Ritz in Paris, which she calls, in what is almost the title of Ralph Ellison's most important collection of essays, *Shadow and Act*: "We—still lived in a—world of light and shadow" (21). As she drifts through these memories, and as the dashes in her speech suggest, she struggles for the language that will describe this quest for God's angry words. The language she settles on is most certainly a racial one, with the sinister, darker secrets of her son's darker passions quite present: "But the shadow was almost as luminous as the light" (21). And this shadow, this seeking for some experience of God, is what will eventually consume her child, her poet, her precious boy who has sexual leanings that cannot be explicitly named except by a literary and religious name that is emotionally activated by a drama of color, of race, indexed by the black birds that will eat the flesh of the helpless turtles.

Catherine's babbling, however, erupts into clarity, interrupting the deliberate obliquity or limits of queer expression used to describe Sebastian's "poetic" sensibilities. She translates the "real" story of Sebastian's and Mrs. Venable's travels. At the end of her own summer trip with Sebastian, after she has served as Mrs. Venable's younger, prettier replacement as Sebastian's decoy, she recounts what happened. She not only knows what they did last summer, she's going to tell all. So we learn that in Cabeza de Lobo, a band of young children decide to pursue Sebastian, with some between "childhood and—older" (88), who are begging for food, making "gobbling noises with their little black mouths, stuffing their little black fists to their mouths and making those gobbling noises, with frightful grins!" (84). Sebastian and Catherine recognize some of the older ones, implying that Sebastian has had some kind of liaison with them, casting the pursuit in terms confusingly situated between eroticism and revenge. But with their black mouths and fists, juxtaposed next to Williams's intense attention to the way that the sun made everything look "White hot, a blazing white hot, hot blazing white" (89), we have the pursuit also characterized as located in a conflict between black and white. And this racialized "band of naked children" pursued Sebastian and Catherine up a "steep white street in the sun that was like a great white bone of a giant beast that had caught on fire in the sky!" (91). Sebastian runs and the naked children begin to scream and are figuratively transformed into those flesh-eating birds: "I [Catherine] heard Sebastian scream, he screamed just once before this flock of black plucked little birds that pursued him and overtook him halfway up the white hill" (91). And in the final moments of Catherine's recollections, the confluence of race, cannibalism, sexuality, and the consuming of flesh are organized by the earlier image Sebastian has of God at the Encantadas, which is not unlike Williams's story of the black masseur:

> When we got back to where my Cousin Sebastian had disappeared in the flock of featherless little black sparrows, he—he was lying naked as they had been naked against a white wall, and this you won't believe, nobody has believed it, nobody could believe it, nobody, nobody on earth could possibly believe it, and I don't blame them!—They had devoured parts of him. . . . Torn or cut parts of him away with their hands or knives or maybe those jagged tin cans they made music with, they had torn bits of him away and stuffed them into those gobbling fierce little empty black mouths of theirs. There wasn't a sound anymore, there was nothing to see but Sebastian, what was left of him,

that looked like a big white-paper-wrapped bunch of red roses had been torn, thrown, crushed!—against that blazing white wall. (92)

Once he's dead, there is no more sound, no more of the children's hideous music, or their gobbling, or their "Ooompa! Oompa! Oooooooompa!" (87), which Catherine cannot help but repeat and babble up to the moment when she reveals the "secrets" of the naked and eaten Sebastian.

We are taken to an awful scene that nobody "on earth" could or should or would want to imagine: the consumption of the queer body by the ravaging forces that will tear apart flesh. We are not supposed to believe this story—it must be a mistake, even though the doctor ends the play with the notion that "we ought to consider the possibility that the girl's story is true" (93). But considering the truth is too much without "help." With no sound, with no horrible shouts, we are just left with a ravaged body that is unbearable to witness in its stark, ultra-white reality, which Catherine cannot endure. So she resorts to a final simile to dress him back up and put him back together in a poetic rather than awful way: his body "looked like a big white-paper-wrapped bunch of red roses had been torn, thrown, crushed!—against the blazing white wall . . ." (93). Significantly, this simile does not end, except in ellipses, implying that there are other figurations that could continue to elaborate his disassembled shape. But more importantly, the rhetorical concern with the white heat, the white wall, against which the naked "black" children lean, seem to be the ultimate collection of figures to describe the tragedy of Sebastian, who is hardly a saint.

I must stress, however, that we cannot just read allegorically in Williams for any coherent account of race relations; the "children" are only associatively racialized by suspect classifications of color and cannibalism. And my own reading of that association is made possible only by recalling Williams's earlier, short story. So we should not try to assign arguments such as: Williams is a racist because he's terrified by the way black bodies will eat white bodies; or that Williams resolved the "race" issue by feeding white bodies to the angry rage of black bodies in hopes of atonement for white guilt. Such explanations, which might be true in some senses, cannot take us as far in our analyses, and they won't activate the more figurative play of color, of blackness's revolutionary star, that writers such as Williams employ to cultivate an emotive dimension in the drama of queerness. Within this figurative object—a play—race, and for that matter, queerness won't bring us to a realist discourse that will guide us into a precise position within any political debate. Within this religious babble, we are at the limits of any formalization (including and especially the formalization of race and queerness) of any identity position. We do not really know much about Sebastian's queerness, other than it existed and was his death sentence. Instead, we are given queer figuration at the extremes of an emotional intensity of Sebastian's story, which might be true. What the rhetorical properties of blackness and whiteness, combined with religious confusion, will produce is a mixed-up, mistaken name for queer sexuality that will make us feel something is wrong. The deplorable protest aesthetic lurks within this story about last summer, but one doesn't know what one did as much as what one felt last summer: and one feels, as Baldwin does when he speaks of *Uncle Tom's Cabin,* "a theological terror, the terror of damnation; and the spirit that breathes in this book . . . [which] is not different from that terror which activates a lynch mob."

Yet this protest need not be at such a grand, social scale as much as a personal fury one cannot ignore: "One need not, indeed, search for examples so historic or so gaudy," writes Baldwin.

> [T]his is a warfare waged daily in the heart, a warfare so vast, so relentless and powerful that the interracial handshake or the interracial marriage can be as crucifying as the public hanging or secret rape. This panic motivates our cruelty; this fear of the dark makes it impossible that our lives shall be other than superficial; this, interlocked with and feeding our glittering, mechanical, inescapable civilization which has put to death our freedom.[51]

The "theological terror" of the protest motivates our cruelty—a motivation of which we should be suspicious, as Baldwin correctly notes. But we still cite and need this terror for people at least to feel, if not understand, that something is wrong and needs to be changed. We cite the terror in the hope that one will perhaps move beyond the terror, move beyond the angry faces and shouts of God that render our best "poems" hideous images that make us feel rather than report the violence that bodies will endure in the white, hot sun.

I am arguing that literary manipulation of the religious, mainly Christian language—a language that is so evocative of race—serves as the cover story for sexuality. Such a rhetorical move can be found in an established tradition of politically charged literature about the heedless babbling that obscures easy or coherent minority confessions, but a religious babbling that still gets the queer point mistakenly across. There is troubled minority complaint here, which we might sense rather than anticipate. In a number of significant ways, the "race card," as the earlier chapters demonstrate, is the "safer" or at least more legible figurative domain of American minority protest, especially in literature designed to provoke political action, notably through the very powerful forms of sentimentality that would have dramatic impact on the social and political settings in which they occurred— in books, for instance, such as *Uncle Tom's Cabin*. Baldwin, despite his literary and political condemnations of Stowe's work (and its inheritance he found in Richard Wright's work), recognized the power of overdone sentimentality, the power of contrived emotion, and he confesses his obsession with Stowe in his essay, "The Devil Finds Work." He "read *Uncle Tom's Cabin* over and over again—this is the first book [he] can remember having read."[52] Baldwin pushes that emotion into the realm of the imaginary that is political even if it is not entirely "realistic." And in an essay that appears at the close of his life, "Here Be Dragons," Baldwin explicitly works out the intricate relationship between "race" and "sexuality," works out the kinds of "revelations" he had been making his entire life:

The American idea of sexuality appears to be rooted in the American idea of masculinity. Idea may not be the precise word, for the idea of one's sexuality can only with great violence be divorced or distanced from the idea of self. Yet something resembling this rupture has certainly occurred (and is occurring) in American life, and violence has been the American daily bread since we have heard of America. This violence, furthermore, is not merely literal and actual but appears to be admired and lusted after, and the key to the American imagination.[53]

The "violence" of sexuality is trapped by traditional values of masculinity, which are figured as the "key" to the concept of both America and one's thinking about America.

By defying traditional forms of masculinity, Baldwin's queers helped push into literary practice the violence that has been present ever since America was first "heard." Something about sexuality is also like something about race, for both are conditions of what he terms American "freakishness," conditions that solicit powerful hatred because they "cause to echo deep within us, our most profound terrors and desires."[54] And he continues without much hope:

But we are all androgynous, not only because we are all born of a woman impregnated by a man but because each of us, helplessly and forever, contains the other—male in female, female in male, white in black, and black in white. We are part of each other. Many of my countrymen appear to find this fact exceedingly inconvenient and unfair, and so, very often, do I. But none of us can do anything about it.[55]

But we can feel something about the violent religious rhetoric always swirling around the queer. Once we break through the religious imagery, once we break down the Tower of Babel, the reified terror of suffering in a Christian nation, we have something else: a painful babbling, a confusion of tongues that is hardly silent, but a racialized collection of deplorable aesthetic noises, sounds, and eroticisms that speak indirectly a language of "hope." There is more to this hope than its aspiration; this language of hope, to certain characters such as Baldwin's John, Crane's reporter, Toomer's Kabnis, and Williams's Sebastian, was not just hope but something else, without an easy name: a difficult and very present feeling that we can only recognize as if they were like "dark fingers," and dark fingers pressed together as if they were like a harsh, difficult prayer.

4 Rights as Wrongs

The Hate State

Baldwin, Toomer, Crane, and Williams are perhaps a strange collection of writers to be considering some of the predecessors and practitioners of strategic political manipulations of the religious hate speech I describe in this book. But by taking us through a tour of these writers, I wanted to emphasize the necessity of thinking about the figurative in contemporary politic actions. My aim is to iterate that the insights garnered from theoretical and literary critical work have been, and will continue to be, critical for queer politics. In fact, I join Lee Edelman, who argues persuasively just how ironical, if not literary, queer politics can be if queers can "no longer disown but assume their figural identity."[1] So, in this chapter, I want us to consider the figural history of Colorado's Amendment 2, and specifically the "like race" comparisons that fueled this religious, political contest. The various strategies that had to be developed in order to stall the sweeping denial of basic civil rights of queers in Colorado were less oriented toward articulating "real" injuries, "real" abuses that might indeed have occurred if Amendment 2 had ever taken effect. Instead, a critical history of these political activities tells us much about how the queer rhetorical spin on religious hate has yielded at least one "success" in the fight over queer civil rights. The secret of this success might help us combat the current attack on queers in the early part of the twenty-first century. Let's begin.

The month following Colorado's passage of Amendment 2 featured abundant commentary by the citizens who were trying to make sense of the fury they had sparked by denying claims of discrimination to lesbians, bisexuals, and gays. Colorado Springs, the birthplace of the voter initiative and the headquarters for so much evangelical activity in the United States since the early 1990s, defensively responded, angered that an international boycott had already resulted in the cancellation of a national conference of the nation's mayors, originally scheduled to take place in the Springs. In the city's daily paper, the *Gazette Telegraph,* conservative editorials, stories, and letters contributed the bulk of the amendment's coverage. Even the very occasional condemnation of Colorado's vote was always overwhelmed by at least twice as many affirmations of the initiative's passage. This one-sided response certainly reflects the extreme conservativism of the city's population; but the commentary also reflects the effectiveness of Colorado for Family Value's campaign tactics, especially its race language.

In the *Gazette*'s December 20, 1992, editorial section, no fewer than two lengthy, angry responses to the amendment's fallout are fluent in the specific kind of racial rhetoric generated by the religious right. Michael W. Rosen's editorial, "Boycott Threats Will Only Harden Majority's Conviction," is particularly instructive: "Contrary to the hysterical ravings of gay activists, the passage of Amendment 2 was not an expression of hate. It wasn't even an expression of intolerance. It was an expression of disapproval. These are important distinctions." Important to these distinctions is that the line between disapproval and hate is a racial one, which marks the so-called social respectability that should not be given to queers. Rosen explains:

In voting for Amendment 2, more than 800,000 Coloradoans also said that they don't regard homosexual behavior as the moral equivalent of

race, religion, gender or national origin when it comes to special protection under civil rights law. In effect, they're tolerant of the homosexual lifestyle but they're not willing to confer upon it the mantle
of social respectability, something they should have every right to
withhold.[2]

There are crucial words to note in this racial morality contest as Rosen
explains his reasoning: the use of the words "lifestyle" and "behavior"
rather than "orientation," the preference of "tolerance" rather than "right."
Such words, and the lines of argumentation they draw, puncture all the
political banter on both "sides" of Colorado's homosexual question. The
choice of these words points to the most crucial elements that made the
passage of Amendment 2 both possible and, through the highest level of
national judicial review, untenable: the politics, language, and laws of racial "civil rights."

Although "civil rights" does apply, of course, to a list including gender,
nationality, religion, and other sorts of "differences," the U.S. history of
civil rights is certainly and centrally perceived to be a racial history, especially with its necessary reference to the equal protections guaranteed
by the U.S. Constitution and specifically the postslavery-inspired Fourteenth Amendment. " 'Like race arguments' are so woven into American
discourses, of equal justice," writes Janet Halley, "that they never can be
entirely foregone."[3] Halley is nevertheless critical of such discourses, especially when lesbians, gays, and bisexual movements have tried to share the
"successes" of racial civil rights arguments by announcing that " 'sexual orientation' is like race, or that gay men and lesbians are like a racial group, or
that anti-gay policies are like racist policies, or that homophobia is like
racism."[4] And as I have remarked, this kind of racial analogizing is often a
faulty strategy, to be sure. But it is *the* central strategy that worried both
conservative Christians and the queers who found themselves having to
respond to Amendment 2.

Something about race discourse, with its purported "mantle of respectability," produces a great deal of anxiety for conservative Christians. Race, in highly qualified and perhaps disingenuous ways, is considered by all sorts of people to be a legitimate form of minority difference, with an established history of injustice that has been, at least in some official capacity, recognized and deemed worthy of explicit government action since the end of slavery and the mid-twentieth-century desegregation rulings and civil rights acts. Whether or not religious and political conservatives were sincerely invested in the preservation of race politics and policies,[5] at least nominal respect of the racial civil rights agenda is a necessary political gesture. Yet more than a gesture, paying lip service to racial civil rights is also a rhetorical maneuver that can be and often is used to sustain civil rights abuses in the realm of queer politics. For instance, one of Colorado's central arguments advanced in Colorado's first trials on the constitutionality of the amendment, proving a "compelling government interest," asserted what much of the pro-Amendment 2 campaign often argued: established "suspect classes"—and the examples used were usually racial and ethnic examples—would be harmed by including queers under the mantle of such suspect respectability. The state claimed that Amendment 2 was necessary in order "to preserve the ability of the state to remedy discrimination against suspect classes by not requiring the state to expend resources prohibiting discrimination based on traits not considered suspect for purposes of judicial scrutiny."[6]

Almost maliciously, we discover at least two things: lesbian, gay, and bisexual folk are morally undeserving of the same protections as other traditionally discriminated groups—protections, incidentally, that have recently come under fire by a born-again Christian U.S. president and Congress. And, second, queers, so the very familiar story goes, would erode both politically and economically the effectiveness of current and "justifiable," morally "approved," and "respected" claims of racial discrimination.

But just as the "like race" status of queers sparked the success of Amendment 2, it was also the main issue why the court system could not let the amendment change Colorado's constitution. U.S. Supreme Court Justice

Kennedy, in his majority opinion of *Romer v. Evans,* which ruled against the constitutionality of Amendment 2, prominently refers to the landmark ruling of *Plessy v. Ferguson,* delivered one hundred years before *Romer.* In that case, which supported and fueled segregation between the United States's two dominant races, one lone dissenter, Justice Harlan, correctly worried about and predicted the kinds of civil rights violations that would be supported by "the seeds of race hate"[7] planted by upholding segregation policies. The Thirteenth Amendment, which outlaws slavery, and the Fourteenth Amendment, which provides guidance in making sure that fundamental rights would be guaranteed to all citizens, seemed to be, according to Harlan, ignored in order for the Court to deliver an opinion in favor of segregationist practices. In 1996, Justice Kennedy used Harlan's dissent to introduce the effects of Amendment 2:

> One century ago, the first Justice Harlan admonished this Court that the Constitution "neither knows nor tolerates classes among its citizens." . . . Unheeded then, those words now are understood to state a commitment to the law's neutrality where the rights of persons are at stake. The Equal Protection Clause [of the Fourteenth Amendment] enforces this principle and today requires us to hold invalid a provision of Colorado's Constitution.[8]

Kennedy, here, introduces the majority opinion on this case of lesbian and gay civil rights with the rhetoric of racial civil rights, making forceful connections to the history of hate that *Plessy v. Ferguson* shamefully recalls. This hate evokes the racist perils of what happens when laws, such as the permission of slavery, create invidious and suspect "classes" among the U.S. citizenry. Kennedy is clear that although that for "practical necessity" most "legislation classifies for one reason or another" people, sometimes to the detriment of that classification, the correct application of the Fourteenth Amendment's "promise that no person shall be denied the equal protection of the laws" should insure that those classifications must not burden "fun-

damental rights," nor "target a suspect class." They must "bea[r] some relation to some legitimate end."[9] But Amendment 2 "lacks," writes Kennedy,
"a rational relationship to legitimate state interests."[10] And what explains
this lack of rationality, according to the opinion's syllabus, is not the state's
primary concerns about the "respect for other citizen's freedom of association" or "the State's interest in conserving resources to fight discrimination
against other groups." Instead, what the irrationality of the amendment
suggests is "the inevitable inference that it is born of animosity toward the
class that it affects."[11] This animosity, in other words, is hatred of queer people, a hatred made legally legible by the kinds of race hate *Plessy* invokes.

The Protection of Hate

Amendment 2's political campaign, organized by concerned citizens from
Colorado Springs and Denver, started in response to the activism of gays,
lesbians, and bisexuals who had wanted to be included in a proposed and
eventually unsuccessful statewide "ethnic harassment bill" (H.B. 1059).
These citizens immediately interpreted bills such as this one as part of a
sweeping "gay agenda" being implemented by a powerful "homosexual
lobby" that would stop at nothing to force people to accept their sinful
"lifestyle." Already, cities such as Aspen, Boulder, and Denver had included
"sexual orientation" in their respective nondiscrimination policies and municipal laws. Increased activity in other cities in Colorado and the United
States gave conservative citizens a sense of deep urgency and need for successful political action. The ethnic harassment bill, which would have
brought increased penalties for hate crimes, was, indeed, defeated. Almost
contemporaneously, Colorado Springs was also considering a queer positive
law, the Human Rights Ordinance, but it was also rejected, in part because of the grassroots organizing of many of the same Coloradans who
had successfully challenged the ethnic harassment bill in Denver. Ever vigi-
lant, these concerned, primarily Christian citizens were winning the battle
against the homosexual agenda.

This group eventually grew into Colorado for Family Values (CFV), led by Christian-minded people such as a well-known Colorado Springs car dealer named Will Perkins. And they designed a bill of their own. With the help of major evangelical organizations, CFV, on July 31, 1991, selected the version of the voter initiative that would prevent the "elite" and "powerful" homosexual lobby from successfully being included in antidiscrimination legislations such as the ethnic harassment bill. The text of the amendment read:

> Neither the State of Colorado, through any of its branches or departments, nor any of its agencies, political subdivisions, municipalities or school districts, shall enact, adopt, or enforce any statute, regulation, ordinance, or policy whereby homosexual, lesbian, or bisexual orientation, conduct, practices, or relationships shall constitute or otherwise be the basis of or entitle any person or class of persons to have or claim any minority status, quota preferences, protected status, or claim of discrimination.[12]

CFV was convinced that a statewide vote from members of the general population, rather than the state legislature that seemed to be favoring the "gay agenda," would be the best way to prevent the further insidious gains of homosexuals. In its place, freedom of religion and freedom of association—and even freedom of speech—would be "restored" to those who could not abide or morally agree with the "lifestyle" they so heartily disliked and believed sinful. The efficiency of this successful initiative is startling. Within one sentence, numerous avenues for a claim of "minority status" based on minority sexuality were effectively barricaded: official, public places of association that need to be open to all—such as public schools and government agencies—need not pay attention to a minority position that cannot position itself "like" a racial/ethnic minority. Queers would not be able to assert that they were denied civil rights; they would not be a suspect class of citizens. The last sentence forecloses the possibility that sexual orientation—deliberately called an "orientation," "conduct," "practice," or "relationship"—could be the basis of a protected identity claim.

Among the right, there was a deep concern about what would happen to a sexual minority if it were to become "like a racial minority" in the eyes of a law. In another December 29, 1992, column in the *Gazette,* syndicated writer Joseph Sobran described the ludicrousness of claiming a "born that way" argument for any cultural or legal push for homosexual acceptance:

Now lately we have been told that homosexuality is implanted by nature not by nurture of free preference. So far, though, the scientific evidence for this is at best tentative. Yet gay rights advocates are already treating this idea as established fact. . . . This strikes me as a case of wishful thinking. . . . Would nature implant a drive for which there is no apparatus of fulfillment and no survival value for the species? Homosexual practices, especially anal intercourse, don't produce life; they induce disease. How can we then think that nature recognizes homosexuality as a distinct biological category? And are we to infer that other sexual tastes—pedophilia, for example—are also biologically decreed?[13]

In order to discredit the possibility that homosexuality is like a so-called biologically determined racial category, Sobran pursued the implications of Amendment 2: homosexual desires are just desires—practices, orientations, and tastes, not something inherent and immutable in the individual. Homosexuality cannot be natural because it is against nature, produces disease, contains no "survival value," or, oddly enough, no "apparatus of fulfillment." Despite the acrimony of this description, with its traditional, conservative refrain of homosexuality's erroneous connection to pedophilia, which we'll encounter more extensively in this book's conclusion, Sobran's simple claim is that homosexuality is not a biological category like

121

race. It is a distasteful lifestyle, not a biological trait, and expressing this distaste is acceptable because the expression is not race-hate based, nor is it targeting a group or class of people who have no choice in the matter of their difference. In other words, homosexuality is simply wrong.

Those who disagree with the homosexual lifestyle, moreover, should feel free to disagree. As fringe writer Stephen Bransford, in his pro-Amendment 2 book, *Gay Politics v. Colorado and America: The Inside Story of Amendment 2,* persuasively argues, much of the concern about whether or not homosexuality is like race was a response to the perceived threat that homosexuality would not only be protected by the Civil Rights Act of 1964,[14] but also that affirmative actions would develop into an unacceptably forced affirmation of the homosexual lifestyle.[15] If homosexuals cloaked themselves in a suspect status like race, then affirmative action and other coercive means of acceptance and tolerance would prevent people from freely expressing their disdain for and disapproval of lesbians, gays, bisexuals, and trans people. If they were like racial minorities in the eyes of the law, queers could force you to hire them, rent to them, or promote them. According to this logic, the advent of desegregation and civil rights has enforced the "affirmation" of racial minorities; the U.S. population is no longer officially allowed to hate racial and ethnic minorities (although that hate might be rerouted into other stances, such as a conservative disdain for affirmative action policies). One of the key figures from CFV succinctly argued, "If having sex becomes all it takes to consider [someone] 'ethnic,' with full minority rights and privileges, the concept of ethnicity will have lost nearly all its meaning and value."[16]

But there is more than the fear that people would have to put up with homosexuals like they have had to put up with and give "rights and privileges" to ethnic and racial others. If gays were to enter into the civil rights arena, it would not only be harder to voice a public opinion against gays, it would be harder, rhetorically, to define a traditional and religious community against the carriers of social decay, of social disease, of social "unnaturalness." Civil rights, at least as they've come to be naturalized by so-called immutable characteristics, would make queers more "natural," and thus more acceptable and less available for the jeremiadic rhetorical forms of hate that need outsiders, that need social contagions that must be phrased out of the nation. No one, then, would be free to hate, at least rhetorically, homosexuals. And the traditional sovereign language of the American nation-state would have lost yet another one of its scapegoats (since gender, race, and religious difference aren't as available as they used to be).

The hysteria about the "like race" argument from conservatives was feverish. Major CFV supporter Bill McCartney stated, quite explicitly, his disdain for gays and lesbians, making controversial comments that drew attention to the implications of the amendment that were not explicit in the wording and battle over the quasi-racial/biological status of homosexuality. McCartney, then a University of Colorado at Boulder football coach, who had led his team to the national title, was a local hero, and as such had the ears of the state. In a February 10, 1992, press conference widely thought to galvanize the petition drive to put Amendment 2 on the ballot, McCartney righteously proclaimed what his faith required him to believe: "I embrace what Almighty God has said about these things [about gays and lesbians] when I read the Scripture. Homosexuality is an abomination of Almighty God."[17] The negative reaction from University of Colorado officials and others, including Representative Pat Schroeder, who declared that McCartney was "preaching hatred" and "hate mongering,"[18] sparked an outpouring of emotions and funds for the CFV cause. According to those sympathetic to McCartney's position, he should be allowed to express his disapproval for a despised minority that should not even be considered a minority. They are an abomination, perhaps an abomination belonging to God. And soon, the right to agree with this anti-gay sentiment was made law by the majority of Colorado voters later that fall. Justice Scalia, in his mean dissent in *Romer v. Evans,* put it succinctly when he argued that Coloradans are "*entitled* to be hostile toward homosexual conduct."[19] And the grim conclusion of this outcry: to be "like race" makes it harder to "not like" queer; so queer is not like race.

Disestablishment

Almost immediately after the success of Amendment 2, a local Colorado Springs religious right watch-dog group, Citizens Project, formed, in outraged horror not only over the passage of the initiative, but all the initiative implied: the religious right had made a comeback, and suddenly it was influencing Colorado Springs's local community in profound and increasingly organized ways. The group's mission statement from a newsletter the summer after the passage of Amendment 2 warns: "In the Pikes Peak area, we are seeing a push toward prayer in schools, pressure to modify school curriculum to reflect religious views, the rise of stealth candidates in elections, increased anti-gay activity, and growing religious intolerance, Citizens Project was formed to challenge those trends."[20] Quickly, a sense of deep urgency was placed on children rather than on the queer rights that had been nullified by Colorado for Family Values. This urgency shifted focus not because gay rights are necessarily subordinate to the concerns with the nation's youth, but because the amendment provoked basic citizenship quandaries posed by religious and minority claims that are often worked out around the very emotional space of children, and specifically where children learn to be citizens in training: the "classroom."

The Citizens Project newsletter claimed that those behind the newsletter were a group of representative citizens from a "broad spectrum of political parties and religious beliefs who are concerned about these attacks [most immediately from the Colorado religious right] to our constitutional freedoms by local sectarian and political extremists." They were thus "dedicated to maintaining the traditional values of separation of church and state, freedom of religion and speech, pluralism, individuality, and tolerance and compassion for others."[21] In short, the concerned citizens were concerned not only for the children in public schools but also for a whole host of issues that the symbols of learning children in public classrooms have long come to imply throughout the twentieth century.

Brown v. Board of Education's 1954 opinion offers concise words that help make sense as to why so many pieces of important civil rights actions have swirled around national, public classrooms: "Education is perhaps the most important function of state and local governments . . . it is the very foundation of good citizenship."[22] Fury around the public classroom is not really about what and who gets taught in the national classroom, but rather what that teaching means for the nation's cultural identity and citizenship, especially along the fault lines of religion, race, and sexuality. At stake, over the nation's "children," are fundamental definitions of who can belong and be protected by the United States, especially in the national classroom that fashions future citizens—especially citizens that will be valued.

John Gallagher and Chris Bull, in their study of the similarities between the religious right and gay and lesbian politics, *Perfect Enemies*, begin their book with one of the more iconic classroom battles: they briefly mention the Scopes trial as *the* event that defines and "prefigure[s] many of the . . . debates over sexual politics starting in the 1960s."[23] The 1925 event took place in a town that, curiously enough, resides in the same county that, in March 2004, asked the state of Tennessee to let them charge homosexuals with crimes against nature.[24] Although lauded as fundamentalism's last stand, the Scopes trial actually functions, at least for some Christian historians such as Martin Marty, as *"the origin* of modern fundamentalism."[25] This origin, however, was never supposed to be just a simple matter about the public school curriculum and the place of religion in that curriculum.

Although a struggle between progressive education and strict religious belief (evolutionary theory versus creationism), the trial was as consciously staged as a large-scale media circus designed to generate notoriety and revenue for a small Tennessee town, Dayton. Citizens at the drugstore owned by the head of the county's Board of Education chose John Scopes, a young physics teacher, to be the teacher who violated the law since he was popular, amiable, not too radical, and without children. Famous attorneys were chosen to make the trial a well-watched event. Something about the debates between church and state, and what those debates implied, had mass appeal, so they convinced the ACLU, which was looking for high-profile cases, to participate, following an approach that was successfully used by other early civil rights groups such as the National Association for the Advancement of Colored People.[26] Various committees, including the "Scopes Trial Entertainment Committee," were formed to promote the influx of trial tourism and industry. And whereas the televised spectacle of racial desegregation, following the *Brown v. Board of Education* rulings, was noteworthy for the way mass communication technologies influenced and shaped important legal and political developments, the Scopes trial was the first radio-broadcasted trial.[27] The conjoining of sensational politics, contested legal terrain, and a very fashionable debate over science versus religion proved to be not only successfully scandalous, it proved to be a legacy that still makes us nervous.

Throughout the 1940s, 1950s, and 1960s, school prayer cases continued the debates of the Scopes trial. Scandals have often erupted when the place of religion in public culture is questioned. School prayer cases, indeed, were not really about what they were supposed to be; whether or not prayers should be taught in a public institution took a back seat to the publicity about who belongs to the nation. Cases such as *Everson v. Board of Education* (1947), *Illinois ex rel. McCollum v. Board of Education* (1948), and *Engel v. Vitale* (1962) are a few of the most important of the period. Any close inspection of these Supreme Court decisions reveals, for instance, enormous contradictions: the heavy and confusing language that relies on the iteration of clichés about American history, culture, and the place of religion in that history; the intent of the Constitution's "framers"; and pleas for either strict or broad interpretation of the original words of the Constitution.[28] But such confusions were not nearly as exciting as the battle over citizenship that inevitably erupted. These cases' stricter enforcements over the church-state divide increased in no small part by the fact that racial civil rights had begun to instruct the United States that it was no longer the WASP culture it thought it was.

Engel v. Vitale (1962), an exemplary case over whether or not religion could remain within public schools, provoked some controversy.[29] The primary issue at debate in this case was a nondenominational, that is generic, prayer that the New York City Board of Regents wanted teachers to lead each morning alongside the pledge of allegiance.[30] Although the board allowed students and their parents to abstain voluntarily from the prayer if they so chose, the Court regarded this devotional activity as a specific violation of the establishment clause, and ruled the prayer unconstitutional. Reaction to the Court was profuse:

> The *Engel* and *Schempp* [another prayer case] touched off enormous public outcry. Many Protestant and Roman Catholic spokespeople lambasted the *Engel* decision. Cardinal Spellman was "shocked and frightened," the Reverend Billy Graham was distraught, and lawyer/bishop James A. Pike lamented that "the Supreme Court has just deconsecrated the nation." Legislative opinion was equally bitter. Senator Ellender referred to the *Schempp* majority as "eight silly old men," Congressman Rooney saw *Engel* as not only "asinine" but a communist threat, and Congressman Andrews summed up the South's reaction to the modern Supreme Court: "*They put Negroes into the schools and now they have driven God out of them.*" The governors of all but New York called for a constitutional amendment to overturn the *Engel* decision, and Congress held extensive hearings on school prayer amendments in 1962 (after *Engel*) and 1964 (after *Schempp*).[31]

Religion and racial civil rights were conjoined as they were pitted against each other, and somehow the removal of God permitted the entrance of "Negroes" into the national classroom, and indeed into full participation in the national citizenry. Religion was cast as the traditional values that are now threatened in a regrettably secularizing nation. If there were no longer room for God, if that's what was jettisoned for an increasing devotion to civil rights and tolerance, then the Christian conservatives were given an obligation to maintain, perhaps at extreme costs, the eroding religious values that are part of not only the traditions of the United States, but also part of its sovereign power that makes the nation a "light unto all nations."

It is certainly striking to see recent events rehearse the stakes over conservative Christianity's ever-precarious last stand. Disestablishment crises continue, especially at a point when queer rights has hit the mainstream. There was the June 2002 controversy over the Ninth Circuit Court of Appeals ruling on the unconstitutionality of the Pledge of Allegiance's clause, "under God," a clause which, by the way, was added the same year as *Brown*. And the summer 2003 scandal of Alabama chief justice R. Moore's refusal to move a Ten Commandments monument he had purchased for the Mobile Judicial Building the same summer that homosexual sodomy was made legal by the U.S. Supreme Court. The 2005 contradictory Supreme Court rulings on the presence of the Ten Commandments in or around government buildings keeps replaying the fight of history against tolerance.[32] It seems that Lisa Duggan, years ago, couldn't have been more on target when she reminded us about the significance of disestablishment for queer politics. In response, she claims, suggestively, that we should "look beyond the language of rights claims for a fixed minority and calls for antidiscrimination (rhetorical positioning largely borrowed from the civil rights movement and feminism), and instead borrow from another liberal discourse, that surrounding the effort to disestablish state religion, to separate church and state," and to disestablish what she calls the "religion of heteronormativity."[33]

Similarly, but in a different and still very suggestive strand, Jakobsen and Pellegrini move away from a rights-based model of sexual politics toward a model of freedom, specifically religious freedom: "We make this shift by switching from the current legal framework, with its focus on nondiscrimination, to one based on the free exercise of religion promised by the First Amendment."[34] Ingeniously, they want to link sexual freedom and religious freedom in order to open up "new political, rhetorical, and perhaps even legal perspectives and possibilities."[35] I appreciate these calls for action. I think both tactics might one day yield productive results, especially since they are among the few scholars who have produced a sustained critique of religion's force in contemporary queer politics. But the story of freedom of religion and issues around the disestablishment of church and sate is complicated and ongoing. Various versions of the Scopes trial happen all the time, fueling anger and hate for holders of "traditional values."

I hope to do more than suggest that the remnants of this disestablishment debate endure. I mean to be more forceful. Church and state issues are the legal and political terrain on which queer civil rights battles often continue to be fought. Since race now has its "mantle of respectability," and people can't be so obvious about their hatred of "Negroes" in the classroom, there still need to be those who are targets of the American jeremiad; the United States needs its inside-outsiders. Thus we begin to see why queers should not be given respectability, not be included in the national curriculum, or at least not made full citizens. The progressive erosion of traditional American family values, which made the United States a sovereign nation, occurred in sites such as classrooms that were being devoted to scientific, secular knowledge rather than the strong religious teachings of Christianity. If even a generic prayer of religious belonging is no longer permitted each morning a child might begin to learn, then maybe religion has, indeed, become anachronistic, and thus is no longer a valued part of the American story.

The religious right in Colorado certainly had this fear in mind, knowing well the "special rights" implications of civil rights. But I must stress that this panic is just that: a panic. Civil rights, not to mention tolerance toward all sorts of people, has never been successful in separating church and state, nor has that been the objective of many civil rights movements. We are just as Christian a citizenry as ever, even if that Christianity means "culturally Christian." But the fear of another Scopes trial, with its possible discrediting of religious belief, is a manufactured fear that enables conservative Christians, not to mention the United States government, to stress the importance, if not the critical importance, of their sovereign values, indeed their sovereign words, in the face of menacing cultural difference.

A Less Strict Race Response

Because the enforcement of disestablishment cases happened at roughly the same moment as the rise of the racial civil rights movement (disestablishment cases started more or less with *Everson* in 1947), and because advocates of Amendment 2 were so worried, genuinely or not, that queer would become "like race," I want us to consider race as the fundamental category for queer politics. I advocate such a position not just because race provides a model of queer resistance, but because race is a necessary category that queers must evoke when they respond to their sacrilization out of citizenship rights and values. In fact, it seems unlikely that any response other than the "like race" argument could have effectively combated the religious rights' radical devaluation of queers as citizens of Colorado in 1992. Thus, I want us to see how race has become, like it or not, the fundamental category of difference in the United States.

Quite controversially, once Amendment 2 was passed, a variety of legal strategies were entertained in order to show off the law's clear violations of the Fourteenth Amendment. Although fraught, the "born that way" *argument* was chosen as the strategy with the most potential. This choice, made by the legal team on behalf of Colorado petitioners suing the state after the successful passage of Amendment 2, makes legal sense, especially in the very complicated and vexed realm of judicial review that needs specific and substantial indications why one group should be considered a class denied equal protections—a denial of rights that can rarely have legitimate state interests, and thus a piece of legislation considered contrary to the Constitution. When laws are based on race and nation, the judicial review must be at its strictest, requiring that the law in question demonstrate, deeply, that it is not motivated by prejudice. There are other review distinctions for other types of laws targeting other segments of the population, referred to as "quasi-suspect" classes, which include the categories of gender and illegitimacy. This intermediate class requires less strict but still important demonstrations that the law targeting such a class is not intended to discriminate, but is necessary for a host of politically and legally legitimate reasons. Sexual-orientation judicial reviews usually fall within the lowest level of class scrutiny, "rational review," requiring lighter justification for the compelling government interest in the creation and execution of a law that impinges on sexual minorities' rights.

The plaintiffs in the original round of court cases in Denver challenging the amendment immediately had to tackle a problem: if they were to pursue an Equal Protection argument, they would then have to define the contours of a sexual minority position; they would have to figure out a manner in which sexual minority status fits into the history of suspect classification legal review that seeks to uphold the Fourteenth Amendment guarantee that no illegitimate classifications of people could be the law of the land. They would have to make the "rational review" status of sexual orientation seem more like suspect class status. Lisa Keen and Suzanne Goldberg explain:

> While even the courts most hostile to gay claimants have conceded that gay people have been historically subjected to discrimination, many of those same courts have also ruled that sexual orientation classifications fail to satisfy the other elements identified by the high court. Often, a stumbling block for courts has been the nature of sexual orientation. Rather than see it as a characteristic that is "obvious, immutable or distinguishing" and irrelevant to the "ability to perform or contribute," many have seen sexual orientation as a choice to behave in a way that is disapproved by society. Some of these courts have also rejected strict scrutiny of sexual orientation discrimination after concluding that gay people have sufficient political power to challenge

discriminatory laws so that such laws do not need additional close reviews by courts.[36]

In what ways can sexual orientation be seen to be more than a chosen tendency, an activity, or even a proclivity? If lesbians, bisexuals, and gays are thought not to be born that way, or are thought powerful enough to combat instances of discrimination, or are not easily identifiable as a legibly minor and persecuted minority, can equal protection claims be a viable court strategy?

In a rather intense, multipronged legal challenge, the plaintiffs spent a great deal of time defining that homosexuality is much more than a choice. The plaintiff's legal team chose, in part, to argue a "like race" or a "born that way" argument, claiming that sexual orientation is immutable—an immutable trait that had exposed LGBTQ people to a long history of discrimination. In testimony from "scientific," "historical," and "philosophical" expert opinions, the status of sexual orientation was somewhat enigmatically, paradoxically, and contradictorily described. Experts included, among others, controversial sex researcher Richard Green, who had written *The "Sissy Boy" Syndrome and the Development of Homosexuality,* in which he argues for the biological markers of homosexuality; University of Chicago professor of history George Chauncey, who had written *Gay New York*; and Martha Nussbaum, a prolific classicist and philosopher. Through their testimonies, the plaintiffs attempted to define the "nature" and origin of homosexuality, thereby manifesting why minority sexual orientation deserved something like the "strict scrutiny" of judicial review. But even though the strategy of a "like race" or "born that way" argument was asserted, the force of the strategy worked not because of appeals to fixed, biological grounds of difference. The "like race" appeal worked (and continues to work) because it provokes emotions that influence law and politics.

Legal review—especially when it scrutinizes the presence of classes or minority groups in a country that is not supposed to have divisive and hierarchical minorities but equality for all its citizens—is a difficult exercise. Legal scrutiny involves well-rehearsed concerns: concerns such as federalist anxiety about the relations between national and state governments; or concerns about whether or not judicial activism runs contrary to "truer" versions of democracy when minority issues assert the possibility that the majority might not have to protect the minority's best interests. But I'm most interested in the concerns about why the racial minority model, solidified by the judiciary's explicit efforts to end American racial apartheid with rulings such as *Brown,* persist as the way to mark the feelings of injustice, exclusion, and persecution of minority groups other than racial minorities.[37] Legal scholar Robert Cover remarks: "The questions associated with the Black experience in America raised, as no others could, the spectre of internal conflict between the values of a free and open political life."[38] I think of this specter as sentimental because questions of the "Black experience in America," as I have noted in the previous chapters of this book, evoke haunting moments of sentimentality that move people into strong feelings about freedom gone awry. Race can be thought of as an emotion haunting the legal scrutiny of all U.S. minorities.

But thinking of race in such a manner is not to dismiss the awful and difficult reality of race relations in the United States. There is incredible force in the emotions of race that course through the letter and the spirit of the law. We recognize as much when we consider the rhetorical quandaries posed by the history of constitutional interpretation, which, as legal historian Charles Miller long ago argued, is a history of how both race and the language used to describe race "[weighs] heavily in the American constitutional tradition."[39] Justice Harlan's dissent in *Plessy,* for instance, recognizes the supreme importance of nomenclature and rhetoric when arguing for racial equality in the interpretation of the Constitution: "It was adjudicated in that [case, *Dred Scott* case] that descendents of Africans who were imported into this country and sold as slaves were not included nor intended to be included under the *word* 'citizens' in the Constitution and could not claim any of the rights and privileges which that instrument provided for and secured to citizens of the United States."[40] The "word" citizen has deep and "real" effects, but requires interpretation, as Harlan writes quite meta-phorically, so as not to "permit the seeds of race hate to be planted under the sanction of law." In fact, what Harlan's dissent and Kennedy's quota-tion of this dissent serve to showcase is an important question of nominal-ism—or what we could call "rhetoric"—about who will be included in a nondivisive manner under the word "citizen." Racial judicial review is not unlike sexual orientation judicial review when some citizens are stripped, for no justifiable or compelling governmental interest, of basic rights or equal protections guaranteed by the Constitution. Important rhetorical ges-tures are made whether or not they immediately translate into an other-wise recognizable reality.

In the confusing realm of sexual orientation's relation to the state and its mediation through the "like race" arguments that eventually helped overturn a pernicious initiative "born of animosity toward the class that it affects," the literary language of racial emotion becomes one method of capturing, or at least suggesting, the confusion of sexual orientation. Justice Scalia's famously acrimonious dissent in *Romer v. Evans* accuses the majority opinion as being "long on emotive utterance and so short on relevant legal citation." The implications are that there is little "real" substance in the simile of "like race," and only the trivial emotion that is often erroneously aligned, through such language, with the heightened protections of racial affirmative actions. Whether we agree with Scalia, and whether or not we could accuse him of similar sentiments and extreme emotional biases against the very class under attack by Amendment 2 (such as the ones ex-pressed in his dissent of the anti-sodomy ruling in the summer of 2003), somehow the emotional, if not heightened language of the case becomes the explanation for the incoherence of argumentation. Sentimental "long utterances" rather than logic persuaded the Court to overrule the majority of voting Coloradans. The emotional impact and the hate bandied about by both sides of Amendment 2 are exactly what moved voters in 1992 and beyond to legislate new words to show that sexual orientation is not at all like race. Fearful or hateful or just misinformed, the controversy over "special rights" convinced voters to vote with their hearts rather than their heads.

It makes sense that political controversies over minority rights are emotionally loaded, especially given the manner in which citizenship status is now negotiated in the contemporary political climate. Lauren Berlant's work on citizenship is quite useful in helping us understand what form of "culture war" was playing out in Colorado—the means "by which mass subaltern [minority] pain is advanced in the dominant public sphere, as the true core of national collectivity."[41] The pain and suffering described by the hateful plight of those who feel oppressed or stripped of basic citizenship rights increasingly takes absolute importance in a conflict over whether or not one belongs equally to the United States. "National sentimentality is more than a current of feeling that circulates in a political field: the phrase describes a longstanding contest between two models of U.S. citizenship," instructs Berlant. "In one, the classic model, each citizen's value is secured by an equation between abstractness and emancipation: a cell of national identity provides juridically protected personhood for citizens regardless of anything specific about them."[42] The Equal Protection clause guarantees as much. She continues:

> In the second model, which was initially organized around labor, feminist, and antiracist struggles in the United States in the nineteenth century, another version is imagined as the index of collective life. This nation is peopled by suffering citizens and noncitizens whose structural exclusion from the utopian-American dreamscape exposes the state's claim of legitimacy and virtue to an acid wash of truth-telling that makes hegemonic disavowal virtually impossible at certain moments of political intensity.[43]

These two versions of citizenship (and noncitizenship)—the abstract/utopian versus the suffering and loud—lead to a form of politics that relies on the functional citation of pain: "Identification with pain, a universal true feeling, then leads to structural and social change." And this citation thus reasserts the value of the classic model of abstract equality:

> In return, subalterns scarred by the pain of failed democracy will reauthorize universalist notions of citizenship in the national utopia, which involves believing in a redemptive notion of law as the guardian of public good. The object of the nation and the law in this light is to eradicate systematic social pain, the absence of which becomes the definition of freedom.[44]

Queer activism and minority complaint most certainly belong to the traumatic model of the pain of citizenship. As victims of hate, as target members of society, injured queers are increasingly used to mark, sentimentally, the failures of the classic citizenship's promise, with an eye on, but perhaps not yet a handle on, eventually becoming "classic" rather than merely a "subject of true [and painful] feeling." Berlant has a host of reservations about these competing models of citizenship, all of which make enormous amounts of sense, especially if one wanted to move beyond the hierarchy and histories of violent exclusion implied in these versions of constitutional personhood, a hierarchy in which "the counterhegemonic deployments of pain as the measure of structural injustice actually sustain the utopian image of a homogenous national metaculture, which can look like a healed or healthy body in contrast to the scarred and exhausted ones."[45]

The system of appeal and complaint is seriously wrong, and Berlant and others, such as Jakobsen and Pellegrini, are holding out for other "democratic possibilities"[46] that acknowledge the complexity and diversity of minority emotion and minority status. Berlant hopes that the subaltern will recognize "that the signs of subordination [minorities] they feel also tell a story that they do not feel yet, or know, about how to construct the narrative to come."[47] The future and the utopian promise of a better, less coercive articulation of marginalization in the national culture fuels much critical queer work, to be sure. Further, there is an understandable mistrust, one I frequently feel, in the deployment of conventional and often abusive forms and relationships of citizenship in advancing any demand for social and structural change. But while we are in the useful and necessary mood to hope and imagine, and to offer excellent criticisms and theories about what could be otherwise, it is also crucial to think about the less detectable, even the less desirable, strategies of "coping" with the confines of dominant culture. There must be strategies of coping with the already established nation-state that doesn't seem to be going anywhere else anytime soon. Amendment 2 was not going to fix itself in methods other than a judicial review that indulged the sentimental politics that brought it into existence in the first place. The hate and pain from "The Hate State's" religious rhetoric is what targeted and made coherent, however dangerously or erroneously, sexual orientation, which needed some method of legal appeal that would deflect the swift theft of even the possibility of claiming any kind of subordinate status, of any possibility that a classic model of being "left-alone" might eventually be attained.

Since we have no choice but to negotiate an emotional, irrational, and abusive public sphere articulated by a language of sovereign security, we have to direct our critical and political energies away, as I've been suggesting, from getting the story right, or realistic. Sometimes we also have to be emotional and irrational while we stall the political sacrilization. In what ways, then, can these coercive narratives of citizenship, pain, race, sexuality, and constitutional personhood be used without the sense that these narratives are actually accurate or realistic accounts of "real" people? In what way is the dominant language of citizen and minority a productive lie about the minority self that can be mobilized by strategic, clever, if not figurative means? When the larger, "hegemonic" culture is not really transforming, or at least fast enough, can the sentimental appeals to a hurt personhood, to the hate that won't go away, be a method of minority complaint that need not detail or even testify about the specificity of social and systematic exclusion? If, as Berlant implies, the two models of citizenship actually reinforce each other through their struggle, then is there a way to work within these models to produce some sort of action that ameliorates, however slightly, the conditions that further marginalize the U.S. minority? Can this nominalistic name game, this sentimental politics, also be helpful in spite of its very "real" pitfalls and dangers? Might the sentimentality, the feeling of hate and its effects be the only way that queers articulate themselves in an oblique and tentative way that still has meaningful consequences, such as the Supreme Court's overruling of Amendment 2?

Rights as Wrongs: An Unreal Citizenship Claim

The American jeremiad wants to hear that its less desirable citizens and noncitizens do not belong to the nation even if they do, and even if they were to eventually acquire basic citizenship rights such as marriage, membership in the armed services, and so forth. The testimony of radical difference from the U.S. nation-state is what is required for the listing of the "array of defects." The minority complaint is anticipated in the sense that there is always something "wrong" with those who do not share in the traditional narratives of national belonging. In Colorado, for example, the religious right called attention to fears that queers were eroding more conservative, national family values by distributing a variety of propaganda videos about homosexuality. *The Gay Agenda* is the most notorious of these videos, highlighting the fabricated militancy of an elite, well-funded program of queer persuasion that not only collects civil, political, legal, and cultural resources, but also convinces and recruits people into a "pleasure-addicted" lifestyle.[48] Despite the over-the-top propaganda techniques one might expect to find in the documentary, the truly remarkable aspect of the video is that the creators of the video did not have to do much to visually impress upon viewers the scary and defective difference and threat of the gay agenda. The most fear-inducing images of the tape came from gay pride parades, with a whole cast of familiar gay characters: drag queens, leather daddies, muscle boys, dykes on bikes, etc. By just showcasing the "radical" alternative elements of the queer life world, which often seem so ordinary to people within the community, the religious right was able to shock its conservative viewers into all sorts of effective hysteria.[49] One might hear in a conservative's mind: "Just look at those homosexuals and their crazy, anti-family, anti-American lifestyle." The pride, the "celebration of difference" (as the blue bumper sticker that immediately appeared on cars of Coloradoans against Amendment 2 encouraged) so easily confirmed, in the conservative minds of the population, the defects of homosexual Americans. This video provided outrageous images for Colorado's voters in November 1992. There should be no "special rights" for drag queens! Surely rational citizens should retain the "right" to disagree, openly, with such flamboyance; gays are not special, they're defective. Indeed, the simple celebration of difference—the spectacle of alterity—does not always shock the system; in fact, the dissent is not only anticipated, but appreciated.

Consequently, the question of representative styles, of the words chosen and the models adopted for queer resistance, is not a frivolous exercise of academic or queer intellectual activity. The concept of minority "realism" once again needs to be profoundly interrogated and critiqued in this context. As we should know by now, even when we are not dealing with explicitly "literary texts," representative politics—and the rhetorical strategies we use, spin, and mediate—are anything but clear views on the world. Legibility, testimony, and political protest cannot assume to be innocent of the more complicated gestures of style, of spin, from any part of the political or cultural spectrum. "Politics is perception," as the saying goes, which we might alter in order to say "politics names how to feel a certain kind of way." When the showcasing of "real" gays so quickly confirms the majority's worst, if not comforting, fears about the minority, we should be inspired to think about the "nature" of representations, and wonder if there's a way not to be so "real," so ready-made and stereotypically legible to the nation-state. And if not, perhaps a stereotypical kind of "realness" can be put to the most strategic and artificial uses that can defy the surveillance and containment of the minority citizen.

What makes the LGBTQ response, filtered through years of "successful" judicial review and culminating in *Romer v. Evans,* an instructive "case study" is the assertion of minority difference as a difference that is traumatized, wounded, and victimized by a hate that one can understand only by simile and analogy. The traumatic and wounded minor citizens are not confessing or testifying "truthfully," nor are they full of authentic realism. They announce their difference by proxy, by a rhetorical gesture that recognizes there are few options of opposition in a nation and a Constitution that transforms its biases very slowly. Something had to be done, had to be said, otherwise basic civil rights, guaranteed all citizens, would have been stripped away from Colorado's lesbian, bisexual, and gay population.

Justice Kennedy's majority opinion reveals a form of legal review that did not go so far as to confirm the immutable and strict status of race to sexual orientation. He does not grant suspect class status to queers. But the "like race" argument, as we've seen, courses through in his opinion. Some legal scholars call the opinion a form of "rational review plus" or "rational review with teeth."[50] Perhaps this "plus" is related to what Spillers calls the "signifying property plus" of some positions African Americans are forced to assume in "the public place."[51] The "plus" is the nebulous, rhetorical position assigned to the racialized subject in contemporary U.S. culture and politics. Kennedy writes:

> Laws of the kind now before us raise the inevitable inference that the disadvantage imposed is born of animosity toward the class of persons affected. "[I]f the constitutional conception of equal protection of the laws means anything, it must at the very least mean that a bare . . . desire to harm a politically unpopular group cannot constitute a *legitimate* government interest." *Department of Agriculture v. Moreno,* 413 U. S. 528, 534 (1978). Even laws enacted for broad and ambitious purposes often can be explained by reference to legitimate public policies which justify the incidental disadvantages they impose on certain purposes. Amendment 2, however, in making a general announcement that gays

and lesbians shall not have any particular protections from the law, inflicts on them immediate, continuing, and real injuries that outrun and belie any legitimate justifications that may be claimed for it.[52]

The animosity of Amendment 2, then, is thought to create injuries not unlike the racial ones Kennedy references in his final Court citation of the difficult and upsetting decisions of the 1883 *Civil Rights Cases,* which overturned the 1875 Civil Rights Act. Kennedy starts and stops with comparison to racial civil rights in overturning Amendment 2, thereby making legally intelligible the sentimental concerns born out of animosity toward this "unpopular group" of sexual minorities. He further concludes that Amendment 2 does nothing more, in a hateful manner, than make them "unequal to everyone else"—everyone has claims of discrimination, regardless of their personal particularities. Amendment 2 would classify, target, and make subordinate lesbians, bisexuals, and gays. It would make, as Kennedy says, the homosexual "class of persons a stranger to [the State's] laws."

Amendment 2, however, never took effect. The initial injunction in the Colorado District Court occurred before the law was scheduled to start. The Supreme Court made sure that its animosity, at least in this instance, would not make queer citizens strangers to the nation's laws. The "real" injuries were not legal facts as much as emotional controversies that have nevertheless had a profound effect on the manner in which gay politics has proceeded in an increasingly "tolerant" climate since 1992. Through the rise and fall of Amendment 2, the "like race" "nature" of queers was iterated in a very intense manner, so much so that a number of lesbian and gay theorists and activists have taken on the concept of "stranger," a concept so in line with the American jeremiad that needed its foreign, stranger, yet still insider elements on which to pin its social and moral decay. The major book on the entire Amendment 2 judicial history aptly echoes Kennedy's assertion in its title, *Strangers to the Law: Gay People on Trial.*[53] In her call to "queer citizenship," Shane Phelan recognizes that "sexual minorities are not citizens of the United States" because gays and lesbians are precluded from equal and full participation in what is guaranteed all American citizens; thus, Phelan uses the productive adjective "stranger" to articulate the unique position queers have within the United States.[54] In fact, in the ensuing years, lesbian and gay activism has mined the "second-class" argument to mark that queers are citizenship strangers, in need of basic citizenship rights, such as marriage, privacy, and family rights.[55] We can conclude that these strangers are hurt by the law, and to be hurt by the law is in many ways to be hurt "like" race.

But I must insist that this injury is not "real," even if its effects are. So let's take a necessary break from reality and return to some lessons provided by James Baldwin. At key moments in *Go Tell It on the Mountain,* written just a few years before *Brown* was decided, John, as we know, resists the evangelical teachings and culture that saturate his life—teachings and a culture that mark his own queer desires as disgusting and sinful. Pitted against a hostile home and church life were John's successes in school that made him feel that he might not have to be a minister like his father; he would be destined for "a world where people did not live in the darkness of his father's house, did not pray to Jesus in the darkness of his father's church. . . . In this world John, who was, his father said, ugly, who was always the smallest boy in his class, who had no friends, became immediately beautiful, tall and popular."[56] The racial darkness of home and church, which, as we have seen, is intricately tied to John's sinful queer sexuality, is alleviated in a space of a more progressive and integrated classroom. In this place, John excels. The classroom allows for John to be reflective about his own posture of defiance within the political conundrums posed by his race, his religion, and especially his sexuality. At one point, after John masters the letters of the alphabet, the principal of the school compliments John's intelligence, leading him to a deep sense of resistance:

> The moment gave him, from that time on, if not a weapon at least a
> shield; he apprehended totally, without belief or understanding, that he
> had in himself a power that other people lacked; he could use this to

save himself, to raise himself; and that perhaps with this power he might one day win the love which he so longed for. This was not, in John, a faith subject to death or alteration, nor yet a hope subject to destruction; it was his identity, and part, therefore, of that wickedness for which his father beat him and to which he clung in order to withstand his father. His father's arm, rising and falling, might make him cry, and that voice might cause him to tremble; yet his father could never entirely be victor, for John cherished something that his father could not reach. It was his hatred and his intelligence, the one feeding the other. (16–17)

Baldwin has another take on "identity politics" here, one which he elaborates more fully in his expository prose throughout his career, making him one of the more noteworthy spokespeople for civil rights. The full and accurate disclosure of John's self is subordinate to the need to be protected against the combative forces that surround him. His "power," moreover, is not a direct product of the classroom; it is not just the distinctiveness and value of John's intelligence, recognized in a secular teaching zone, that shields John from his father's (and his father's religion's brutality). His shield is a combination of his smarts *and* his *hatred*, which has something to do with the unspecified, unnamed "wickedness" or sin lurking within him. It is his "power" or his "feeling" that allows him not to be saturated by their hatred. He has another structure of feeling, one that will remain deliberately nameless. "And this was why," the text continues, "though he had been born in the faith and had been surrounded by the saints and their prayers and their rejoicing. . . . John's heart was hardened against the Lord" (17). This hardening of a deep emotion will save him from his own potential loss to the darkness of their traditions, their family and religious values. The terrible landscape of religious words, viewed from the perspective of the classroom, provides the occasion and the text of an alternate story of the feeling lurking within John, as he exists as a queer stranger within the religious people and prayers that shape his everyday.

For he is a stranger to their laws, especially his "father's [long] arm [of the law], rising and falling, [which] might make him cry," so much so that it is apparent that he is a minor, sexual second-class citizen. John must nevertheless sing some tune with the words they have given him. We certainly can relate this novel to a quotation from his expository writing: "The favorite text of my father, among the most earnest of ministers, was not 'Father, forgive them, for they know not what they do,' but 'How can I sing the Lord's song in a strange land?' "[57] As I showed in Chapter Two, *Go Tell It on the Mountain* is an attempt to learn how to sing about queerness using the religious words that racialize this sexuality in a land that relies on making the queer a stranger to the religious nation's laws, phrasing them out, by beating them out, with the repetitive concern that queers are bad for the family, sinful for the family, and deserving of the second-class status they continue to occupy.

But what I did not emphasize earlier is that Baldwin's novel is not fighting for yet another deep description of an outsider status for the queer who is expected to be outside of the law. Instead, something more peculiar emerges in John—an emotional force that cannot be effortlessly located, quickly stereotyped, or even accurately named. The emotional force of his difference, his queer difference, finds expression in a quest for racial civil rights that are not necessarily appropriate for the condition that most vexes him. After all, John struggles most with the members of his African American family and community, all of whom believe in a sovereign religious tradition that deems African American flesh evil, dark, and sinful. I want to remark that John's defiance against his family, community, and religion is not in the service of his coming to terms with a legible queer self that can be disclosed; he is certainly not coming "out of the closet." His resistance emanates from his ability not to be saturated by the hate that surrounds him, while simultaneously relying on that hateful, racial feeling to remind him that he has a value that needs to be opposed to the forces that try and strip him of value.

Such a confusing political gesture, especially in the realm of civil rights, deepens our understanding of the nebulous quality of rights-based minority positions in the United States. John's affective activism is not explicit, nor official, but something more confusing, something more emotive than rational. His activism is also not about explicit structural change as much as it is about survival amid so much hatred and defeat. His relationship to rights, inasmuch as anyone who exists in a rights-based nation-state has some kind of relationship to rights, brings us numerous questions about civil rights.

Dissatisfied by the current queer focus on civil rights, Jakobsen and Pellegrini question the "nature" of rights, and whether or not a rights-based politics is worth pursuing.[58] For "rights" are perhaps some of the oddest things in the judicial-political system, animating the official and not-so-official U.S. public sphere. Robert Cover traces the rise of judicial minority protections and the ballyhooed "origins of judicial activism" in the landmark 1938 *United States v. Carolene Products Co.*, a case that, through a footnote, guides the development of the judicial protection of minorities. With the acknowledgment, especially in the late 1930s context of the terrible effects of fascism and an even clearer sense that the majority of a democracy might not protect the minority, judicial protections of minorities, especially African Americans, were articulated in legal review. Civil rights, moreover, if I am not mistaken, frequently emerge not as things in themselves, but as indexes of something at risk: the 1938 case "extend[ed] the scope of judicial review not in terms of the special *value* of certain rights but in terms of their *vulnerability* to the perversions of the majoritarian process."[59] That is, the rights one has in a political culture emerge less as a definable value one protects as much as they become the sign of one's defenselessness. Rights are often at question when they are not available, not allotted—such as the question of same-sex marriage rights in the United States—or when various legal and legislative processes are infringed upon. If we remember Berlant's characterization of pain and suffering as one competing model of citizenship, can we then begin to conceptualize a civil right as a *figure* of pain, suffering, and vulnerability? Can a civil right be considered a judicial and political sign of weakness, complaint, anxiety, and trauma that names, in the negative, minorities who do not have the rights and citizenship status they crave? Put simply: Are rights, as they now operate within contemporary minority politics, the rhetorics of suffering and pain, the articulation of minority emotion, that can be used by the politically and culturally disenfranchised to announce and bother people into some kind of transgressive action? Are rights the language of wrongs?

There can be no comprehensive answers to these questions that would suffice. I have no interest now in rigidly defining the "nature" of rights.[60] Instead, I want to characterize the constellation of ideas about minority legibility, as they emerge using the language of rights, which, in turn, produce the sentimental sense of the minority's disenfranchisement, especially the queer's disenfranchisement. The pursuit or protection of civil rights, usually articulated by the analogy to racial civil rights, produces not a "born that way" argument as much as a political name, nomenclature, a rhetoric of representation. The subject of "true" feeling is then the subject of "figurative" feeling—a feeling that relies on what we might as well call the universal-minority rhetoric of racial minority status. We are not talking about realism here. We are not searching for accuracy, or truth, or even full minority disclosures. We are not even discussing the best kind of politics, which are certainly better imagined in much more sanguine and optimistic proposals set out by scholars such as Berlant, Pellegrini, Jakobsen, Halley, and Duggan. Instead, we are pausing to note that queers take on the language of injury that conforms not with a biological model of minority status, but with an impoverished metaculture legibility that cannot and will not describe too much difference. The figurative language of rights as wrongs does not conform to the actual or accurate description of sexual orientation's lived experiences. Instead, it is a form of rhetorical shorthand that is certainly dangerous; but living without this shorthand is perhaps just as dangerous.

I have used the example of Baldwin and a number of imaginative writers who affiliate queerness and race through the hateful language of conservative Christianity to suggest that we might want to consider current minority movements in less rigid, less detectable, and less congealed ways. The LGBTQ response to Amendment 2's legal confusions over the status of sexual orientation—nature or nurture—did not resolve them; in fact, they were made more confusing and relied on many rhetorical flights of fancy that veer from the "truth" of *realpolitik*. Which is not a bad thing when working with a system that only understands simplistic notions of sexuality, not to mention citizenship or personhood, or feeling.

Interestingly, Berlant, while worrying about the suffering/feeling model of sentimental politics, wonders if "it may be that the sharp specificity of the traumatic model of pain implicitly mischaracterizes what a person is as what a person becomes in the experience of social negation."[61] Although she sees the mischaracterization as potentially damaging for minority politics, I'm curious about the mischaracterization, about how the "like race" model gives us not specificity as much as a gross generalization that helpfully obscures the "real" queer self from entering into the toxic and pathological public arena where queer negation must always be expected. When queers then take on racial similes, inspired if not provoked by the religious hate speech of the conservative right, to describe themselves, a certain pernicious realism assigned to either race or sexuality is momentarily evacuated, or at least contested.

Thus, I grudgingly like "like race" arguments. A particularly useful space for thinking critically and acting strategically occurs within the fury around the comparison, especially during insurgent moments such as the activity and activism in Colorado. Moreover, the "like race" simile usually implies a "structure of feeling," a hypothesis rather than explicit statement of fact or confession of identity that tentatively enables the inarticulate to find some kind of momentary legibility. Perhaps this flight of fancy resists the kind of jeremiadic legibility required of the state's minority populations. Religious hatred, then, becomes an opportunity for the comparison between sexuality and race; religious hatred operates as a racial feeling that is "a kind of feeling and thinking which is indeed social and material, but each in an

147

embryonic phase before it can become fully articulate and defined ex-change."[62] Queers certainly belong to a minority category that suffers and benefits from the ways it is always "embryonic." But in the realm of insurgent politics, they must find some language, some nominal claim of difference that will make a greater difference that can sidestep the treachery of the American jeremiad.

The hatred of race, persistently and rhetorically used as the hatred that is kind of like the hatred experienced by queers, is, as the raging debates about gay marriage reveal, still in heavy rotation. This racial feeling, made possible by a religious language that targets and hurts, puts the queer minority complaint into a language of subaltern citizen that is a not-so-true "subject of true feeling," who then is part of the sentimental politics that dominates so much theory, criticism, and activism from the American left. This feeling, this worry over systematic hatred, carries hope by recognizing, if not overemphasizing, the hate, the degradation, and the pain one feels when disenfranchised by the state. It is in the queer's best interest to lie because lying about oneself makes more complicated, and perhaps more subversive, the ways that minority citizens will figure out how to deflect or shield themselves from the dominant radar that anticipates any complaint or defect they might want to share. Sure, we sacrifice historical, ontological, and faithful clarity about who we might be. But with that sacrifice we become sacrifices, martyrs. And then we become a bit more valuable and make it harder to make us *homo sacer*, make it harder to dispose of us as if we don't matter.

Conclusion

Our Aberrant Future

... and a great many people who came out of the closet should reconsider.

—JAMES BALDWIN[1]

Family Disasters

Although critics and activists discovered that they could use the hateful Christian rhetoric to make queers "like race," the religious right has been quick to notice as much.[2] They've figured out that their "special rights" campaigns backfire—that accusations of hate and homophobia have enabled queers to make a claim that they are a targeted minority, much like a racial minority. In 2003, less than a decade after *Romer v. Evans,* Mission: America, just one of the many cyber evangelical ministries on the Internet, asked its readers to be on the watch for queer accusations that the religious right is hateful. One of its diagnostic tools, created in 2002, "A Checklist to Assess Your School's Risk for Encouraging Homosexuality," wonders if your local school has a "Non-discrimination policy" based on "sexual orientation" or programs to stop "homophobia," "hate," or "bias"? If so, there are "problems" and "assumptions" that Mission: America helpfully delineates:

Assumptions: That there is something wrong with objecting to homosexuality. That homosexual behavior is a minority issue like racial status. Any objections to homosexual behavior are said to originate from "hate" and are connected to violence against homosexuals. Such programs claim there is no difference between expressed hatred of homosexuals and commonplace moral objections.

Problems: Puts those who object to homosexuality for any reason on the defensive. Causes those who have objections to remain silent, leaving an open field for radical student, teacher or outside group to define "hate" and discrimination however they wish. Flies in the face of freedom of religion, freedom of association and freedom of speech.

. . .

Results: Christians, conservatives and in fact, all supporters of traditional values are accused of "hate." Instances of harassment are linked to those who would never commit such acts. Students are not warned about homosexuality, so more will experiment with this high-risk behavior."[3]

Whether or not we agree with the ministry's full logic (which is actually quite on target), we should note how the discourse of hate now signals to the religious right that the homosexual "agenda" has not been stopped; despite the right's best efforts, the gay agenda is putting the right on the defensive. Moral objections to homosexuality risk exposing those who oppose homosexuals to accusations of intolerance, avarice, and violence, perhaps silencing the expression of those objections. It has become harder to be so open about one's disdain for the homosexual lifestyle, especially since the hatred is helping mark queers as like a racial minority. One implication of this line of thinking is that the social attack on queers can no longer be so explicit. Otherwise one might be violating school policies that might, given time and the power of the "gay agenda," become municipal, state, and federal policies. Religious hate has had to go into the closet, as it were. Lest conservative Christians further aid queers in becoming "like race," disagreement with and disapproval of homosexuality have to be more "diplomatic" in a rhetorical and political world that appears to be more open-minded about queers.

Certainly, cultural and some political developments since Amendment 2 cast queer politics and visibility as a more common phenomenon, inviting the perception that there's more social acceptance and thus less "tolerance" for an anti-homosexual sentiment. In the words of John D'Emilio, "the world turned," and now the previously marginal and reviled queer has become a central focus of mainstream politics and culture.[4] The examples of an increasingly queer mainstream are abundant: popular television programs such as *Will and Grace, Queer Eye for the Straight Guy, The L Word,* and both of Ellen DeGeneres's shows have crowded the airways; homosexual sodomy was legalized in the United States by the U.S. Supreme Court decision in *Lawrence v. Texas*; and then there is the same-sex marriage issue. Ah, marriage! It is possibly the queer's necessary Achilles' heel, a question that troubles both the right and the left.

Often cast as an ultimate push for social and political legitimacy, marriage has gotten many activists and scholars worried about the mainstream directions of LGBTQ activism. We should recall the work on the perils and pleasures of the mainstream by Urvashi Vaid, Andrew Sullivan, and Michael Warner.[5] In 2003, Lisa Duggan offered a critique of the mainstreaming of queer politics in *The Twilight of Equality?* In this study, she understandably worries about the pro-business, "neoliberal" tendencies of so much left-based politics, which frequently includes the "false promises of superficial 'multiculturalism.'"[6] The "neoliberal" politics have eviscerated the radical action she watched develop and devolve during her adulthood of activism. Duggan argues, in an explicitly polemical manner, "As long as the progressive-left represents and reproduces itself as divided into economic vs. cultural, universal vs. identity-based, distribution vs. recognition-oriented, local vs. global branches, it will defeat itself."[7] Her critique might very well be a wake-up call for those moments when we think we are being radical in our attempts to access national membership using traditional models of liberal action, especially when those attempts are divorced from economic considerations. Just because one has the right to marry does not really change the world all that much. Even when we demand equality, especially equality in marriage, we might also be reinforcing an increasingly homogenized "neoliberal" state. The state, after all, has the capacity to normalize and sanitize what is "minor" and countercultural about queers who should otherwise resist the traditional forms of the nation— forms that are globally inflected by the late American empire formations, which in turn make us supine consumers in the circuits of post-Fordist, late-finance capital that only offer further imprisonment in cultures and states of damaged and damaging consumption.[8]

Yet the right to wed, rightly or wrongly, is considered fundamental to the what it means to count as a person who is free in the United States. The majority opinion in *Loving v. Virginia,* the case that outlawed miscegenation and permitted people of different races to wed, tells us that "the freedom to marry has long been recognized as one of the vital personal rights essential to the orderly pursuit of happiness by free men."[9] So that which is at stake in the fight over marriage is not just a frivolous question of assimilation, not just the desire to be comfortably and officially partnered in a binding financial, religious, and statutory manner; it is also a fight to be counted as valuable as a citizen, as one with access to the cluster of rights and freedoms that may or may not include the official recognition of same-sex marriage. To have that right as an option gives value to the people whether or not they wish to exercise that right. Sure, this is a lousy predicate of personhood, and I don't particularly enjoy watching queer politics being dominated by the marriage issue. But when there is a fundamental restriction to "one of the vital personal rights," people should be alarmed, even if they hate, as I do, the institution of marriage, even if they despise, as I do, the system that makes freedom and marriage so interlaced. At issue is not wedlock so much as counting as a person in a sovereign system that wants to strip people of personhood in order to consolidate and augment political power. Whatever the eventual outcome of the marriage issue, just the fact that there has been so much outrage and resistance to queer marriage demonstrates the strong desire not to give queers fundamental value in the United States. The stakes of this debate, no matter how poorly this contest is being waged, are enormous.

More distressing, however, is what the conservative, Christian right can do with this issue. A massive fund-raising and activist initiative by the Family Research Council, "Family, Faith, and Freedom: The Battle for Marriage," has been created to help push for the Federal Marriage Amendment. The same-sex marriage issue, one of many issues dear to the council and the religious right (such as abortion, the right to die, contraception, stem-cell research, Internet pornography, decency laws), reactivates the revulsion many still feel against queers. Whereas open hostility toward queers might get some conservatives into trouble, which might then help queers pursue their "like race" agenda, concern over marriage allows queers to be attacked, to be the object of jeremiadic disdain, but by proxy. To put it most simply, same-sex marriage debates have enabled the right to bring us right back to the longest-standing association with what's wrong with homosexuality: homosexuality's connection to pedophilia and incest.

Lawrence v. Texas, which overruled the criminalization of homosexual sodomy, paving, as Scalia warned, the way for gay marriage to come to the United States, echoes the anxieties that everyone seems to have when the rights of queers are at issue: "This case does not involve minors, persons who might be injured or coerced, those who might not easily refuse consent, or public conduct or prostitution. It does involve two adults who, with full and mutual consent, engaged in sexual practices common to a homosexual lifestyle."[10] The conservative rehearsal of the pedophilic association as the object of the jeremiadic lament enables a more "sensitive," less coercive conservative constituency to still traffic in hate, still devalue and strip the queer—banning him or her through the form of religious attention and sacrilization that Agamben warns us about.

David Sedaris describes this incest and pedophilia paranoia while reflecting on his relationship to the Catholic Church sex scandals that have intensified since the beginning of the twenty-first century.[11] The anxieties about the Church and homosexuality could become an anxiety about religion and sexuality that all could share, regardless of whether they are Catholic, Protestant, Jewish, or of any other faith, or atheists. The scandals offer a contagious moral outrage, which permits people to say mean things about queers. While listening to one radio program that had been discussing the scandals, Sedaris reports:

> The Catholic Church scandal had been front-page news for over a week, and when the priest angle had been exhausted, the discussion filtered down to pedophilia in general, and then, homosexual pedophilia, which was commonly agreed upon to be the worst kind. It was, for talk radio, one of those easy topics, like tax hikes or mass murder. "What do you think of full-grown men practicing sodomy on children?"
>
> "Well, I'm against it!" This was always said as if was somehow startling, a minority position no one had dared lay claim to.
>
> I'd been traveling around the country for the past ten days, and everywhere I went I heard the same thing. The host would congratulate the caller on his or her moral fortitude, and wanting to feel approval again, the person would rephrase the original statement, freshening it up with an adverb or qualifier: "Call me old-fashioned, but I just hugely think it's wrong." Then, little by little, they'd begin interchanging the words *homosexual* and *pedophile,* speaking as if they were one and the same. "Now they've got them on TV," Audrey said. "And in the schools! Talk about the proverbial chicken in the henhouse. . . . These homosexuals can't reproduce themselves, and so they go into the schools and try to recruit our young people."[12]

Sedaris's reaction, given this persistent association and easy substitution of "pedophile" with "homosexual," is to think, nervously, about the implications and suspicions queers, especially queer men, must occupy in a nation that can so quickly hate them, or deem them wrong, or proclaim them dangerous. Anxieties about priests quickly translate into anxieties about gay people. Gayle Rubin taught us years ago about the quick and highly effective moral panics provoked by the association, if not the fungible quality, between homosexuality and pedophilia, and Sedaris humorously comments on the link's recent incarnation.[13] He unavoidably must sort through this link, for indeed, most queers, especially queer men, must always worry about the connection.

Sedaris's observations are not idiosyncratic; there are other "haters," more dangerous than radio call-in pundits. For instance, in 2003, Joseph Druce murdered John Geoghan, a notorious "pedophile priest." Druce, a man whom the Worcester, Massachusetts, district attorney described as being "so consumed with hatred toward homosexuals," considered Geoghan a "prize" worth killing.[14] Druce was already serving time for the strangulation of a man he had believed was gay. Geoghan's murder, which occurred within the confines of the Souza-Baranowski Correctional Facility, was gruesome and has been reported in vivid detail, but, curiously, the moral outrage one often expects from details of a homicide have not been abundant. After all, it was a pedophile who was killed, a man convicted in January 2002 for groping a ten-year-old boy in 1991, just one incident among many he allegedly committed. In September 2001, the Boston archdiocese paid a reported $10 million to settle a suit comprised of eighty-six plaintiffs, all charging Geoghan with sexual assault. Notre Dame historian Scott Appelby told CNN that Geoghan was "clearly a troubled soul," a "sick man and a predator priest. An icon for the scandal that has rocked the church."[15] The defrocked priest was certainly no martyr, and so his gruesome end, at the hands of an unrepentant homophobe, is not easily mourned. He was a "sick" and "perverse" icon of the increasingly infamous Catholic Church.

Certainly it is hard to defend the actions and life of a pedophile, especially with all the harmful and tragic stories of real abuse that comprise Geoghan's history and the many histories within dioceses throughout the world. Among numerous quarters and in casual conversations, however, a knee-jerk response to the outrage over pedophilia has overshadowed the fact that a man had been killed, and by someone who has long hated homosexuals. Real justice, as I have repeatedly been told, was served behind bars.[16] Appelby explained, "While some may say, sadly, he got what's coming to him. I think the prevailing feeling is one of sadness for what he did, for the state of his own soul."[17] In statements such as these, instead of the prevailing feeling being one of shock and anger over the actions of Druce, we are directed to the "real" story—one with priests who pray and prey on little boys, priests whose sicknesses must be lamented, if not "cured" by death. What often escapes our attention is the fact that Druce made the mistake that many often willfully make: there is an assumption that pedophilia is just another example of homosexuality, and that some kind of hatred toward gays can find an acceptable expression in the violent punishment of the predators, the pedophile priests. The lack of consent of Geoghan's sex abuse should not be diminished; nor should we be unconcerned with the after-effects of any act of sexual violence. But that kind of abuse cannot be so easily conflated with homosexuality; nor should the hatred of homosexuality be permitted, or even celebrated, when the homosexual victim is considered to be a pedophile. We should be worried about the public uses and abuses of pedophilia and wonder why so much hatred can be deemed justifiable or acceptable when questions of children, of religion, and of family seem threatened—usually threatened by someone thought to be "homosexual."

This murder and the reactions it elicited are by no means isolated. The proliferation of church sex scandals, along with the regimented outrage that even permits homophobic violence to occur within state institutions such as prisons, are not just accidental occurrences, aberrations in a public that *seems* to be more tolerant and accepting of gays. One should look at the not-infamous-enough comments of U.S. senator Rick Santorum, who made many of the links between homosexuality and pedophilia that contemporary queer politics should worry about. In an April 7, 2003, interview with the Associated Press, Santorum connected the decline of the traditional, heterosexual family with the "moral relativism" brought on by "liberalism," which is, according to the senator, one of the root causes why there are so many Church sex scandals. With the acceptance of a variety of "different lifestyles," Santorum explained that you make the dangerous case that "you can do whatever you want to do, as long as it's in the privacy of your own home." When he made these remarks, he was concerned about the then impending *Lawrence v. Texas* ruling, with its specific issues about who has the "right to privacy." For Santorum, there's the dangerous possibility that privacy granted to all, twinned with consent, would allow for any type of behavior: "You're sending signals that as long as you do it in private and consensually, we don't really care what you do." Bizarrely, this fear of private permissiveness inspired Santorum to characterize the Catholic Church scandals as sex scandals that featured relationships that were "basic homosexual relationships" between consenting, private adults: "We're not talking about priests with 3-year-olds, or 5-year-olds." If we think about this assertion, suddenly, the pedophiles are no longer pedophiles, they are homosexuals, and Santorum quickly made the association Druce made: pedophilic priests engage in "basic homosexual relationships," which are revolting and worthy of our disdain.[18]

When questioned by the AP reporter about his bias against homosexuality, Santorum parroted a typical Christian response that, as a Christian, he "has no problem with homosexuality" per se. His problem is actually with "homosexual acts." And homosexual acts done privately and with consent signal the descent of decent, American society. I must quote this passage at length:

> We have laws in states, like the one at the Supreme Court right now, that has sodomy laws and they were there for a purpose. Because, again, I would argue, they undermine the basic tenets of our society and the family. And if the Supreme Court says that you have the right to consensual sex in your home, then you have the right to bigamy, you have the right to polygamy, you have the right to incest, you have the right to adultery. You have the right to anything. Does that undermine the

fabric of our society? I would argue yes, it does. It all comes from, I would argue, this right to privacy that doesn't exist in my opinion in the United States Constitution, this right that was created, it was created in Griswold [v. Connecticut]—Griswold was the contraceptive case —and abortion [*sic*]. And we're just extending it out. And the further you extend it out, the more you—this freedom actually intervenes and affects the family. You say, well, it's my individual freedom. Yes, but it destroys the basic unit of our society because it condones behavior that's antithetical to strong, healthy families. Whether it's polygamy, whether it's adultery, whether it's sodomy, all of those things are antithetical to a healthy, stable, traditional family.

Every society in the history of man has upheld the institution of marriage as a bond between a man and a woman. Why? Because society is based on one thing: that society is based on the future of the society. And that's what? Children. Monogamous relationships. In every society, the definition of marriage has not ever to my knowledge included homosexuality. That's not to pick on homosexuality. It's not, you know, man on child, man on dog, or whatever the case may be. It's one thing.[19]

The persistent and all-too-familiar connections between homosexuality and the decline of the family seem inescapable. For Santorum, as well as many others, homosexuality, as conservatives rarely tire of saying, is the family's apocalypse; the basic foundation of "family" as a monogamous, heterosexual union will shake as we become more private and tolerant. Most worrisome is that children might be most at risk. Of course, children are not just children, they are the future, and these children should not be hurt by the progressive move to change the nation's most cherished institution—marriage.

Perhaps this is one reason, beyond the scandal of sexual abuse, that pedophilia so quickly becomes the story of homosexuality. Homosexuality, in its illogical conflation, is always an affront to children—it is pedophilic preying on the nation's future voting citizens, who might otherwise learn to tolerate and accept any social behavior, who might allow for Gayle Rubin's long-held wish for "benign variation" of sexual identities and behaviors.[20] Or, these children might simply not be "there" at all, if we ignore the realities of queer parenting and reproductive technologies and, instead, believe the conservative Christian lie that homosexual families are nonprocreative families. In any case, we are led to worry, in a sentimental way, about the future loss of children. We are told to worry about the violent world they will be forced and coerced into accepting if homosexuals were permitted to thrive in privacy, in consensual relations, in marriage, and, *especially*, in the Church, which, as we know, is increasingly synonymous, through the pervasive presence of conservative evangelicals in the United States, with "the Family."[21]

But we shouldn't stop there with a critique. Santorum suggestively makes leaps of logic that help mask the hatred of homosexuals as base and raw exercises of sovereign power. He confuses homosexuality not only with pedophilia, but also pedophile homosexuals with a demand for incestuous rights. Incest has certainly long been a vexing issue, a constitutive taboo, which has touched most arenas that are engaged in understanding the makeup and maintenance of family, if not all other social structures. A great deal of fascinating work in psychoanalysis, anthropology, and feminist anthropology, as well as American literary criticism has already investigated the "right" of incest and its precious placement in the constitution of families, societies, nations, and individual psyches.[22] In a study of Greek tragedy and *Antigone*, Judith Butler, in an example that understands Santorum's hysteria, explains:

Alternative kinship arrangements [such as same-sex kinship relations] attempt to revise psychic structures in ways that lead to tragedy again, figured incessantly as the tragedy of and for the child. No matter what one ultimately thinks of the political value of gay marriage . . . the public debate on its legitimacy becomes the occasion for a set of homophobic discourses that must be resisted on independent grounds.[23]

I agree with Butler. Such resistance, however, is increasingly difficult to resist on "independent grounds." The tragedy of queer rights is a tragedy for the child, and this figuration of tragedy engenders the kind of hateful rhetoric so laboriously used by religious politicians such as Santorum. Church sex controversies so quickly transform into homosexual controversies, then into gay marriage controversies, threatening traditional, very national and patriotic kinship systems, which are "incessantly," or "incestantly," the child's, and thus the nation's potential loss.

We most certainly can describe this tragedy as sentimental, providing conservative politicians with an emotive occasion to become quite hateful toward the pedophilic, if not incestuous, "Father" of the child: the homosexual. Butler rightly states:

> [C]onsider that the horror of incest, the moral revulsion it compels in some, is not far afield from the same horror and revulsion felt toward lesbian and gay sex, and is not unrelated to the intense moral condemnation of voluntary single parenting, or gay parenting, of parenting arrangements with more than two adults involved. . . . These various modes in which the oedipal mandate fails to produce normative family all risk entering into the metonymy of that moralized sexual horror that is perhaps most fundamentally associated with incest.[24]

Santorum's comments certainly experience and manipulate that sexual horror. I would push Butler's argument even farther: that incest—which is so closely aligned with pedophilia—and homosexuality are so frequently thought together, that the horror of incest is now also the horror of homosexuality, the horror of what a permissive, private, and queer-friendly society might permit. In other words, the horror of incest and its twin, pedophilia, is the current way to mark, to figure, the limits of what kind of sexual tolerance toward gays, lesbians, bisexuals, and trans people the current, *extremely* conservative political climate can accommodate.

It is thus perfectly acceptable for a leading politician to voice, in a national way, his hatred of homosexuality, in part because the specter of homosexuality is not "far afield" from the destruction of the family, the fabric of a great nation, and the onslaught of a too permissive liberalism that believes "anything goes." Furthermore, it is perfectly acceptable for Supreme Court justice Antonin Scalia to fret, similarly, over the foundations of the American nation in his dissent in *Lawrence.* Anxious that the Court's anti-sodomy ruling might deform the United States' marriage laws, Scalia believes that the "homosexual agenda" now hurts many Americans who "do not want persons who openly engage in homosexual conduct . . . as scoutmasters for their children, as teachers in their schools"; indeed, these Americans are in peril and will not be able to protect "themselves and their families from a lifestyle that they believe immoral and destructive."[25] The new social tolerance of the homosexual agenda, again and again, puts our moral/religious country, our moral/religious families, and *especially* our moral/religious children at destructive risk. The specter of the pedophile, the specter of incest, is lurking perniciously within this apocalyptic vision of the nation's future. This jeremiadic position does not cause enormous outrage because the hateful connections between the homosexual as sexual predator on children are always so present, always so potently upsetting, that no amount of flair and comedy from the "Fab Five" Queer Eyes can yet alleviate the country's rhetorical convulsions over the possibility that homosexuals might come into destructive contact with children.

The Shadow in the Word

Luckily, this emphasis and exploitation of the incestuous and pedophilic connection to queerness cannot derail the queer use of religious hatred in its argument for the value of queerness. Given the incestuous and pedophilic affiliation we have not chosen and cannot avoid, we can still work through the manner in which queers have long had to address the nation from this pedophilic, incestuous position. By traversing some key moments in queer writers' necessary exploration of the religious link between incest/pedophilia and queer sexuality, I hope to point to yet another series of "like race" analogies that create occasions for political coping, egress, and sanctuary when there are very few other options. Once again, the religious but now incestuous word on homosexuality permits the queers to become gray, become hard to detect, and harder to phrase out conveniently from the conservative nation that needs to hate. As such, the words force us into a deeper appreciation of the holy war of words' emotions, a political structure of feeling that has been and will continue to be the primary terrain of political and cultural contests over who will count and not count as protected citizens of the United States.

While Santorum, through incestuous and pedophilic substitutions, rhetorically casts the queer as *homo sacer,* the rhetoric cannot contain every kind of sentimental hysteria. That is, Santorum and other conservatives can't control the structures of feeling that respond to the vexing questions of queer tolerance. Although this attack is only slightly more oblique, its take on tolerance symptomatically manifests the desire not to mark queers as "like race." He has chosen to absorb the oppositional strategies of queers who present their concerns as if they were racial concerns into the larger feelings of what we will get if too much equality is extended: the fear of a planet of destroyed families, of abused children, of Godless freedom. His comments were not as effective as they might have been because he did not stop with incest and pedophilia on that associative chain—he included bestiality as a potential outcome. His comments went straight to the dogs, as it were, making his ideas seem ridiculous, making them sound like angry and irrational rhetoric.

If we are then free to associate in whatever way we feel fit, the sentimentality of the "like race" analogy can still be deployed, even if incest and pedophilia are code words for homosexuality. Think, for instance, of queer moral outrage—even my own personal outrage—over Santorum and over Geoghan's killing. My rhetoric must also be questioned as a strategy dedicated to my own left and prohomosexual agenda. Curiously, "Godhatesfags.com" is correct when it asserts, "Fags shamelessly use the deaths of fags to promote their sodomite agenda,"[26] for I am using the moral panic of unjust deaths, the manifest expressions of queer hatred, to a perverse, queer advantage. I am putting on display conservative worry over restricted national notions of families and especially children. I can then reassert what is still minor about queerness, especially at a moment when "gay visibility" has been heralded as winning the battle, especially at the moment when tolerance seems to be so readily extended to queers.

I am thus indeed using the horror of incest and pedophilia, but for a different purpose. By drawing attention to the hysteria of people such as Santorum, by drawing attention to the perversity of religious commentary on national futurity and the nation's important children, I make room in the hateful words of the religious right in order to describe negatively the position of queer in contemporary U.S. politics and culture. I can take on that form of hate speech as a form of self-expression of the queer as a minority by asserting something as strange as: I'm still a minority because I'm so quickly affiliated with incest, pedophilia, and the destruction of functional, productive families. I'm still a minority because I have to figure the apocalyptic vision of liberal ruin, and as an incestuous, pedophilic figure, I can readily and calmly be defiled at the lowest and highest levels of U.S. government and culture—on the floor of the Senate or on the floor of a jail cell, as it were, all while the conservative and religious public sphere gives such derision its religious blessing. What's more, as representative of the nation's limits, I have no choice in the matter—the associations and anxieties are there, no matter how much I wish they weren't. So, in negative, in obverse, I'm still using, and not really changing, the religiously inflected terms set by the Christian right, if not the religious righteous: my claims of recognition also cause worry over the family, child loss, and the future of the nation—a nation so predicated on conservative, Christian values.

George Chauncey, in the *New York Times,* is quoted as saying: "What strikes me . . . is how closely the resistance to same-sex marriage resembles white people's fears about interracial marriage, which were the emotional core of their fears about integration in general. Now, as in the 1950s and 60s, much of the objection to legally extending marital rights takes the form of religious warnings about a declining 'moral order.' "[27] Chauncey, referring to the sexuality anxieties legally but by no means fully resolved in the 1967 *Loving v. Virginia* case, brings the current concerns over queer rights once again into alignment with the emotional core of race relations. This "emotional core" of race is also the emotional core we can quite simply find in the generic Christian Word. Inside the Word, we have dangerous, resisting emotions about race that bother us, propel us, into a language that is more capacious than literal, open to all sorts of figurations that refuse the explicit articulation of queerness.

No wonder that Butler, soon after she argues that the horror over incest is so often associated with the horror of gay sex, rushes into a discussion of Orlando Patterson's influential book, *Slavery and Social Death,* and his useful concept of "social death," a "status of being a living being radically deprived of all rights that are supposed to be accorded to any and all living beings."[28] The social death of slavery is a social death that can be applied to the kinds of death queers are given in the United States, especially when they are so closely aligned with the horrors of incest, also known as the horrors of the eroding tradition of the American family. In the current queer political and cultural climate, the rhetoric of these kinds of emotions provokes us into politics; we are struggling, as we long have, with social injustice in terms of loss, of slavery, of incest, and strong feelings that aggregate the queer with race. So let's chart that struggle with a few instructive queer instances. Please note that the following examples are created by and about women. I pursue these examples because they highlight a crucial gendered element in the political manipulation of the anxieties of incest and queerness.

Alice Walker's epistolary novel, *The Color Purple,* is a race story about social deaths played out in plots involving pedophilia/incest, religious faith, and lesbian sexuality, among other things. The protagonist, Celie, through letters belonging to her and her sister, describes a hard existence that is most profoundly indexed by family situations that are so disastrous that one should, as the beginning italicized phrase above the first letter warns, *"not never tell nobody but God. It'd kill your mammy."*[29] Indeed, the tragedies are so awful that Celie needs God as her confessional interlocutor, enabling the articulations of horrible things too lethal for even a mother's ear. But we, the readers, hear about them, and what we learn is that the ravages of a rural, poor black life have taken their toll on Celie, who does not belong to a functional family. Her father, or the man she believes to be her father during much of the novel, is the original culprit for her kinship troubles: he repeatedly rapes Celie, making her children also her siblings; he beats Celie's mother; he has an intense attachment to Celie's sister, Nettie; and he eventually marries Celie off to an abusive and unwanted husband, Mr. ——, who grudgingly allows Celie to serve as a caretaker of his children, house, and farm. This patrilineal tour from one bad family structure to another is only about sexual and physical violence, with her early sources of delight and love—her children and her sister Nettie—persistently banished by the men who order her into all sorts of submission.

This state of submission is most intensely communicated by "father-daughter incest" that is perhaps the most potent way Walker exposes and articulates, through epistolary address, the awful things that can only be said to God. Spillers, in a piece about Walker and other African American writers working *fictionally* with incest, explains something helpful: "It seems that parent-child incest, in its various ramifications, remains the preeminent dream-thought that not only evades interpretation (or dreaming), but is so layered itself in avoidance and censorship that an interpretive project regarding it appears ludicrous."[30] Perhaps because of this ridiculousness, "incest translates into the unsayable which is all the more sayable by

the very virtue of one's muteness before it."[31] For Walker's novel, which fix-
ates on Celie's sexual trauma and the lack of coherent family structure
made possible because of incest, says so much, indeed shouts so much,
about what the incest narrative allows her to achieve: "an enclosure, a sort
of confessional space between postures of the absolute."[32] Incest, that is,
provides a verbose and muddy area of articulation, permitting the affect of
families gone awry to be expressed, kind of. The fictional detail that we
learn well into our reading of the novel further proves my point—Celie's
father was not actually her father: "My daddy lynch. My mamma crazy. All
my little half-brothers and sisters no kin to me. My children not my sister
and brother. Pa not pa" (163). The parent-child incest within the text's die-
gesis is entirely fictional, which resolves some of the bad family feeling in
the novel but, more importantly, points out that incest serves, for Walker,
as an important, shadowy trope—incest is the way that the unsayable can
be said, some confessional enclosure that cannot be clear or absolute, but is
terrible and poignant nonetheless.

That something terrible and poignant has something to do with lesbianism, so Walker, like so many other queer writers, is also guilty of making
incest a key but shadowy part of a fictional representation of queerness. She
combines incest with violent, Christian language to make the queer's plight
felt. For example, not too long after Celie, who has had lesbian sex with
Shug Avery, learned that her important family members (her sister and her
children) are alive and not sullied by incest, she chooses to write her confessional letters to her sister instead of God. In the long letter that gives us
the explicit reference to the book's title, Celie recounts a theological discussion she has with Shug—a discussion Celie has while she sorts through her
resentment of Mr. ——, a resentment most vividly felt by deliberately
allowing Celie to think that her ravaged family was forever gone, forever
marked by the toxic nonrelations of incest. Celie's faith in what she has
learned to believe, her faith in the awfulness of a life with things so terrible
they could only be addressed to God, has shook, and Shug gives her a new
way to approach religion. The letter reads:

Here's the thing, say Shug. The thing I believe. God is inside you and inside everybody else. You come into the world with God. But only them that search for it inside find it. And sometimes it just manifest itself even if you not looking, or don't know what you looking for. Trouble do it for most folks, I think. Sorrow, lord. Feeling like shit.

It? I ast.

Yeah, It. God ain't a he or a she, but a It.

But what do it look like? I ast.

Don't look like nothing, she say. It ain't a picture show. It ain't something you can look apart from anything else, including yourself. I believe God is everything, say Shug. Everything that is or ever was or ever will be. And when you can feel that, and be happy to feel that, you've found it.

Shug a beautiful something, let me tell you. She frown a little, look out cross the yard, lean back in her chair, look like a big rose.

She say, My fist step from the old white man was trees. Then air. Then birds. Then other people. But one day when I was sitting quiet and feeling like a motherless child, which I was, it come to me: that feeling of being part of everything, not separate at all. I knew that if I cut a tree, my arm would bleed. And I laughed and I cried and I run all around the house. I knew just what it was. In fact, when it happen, you can't miss it. It sort of like you know what, say, grinning and rubbing high up on my thigh.

Shug! I say.

Oh, she say, God love all them feelings. That's some of the best stuff God did. And when you know God loves 'em you enjoys 'em a lot more. You can just relax, go with everything that going, and praise God by liking what you like.

God don't think it dirty? I ast. (178)

God is always difficult to talk about. But Shug has devised a way to incorporate something like God into her worldview—a worldview, with her

God's help, that permits her to cope with the kinds of racial and gender oppression that otherwise threaten to sully and reduce her own attempts at having a vibrant life. Obviously, the very unorthodox spirituality she has devised to translate the violent, white Christian God ("the old white man") into something more equitable and life affirming is most pronounced about Shug's theological invention. In an Eastern mysticism way, suddenly God is everything, every feeling, and an organic whole one only needs to notice, one only has to feel. But what is more interesting, I think, is her rhetorical innovation that exceeds the desire for a gender and racial-neutral language about God: "God ain't a he or a she, but a It." If God is an "It" rather than a gendered (and white) being, then something incredibly powerful and vague can happen to the God: "It" describes everything, with absolutely no precision or logic. And "It," furthermore, is an emotional language that relies less on divisions ("the feeling of being part of everything, not separate") and more on an emotional punch.

Even though Shug makes the God *qua* It deeply unspecific, her desire to impress the point of "It" relies on a very important example of what "It" is: "It" is like "you know what"—the sexuality and eroticism of which Shug reminds Celie by rubbing Celie's thigh. What resonates here is the significance of Baldwin's queer "It" in *Go Tell It on the Mountain.* Like Baldwin, such an unspoken and inarticulate reference immediately recalls, for Walker, shared sexual experiences, which are fully framed and implicated in Celie's difficult family circumstances:

My mama did, I tell Shug. My sister Nettie run away. Mr. —— come git me to take care of his rotten children. He never ast me nothing bout myself. He clam on top of me and fuck and fuck, even when my head bandaged. Nobody ever love me, I say.

She say, I love you, Miss Celie. And then she haul off and kiss me on the mouth.

Um, she say, like she surprise. I kiss her back, say, *um,* too. Us kiss till us can't hardly kiss no more. Then us touch each other.

I don't know nothing bout it, I say to Shug.

I don't know much, she say.

Then I feels something real soft and wet on my breast, feel like one of my little lost babies mouth.

Way after while, I act like a little lost baby too. (109; emphasis in the original)

As queer novices, Shug and Celie confess not knowing much about what seems like lesbian sexuality, "It," and instead use a very vague language that is sometimes marked only by an inarticulate sound, "*Um.*" These instances of "It," these moments of kind-of-articulate rubbing and touching, are something like the feeling of Shug's sense of God. Moreover, these instances are also given crucial analogies that help Celie describe the feelings of sex: it "feel like one of my lost babies mouth." The language of sex, here, is quite literally at the tip of their tongues, close to their mouths, but not only their mouths. Instead, their mouths feel like the things that carry the most complicated, emotional weight of Celie's shattered, incestuous family—her lost babies, the babies she thinks are both her children and her siblings. That is, for the moment Celie can only experience the connection to her family in the "like" quality of her sex acts with Shug. Her own literary grasps for sexuality's articulateness is thus made possible by an ambivalent language of love and loss that her not-normal-enough family structure, however tragically, has provided her.

For Celie, then, her sexuality, with its attendant emotions of love and connection to Shug, is best expressed by an ambiguous set of analogies that refer to her own affiliations with incest, with a dysfunctional family life that punctuates just how bad her life has been, being black, poor, and female in a very inequitable America. The *Um*-quality of her sexuality is incestuously a*kin* to the "It" quality of God—a God responsible for all sorts of experiences of connection and division, belonging and not belonging, racial inclusion and racist exclusion, gender parity and male supremacy that Celie and Shug and the novel's characters must accept. For lesbianism, incest, sexuality, and unorthodox religious beliefs, although sometimes troubling, are the circumstances, stories, and words that Celie has been given, which in conversations and reflection she turns into something else —a language and a story of "It" that she first addresses to God and then to her sister, Nettie—first God-talk, then dysfunctional family talk.

Walker has Celie tackling some of the biggest issues facing her African American characters by interlacing queer sexuality, incest, and religion for a reason: at key moments in the novel, she is condensing many dramas of oppression and violence into a drama of a family gone wrong, only to be made right or given some kind of civil right, fictionally accomplished by relying on a terribly ambiguous word, "It," which is a word for God, but which is a word much freer than one had previously thought or felt. So much of what should not be said can be said by a religious language of "It," which inaugurates the important project of making the stories open to re-vision, reflection, play, and impression. By choosing an epistolary perspec-tive with an interested and biased narrator, Walker calls attention to the invested kinds of inflections a character has in presenting the "facts" of her life as words, or as an "It" she can manipulate so she can do something with the terror of "It's" feelings. As figurations, Celie can write the feelings, figurate the feelings, and fix her feelings in order to allow for more that will not be said. Walker's race story to God, then, which is also a story about incest and queer sexuality, is just that: a story. But this story harbors an emotional race core, capable of communicating inarticulate things about queer sexuality through an incest association, which we learn is not true. But it is an association that must be thought true, proven false, and still very much a part of the way Celie imagines the sequence of events and emotions she wants to commit to the page.

I don't mean to say that this novel has nothing to do with reality or even realism. Certainly Walker's story has plots and instances that resonate with "the real world." But Walker is making up the story, featuring key parts, such as incest, as fiction that still makes possible the articulation of a happier story of hard-earned love and connection. We can then consider

Walker's book to God as a *fictional* argument, an argument reliant on the play of words in order to make the harshness of one's social position more malleable, more evocative, and more moving than just the production of a testimony that can only be addressed, as the book's opening and broken prohibition warned (*"You better not never tell nobody but God"*), with extreme and reverent seriousness, with pious and deeply held secrets that carry the theological terror that cannot be played with, transformed, or made into something other than terrible testifying. In other words, inside the ambiguous but authoritative religious Word, once it becomes an incestuous *word*, literary play can occur, twisting the known world into something quite unfamiliar and harder to grasp.

The last letter is addressed to a Whitmanesque world: "Dear God, Dear stars, dear trees, dear sky, dear peoples. Dear Everything. Dear God" (249).[33] For Walker has Celie learn to write to her sister, to others, offering the possibility of a sinister and terrible formulation of the representation and recognition (like race, like incest) of sexuality that is nevertheless an ambiguous language of God—a language that is strangely productive of unimaginable pleasure and connection. At novel's end, her family, although peculiarly constituted, lives together during the national holiday when "White people busy celebrating they independence from England July 4 . . . so most black folks don't have to work. Us can spend the day celebrating each other" (250). In spite of the violence, destruction, heartbreak, and inequality, they still celebrate. God, who has been so hateful, is also like love, God is also like queer feeling, God is also like incest, God is also like the families we make, but mostly God is an "It," a language of an inarticulate emotional race core, an oppositional language of blackness, full of all sorts of terrible things that will be indexed but not fully expressed. God is a terrible "It," God is sort of like a vague race pronoun, permitting the worst of life's occurrences to find a form of address that can communicate bad things while still providing for much more than the bad.

Walker, of course, is not the only one to connect the racial "It" quality of God through a fiction about race and incest. Take, for another example, the book Ann Cvetkovich describes as a "powerful" examination of "the intimate connections between sexual trauma and sexual pleasure, and by implication the connections between incest and, if not lesbianism explicitly, then, perverse sexuality":[34] Dorothy Allison's *Bastard Out of Carolina*. For this "lesbian" narrative—and I will, for the sake of convenience and clarity, call it such—does express some difficult connections that belong to this constellation of homosexuality, incest, hate, and, quite poignantly, race and religion that I have been describing. The central character, Bone, a victim of "real" incest and a failing and poor white family, struggles and embodies a "hardscrabble" existence. At key moments, nevertheless, Bone is overcome by the power of gospel music, by the power of preachers' words, wondering how she could possibly belong to these moments of public, collective expression about what is supposed to be private: one's soul, one's personal story, or one's faith. The words she hears during one church gathering are characteristically religious in that they are both obscure and yet very potent: "Revivals are funny. People get pretty enthusiastic, but they sometimes forget just which hymn it is they're singing. I grinned at the sound of mumbled, unintelligible song."[35] Despite the lack of specific words and message, and despite the way that this mumbling occasions men close to the Revival tent to "punch each other lightly and curse in a friendly fashion," Bone finds the religious utterances deeply moving:

> *You bastard.*
>   *You son of a bitch.*
>   The preacher said something I didn't understand. There was a moment of silence, and then a pure tenor voice rose up in the night sky. The spit soured in my mouth. They had a real singer in there, a real gospel choir.
>   *Swing low, sweet chariot . . . coming for to carry me home . . . swing low, sweet chariot . . . coming to carry me home.*
>   The night seemed to wrap around me like a blanket. My insides felt as if they had melted, and I could taste the wind in my mouth. The

sweet gospel music poured through me in a piercing young boy's voice, and made all my nastiness, all my jealousy and hatred, swell in my heart . . . The world was too big for me, the music too strong. I knew, I knew I was the most disgusting person on earth. I didn't deserve to live another day. I started hiccupping and crying. (135–136)

Initially, it might be hard for a reader to see how on earth the language provoking the feelings of being "the most disgusting person on earth" might actually foster a radical politics. But surely the redeployment of the word "queer" demonstrates that negatives still might generate some unforeseen and positive developments. Emotionally charged language can be twisted and wrestled in some very curious ways, especially religious language.[36] Thus, Allison here emphasizes such emotion through italics the song-quality of gospel music, just as she also starts the quotation of meaningful rhetoric with curses that call attention to Bone's status as a "bastard," as someone outside of legitimate kinship systems. With italics, Allison grants a significant status to the religious words that are drawn into equivalence of the "friendly curses" to give importance to the form and rhetoric of gospel rather than to the message of the words. Direct religious words from the preacher—theological messages—are not understood; precise meaning is not as important as the visceral, affective state the gospel words provoke in Bone. She is wrapped up by the night, her insides melt, her spit sours, her nastiness and jealousy and hatred swell in her heart. She has an extreme emotional response that is signaled by her intense, corporeal reaction, which calls forth all the feelings of shame, abuse, and anger that make her feel at once full of grandiose self-disgust and empty of significance. Moreover, the gospel music leads her through a series of images of her family into a realization of the way the world is "too big": "I remembered Aunt Ruth's fingers fluttering birdlike in front of her face, Uncle Earle's flushed cheeks and lank black hair as they'd cried together on the porch, Mama's pinched, worried face and Daddy Glen's cold, angry, eyes" (135). It is significant that the eyes that give Bone her particularly confusing insight into her own complicated disgust are the eyes of her incestuous abuser. His eyes enable her perspective; his eyes give her eyes. This victim of incest has a family that has quite simply made her feel terribly wrong, out of place, out of scale, not belonging to this large, strong world.

But Bone's response to gospel is not simply witnessed by either the reader of the novel or Bone herself. She outlines a linguistic structure of these provocative emotions. The religious words are not merely vehicles for the expression of a paralyzing hatred and self-disgust. For Bone astutely tells us something important at another point in the novel: "Salvation was complicated" (148). And part of that complication, Bone explains, are the religious words, exemplified by gospel, which are there to "make you hate and love yourself at the same time, make you ashamed and glorified" (136). It is a musical language of ambivalence that provides a particularly important form in which to express extreme emotions. Listen to the way Bone describes her Uncle Earle's insistent need to blaspheme:

> What I really liked was how he talked about Jesus in a way I understood even when I couldn't put it together with all he said. He talked about Jesus like a man dying for need of him, but too stubborn to sit down to the meal spread within his reach. Earle talked the language of gospel music, with its rhythms and intensity. I heard in his drawled pronouncements the same swelling rough raw voices, the red-faced men and pale sweating women moaning in the back pews. "Lord, Lord!" Moaning and waiting, waiting and praying, "to be washed, Lord Jesus! washed in the blood of the Lamb!" The hunger, the lust and the yearning was palpable. (148)

Bone's sense of words that "could not be put together" into a coherent theological message is subordinate to the fact that she understands the "language of gospel music" to be a language of intensity, moaning, waiting, lust, hunger, and yearning—emotional states that are somehow made "palpable" by the music. Bone needs this language of love and hate because it helps her to understand. More importantly, this language of love and hate, "It," helps her to feel.

Tellingly, the moment in the novel when Bone most feels the power of gospel, what she immediately describes as "real gospel" (169), is when she encounters a clapboard church in the woods. This church provides the occasion for Bone to hear where gospel comes from—from the overwhelming sentiment of African Americans. "At that I froze, realizing that such a church off such a dirt road had to be . . . a colored church" (170). And this moment also provokes a difficult instance of Bone encountering racist hate speech. Her companion, Shannon, uses the slur, "Nigger." In response, Bone acknowledges, "My voice was shaking. The way Shannon said 'nigger' tore at me, the tone pitched exactly like the echoing sound of Aunt Madeline sneering 'trash' when she thought I wasn't close enough to hear" (170). Bone's white-trash status—a status that is most tragically marked by her status as a victim of incest—has made her vulnerable to the kinds of hate speech attacks she so readily identifies as sharing the same pitch as "nigger"; both are slurs that are also experienced as the language of injury. But it is the African American slur in particular that helps her understand that language can tear. The language of slur is so closely associated with the language of "real gospel," and Bone, here, can feel and understand the kind of hate she must also endure as a subject who is systematically blocked from full or legitimate status in the hostile world that hates its "niggers" and its "trash."

Spillers regards "African American sermons [and the religious language they contain] as a paradigm of the structure of ambivalence that constitutes the black person's relationship to American culture and apprenticeship in it."[37] Bone similarly regards sermons and gospels, particularly African American gospels, as paradigmatic of the ambivalence she must confusingly negotiate as she circulates within a culture and society in which she is not legitimate (she's a bastard, an incest victim, a minor girl, and white "trash"). The agony of African American experience so deeply feels *like* Bone's agony. There are powerful analogies, occasioned by the penetrating feeling and power of religion, between "race" and other forms of social exclusion that are hard to articulate, especially if one is a young girl without any status at all.

No wonder that theorists and activists, and not just characters in a book, excavate this emotive connection, this high pitch of hatred, feeling, agony, hunger, and lust, to communicate the "tragedies of a child." Butler, as I mentioned above, suggestively manipulates childhood traumas such as incest to propose the productive qualities of an unexpected resistance we can and should call a racialized politics. She concludes her arguments with a lyrical appeal to the "social death" and the "shadowy realm" of those who fall outside of the boundaries of normative, public sphere. "Giorgio Agamben has remarked that we live increasingly in a time in which populations without full citizenship exist within states; their ontological status as legal subjects is suspended," writes Butler. "These are not lives being genocidally destroyed, but neither are they being entered into the life of the legitimate community in which standards of recognition permit for an attainment of humanness." But rather than see these populations as helplessly moribund, something about this status is productive, or useful. Butler wonders:

> How are we to understand this realm, what Hannah Arendt calls the "shadowy realm," which haunts the public sphere, which is precluded from the public constitution of the human, but which is human in an apparently catachrestic sense of that term? Indeed, how are we to grasp this dilemma of language that emerges when "human" takes on that doubled sense, the normative one based on radical exclusion and the one that emerges in the public sphere of the excluded, not negated, not dead, perhaps slowly, yes, surely dying from a lack of recognition, dying, indeed, from the premature circumspection of the norms by which recognition can be conferred?[38]

The shadowy realm, the realm of a haunting death of those who do not belong to the public sphere, poses a "dilemma of language" that is summarily described as the "melancholy of the public sphere." Bone feels this melancholy of her own lack of positive recognitions that are more valuable than derivative, palpable appellations of "trash," which are akin to "nigger." But through love-hate gospel, her existence in the shadowy realm of non-or-not-quite citizenship produces a melancholy language, full of the ambivalence that cannot let go of the pain, that must love and hate, and that must produce a rawness that is not as intelligible as much as it is felt.

Somehow this religious language—which functions more as a dilemma of language rather than a clear, theological message—produces defiance in Bone. She describes, in terms that could be the very definition of melancholy,[39] what she likes about the way religion expresses the incoherency of her shadow existence. Bone responds to her inability to be "saved" in various Baptist congregations; she knows there was no magic or guilt that would be purged from herself. Nevertheless, religion provides some kind of comfort, and it is a hostile comfort:

I sneezed and coughed for a solid week, lying limp in my bed and crying to every gospel song that came over the radio. It was as if I were mourning the loss of something I had never really had. I sang along with the music and prayed for all I was worth. Jesus' blood and country music, there had to be something else, something more I could hope for. I bit my lip and went back to reading the Book of Revelation, taking comfort in the hope of the apocalypse, God's retribution on the wicked. I liked Revelations, loved the Whore of Babylon and the promised rivers of blood and fire. It struck me like gospel music, it promised vindication. (152)

What Bone enjoys, here, is that religious words provide a reversal of the dire circumstances in which she finds herself, in which she experiences those around her as the wicked who tear into her, much like Shannon's disdain for "nigger," which is so much like the disdain thrown at her by other words. Rather than be "saved," Bone enjoys the power and force of the words that promise some kind of intense opposition to those who oppress her. In this way, she affiliates herself with something that, as we must anticipate by now, the "shadowy realm" of non-or-not-quite-citizen often deeply evokes: a language of blackness. Blackness, even from a position of incest, once again functions most as a powerful language of critique. And Bone speaks as if she's black in order to make a forceful opposition to the public sphere—the liberal nation-state that despises and excludes her.

Butler's own writing reveals similar rhetorical emphases, optimistic about what the shadowy realm of confusing language might permit in terms of its oppositional potential. In describing Antigone's incestuous, promiscuous claim on the human, when she is supposed to be excluded, we know that Antigone "is not of the human but speaks its language. . . . She speaks within the language of entitlement from which she is excluded, participating in the language of the claim with which no final identification is possible."[40] Antigone, much like Bone, has no right to speak in the ways she does, but nevertheless, she does, and as she does, produces the possibility of her own dark, blackening opposition to the language they are forced to inhabit. Antigone speaks the language of the state, and Bone, we can argue, does the same: the language of the American state, a religious language. Both female figures of incest speak the authoritative languages but undermine those languages, forcing them "into perpetual catachresis, showing . . . how a term can continue to signify outside its conventional constraints."[41] An outlaw figure such as Bone or Antigone or even Miss Celie "acts, she speaks, she becomes one for whom the speech act is a fatal crime, but this fatality exceeds her life and enters the discourse of intelligibility as its own promising fatality, the social form of its aberrant, unprecedented future."[42]

Amen

I could conclude this book by calling attention to relatively recent legal "successes" that demonstrate the "like race" arguments still being made by courts, in much the same fashion as they were made in Amendment 2, but now with marriage as the major rights contest. It is true that members of a 400-something coalition of progressive clergy called the Religious Coalition for Freedom have signed a declaration that states, "From the shameful history of slavery in America, the injustice of forbidding people to marry is evident as a denial of basic human rights."[43] The Supreme Court of Massachusetts, in their second ruling on same-sex marriage, rhetorically and explicitly reference the history of segregation, racial civil rights, and *Brown v. Board of Education,* in the majority opinion, issued on February 4, 2004: "This history of our nation has demonstrated that separate is seldom, if ever, equal."[44] But such citations of the prevalence of sentimental race rhetoric would not necessarily count as sufficient evidence that this strategy is actually working or will continue to work. Instead, as the nature of this chapter's primary examples of queer resistance suggests, I find more that's suggestive for the attitudes we should have toward politics is explicit work that foregrounds the rhetorical and its shadowy emotions—selections of queer literature that offer not a commentary on "truth" or the way things "are." I move into a genre of writing that quickly accommodates emotion and lies. In the current climate where religious opinions about homosexuality's dangerous connections to incest, pedophilia, liberal ruin, family destruction, and moral decline flourish at the same time as queers have "achieved" greater acceptance and exposure, it is especially important to understand that words with great political import can be merely and "only words," a literary "dilemma of language," and that those words make queers hated in the most sentimental ways. As I have tried to communicate, the violence of the religious nation-state's rhetoric does not have to be only violent. Figuring out as much, however, does not guide us into a clear, political direction.

So I must conclude this chapter and book by *not* leaving us with a pro-grammatic, directed project of political resistance and change that can transform the nation that is, in the words of Belize from Tony Kushner's *Angels in America*, "[t]erminal, crazy and mean."[45] To attempt otherwise, I would have to imagine that the current system of sovereignty, government, and publicity operates in a consistent and rational manner. As I hope this chapter's examples emphasize, many people are making up much of the homosexual, incestuous, pedophilic panic; they are being effectively inven-tive, fictitious, and rhetorical, with very "real" consequences that can't be predicted in advance. They keep finding ways to hate queers, to strip them of value, even when there are hollow gestures of tolerance, if not amuse-ment, in the culture at large. So what I want to offer instead is an urge not to reproduce the awful logic of subordination by believing too much in the assertions of identity difference for a coercive political sphere that has already determined those differences well in advance. The "freedom" offered by the current system of government, the current public sphere, and the culture surrounding queers as they seek protection from those sys-tems is probably impossible to achieve. But that doesn't mean that we can't find ways to stall the destructive sacralization of the queer and live, and even thrive, within rhetorical impossibility in the fatality of our "aberrant, unprecedented future."

It was moving to watch the HBO adaptation of Kushner's *Angels in Amer-ica* plays, which gained large audiences and many awards soon after its debut in 2003. The plays, which take place during the Reagan era and the earlier days of the AIDS epidemic, resonated greatly with my own sense of the political tenor of the Bush administration and the continuing queer fight for full enfranchisement. Kushner's final words, which make their way into the film adaptation, are words that capture the minority complaint I have been pursuing throughout this book. While queers have been made sacred—in Agamben's sense of the term—by God's hate and their lives, by the sovereign's will, are considered disposable, which can then be killed but not mourned or sacrificed, queers, nevertheless, can still use that hostility to their advantage. The final words of Kushner's two plays urge: "This disease [AIDS, Republicanism] will be the end of many of us, but not nearly all, and the dead will be commemorated and will struggle on with the living, and we are not going away. We won't die secret deaths anymore. The world only spins forward. We will be citizens. The time has come."[46]

How we are to make sure that queers are no longer without value, and that the dead will be commemorated, is not entirely clear—which is perhaps why the play ends with the proclamation, punctuated by "And I bless you: *More Life* / The Great Work Begins."[47] We might read these words, in the light of my study, as a desire to take back religious language from a language that enables the sovereign's power to decide who lives and dies. The routes into a more blessed life, perhaps, can be achieved less through a blessing and more through the persistent acknowledgment of its curse.

I think here of Belize, who has a speech that takes place in front of a statue of an angel, which I used as the epigraph starting this book. I return to it now, because Belize's words capture much of the revolutionary emotion I have been pursuing throughout *God Hates Fags*. The speech ends a confrontation he has with another character named Louis, a homosexual Jew who, as a leftist, still believes, despite all evidence to the contrary, that freedom, equality, and political transformation are truly possible within the United States. The ex-drag queen Belize, both queer and African American, is pushed over the edge with Louis and his "big ideas," so he accuses Louis of loving America and then offers the following sentiment:

BELIZE: Well I hate America, Louis. I hate this country. It's just big ideas, and stories, and people dying, and people like you.

The white cracker who wrote the national anthem knew what he was doing. He set the word "free" to a note so high nobody can reach it. That was deliberate. Nothing on earth sounds less like freedom to me.[48]

Belize understands the predicament of Americans' love of freedom. The "white cracker" who set the note "free" was not interested in freedom as much as in power, sovereign power, if you will. So Belize does not respond with an explicit politics of resistance; he doesn't produce "big ideas" that could get us out of the conservative regimes holding onto the lives of American citizens and noncitizens. Belize is skeptical of America. But not saying what he thinks is possible doesn't mean that he doesn't have optimism for our despised future. Instead, he tells us about his hate, an emotion that frames what he next admits, "I *live* in America, Louis, that's hard enough. I don't have to love it."[49] The boldness of his statement of hate, the anger of the statement, is what circumscribes yet permits his living. His emotions don't have to be directed at major revolutions but rather at the difficult job of living—not just bare living, but perhaps even living well and justly amid so much difficulty and struggle.

Hate is often called a negative emotion, and I have been valuing its negative qualities by aligning the emotion with a form of sentimental, oppositional blackness that has run throughout my examples of Baldwin, Toomer, Williams, Walker, and Allison, not to mention all the queer activists and politicians who have struggled with pernicious laws such as the lynching of Matthew Shepard, Amendment 2, same-sex marriage debates, and other instances that are all part of the continuing American jeremiad. Much like Lee Edelman, albeit differently, I want us to consider the value of articulating politics in the form of negation. Edelman puts it this way: "Rather than rejecting, with liberal discourse, [the] negativity to the queer, we might . . . do better to consider accepting and even embracing it."[50] Belize is an even more suggestive figure in this play because he calls himself the "negation" of the conservative Republican, who, although gay, has chosen to pursue power and prestige over all other concerns of a queer community—Belize is "the shadow" on his grave.[51] But as a negation, he does not mean to claim that he's nothing, or that he has given up on improving the conditions in which he finds himself and his friends. In fact, Belize is the most strategic and politically minded character in the play: he nurses and loves everyone around him, still respects the final religious rights of his enemies, and steals in order to provide life-saving drugs for those who can't get the drugs by legitimate channels. I want to have his example, with the associations of negativity, race, and hate, operative for political actions. The fact he appears in a play, a fiction, about queerness, America, and religion makes him, in some ways, ideal.

Further, I hope that the queer uses of religious hate speech, which work as "like race" analogies, instruct us not to dwell on either side of the comparison between queer and race, or to dwell within the way the sovereigns of this terrible America ban us from citizenship and life. We can certainly be defiled by the religious rhetoric that needs us to be the inside-outsiders, the enemies, of America, and I don't want to diminish the important scholarship that defines and elaborates that kind of identity-based political, intellectual, and cultural work. But since radical transformations of our government and economics are nowhere in sight, we still have to negotiate the toxic field of difference in the United States, which relies not on freedom, but inequality, to keep moving forward into unprecedented accumulations of power and wealth. But here is where I am most optimistic: we can be much more than the rhetoric—we can be much more than the names we have been forced to assume. A point I must stress is that we are not dealing only with sovereignty but also with sovereignty's language; we're not just dealing with hate but also with hate's language.

When we take on the negativity of religious hate speech, then, we can remind ourselves of the intricate and nonsaturated way that the speech and style of representation we engage in important exercises of political and cultural recognition might not be so literal, so real, and so closed to manipulation. When queers reference the hate of the religious righteous to make the racial analogy, we demonstrate that the religious hate of queers is a position in rhetoric as much as it is an immediate and upsetting emotion. Religious hate is a position that affiliates us with the kind of oppression that is more legible within a public sphere that is religious and not ready to transform and lend full civil rights to queer people: a raced position that has captured at least the emotive attention of a nation that has made some —but not nearly enough—strides to make racial minorities more full and valued members of society. Race's negativity—the oppositional power of blackness—rather than only offering realistically and rationally described histories of differences also offers an important political mode of critique and sentimental protest, which gives us a rhetorical opportunity to engage the political and cultural sphere at an important, linguistic remove. Our claims of negation don't mean our end; in fact, negation can be a point of linguistic departure for daily, important feelings that can strategically move us toward making our everyday lives livable and valuable. It's okay to say that we are hated and thus we hate. God blesses America, but hates me while it blesses. So I appreciate Belize's candor. I can finally confess: I, too, hate America.

And now: here's to more than life. The Great Work Begins.

Notes

Notes to the Introduction

1. For a detailed account of this phenomenon, see the very readable *Losing Matt Shepard: Life and Politics in the Aftermath of Anti-Gay Murder* (New York: Columbia University Press, 2000) by Beth Loffreda. More recently, this "aftermath" has been the subject of a very sentimental made-for-NBC movie starring Stockard Channing called *The Matthew Shepard Story* (dir. Roger Spottiswoode), which originally aired on 16 March 2002, and the 2002 HBO filmic adaptation of *The Laramie Project* (dir. Moises Kaufman).

2. Thanks to Janet Jakobsen for reminding me of this event's activist impact. See Loffreda, *Losing Matt Shepard,* 92.

3. Rocky Mountain Collegian, 16 January 2001; found on http://www.lambda.10 .org/antigay_protests.htm, accessed 10 May 2002.

4. www.godhatesfags.com/memorial.html, accessed 24 April 2002. A companion memorial has been set up for Dianne Whipple, the "filthy dyke" who was mauled and killed by dogs ten days after Westboro's protest.

5. In her book *Between Jesus and the Market: The Emotions That Matter in Right-Wing America,* Linda Kintz persuasively demonstrates the persistent connections between religious and right-wing conservative movements in the contemporary United States. Kintz argues that "the tenets familiar from religious conservativism help shape market fundamentalism by sacrificing certain groups to the purity of the market while displacing attacks on workers, people of color, gays, and lesbians into the abstractions of economic theory" (Linda Kintz, *Between Jesus and the Market: The Emotions That Matter in Right-Wing America* [Durham, NC: Duke University Press, 1997], 4). This market focus is very important to keep in mind. My study is more involved in detailing the ferocity of the rhetoric of Jesus and should be read as a companion piece to Kintz's work.

6. For an excellent discussion of the limits of tolerance when Christian conservatives advocate the "love the sinner, hate the sin" position, see Janet R. Jakobsen and Ann Pellegrini, *Love the Sin: Sexual Regulation and the Limits of Religious Tolerance* (New York: New York University Press, 2003), 45–72.

7. http://www.family.org/welcome/aboutfof/a0000078.html, accessed 24 June 2002.

8. This list came from "Q&A: Amendment 2," a pamphlet distributed by the ACLU of Colorado in March 1993. On file with the author.

9. Ibid. Emphasis in the original.

10. In the *Gazette Telegraph,* then CFV chairman Will Perkins insisted that the outrageous reaction of gays and lesbians was producing this boycott: "Gay activists have spread the word nationwide that Colorado just suspended civil rights for homosexuals. And that's nonsense" (Ray Fleck, "Perkins Rips Growing Boycott," Section B, 10 December 1992).

11. John Gallagher, "Colorado Goes Straight to Hell," *The Advocate,* 23 February 1993, 34.

12. Thanks to Ann Pellegrini for reminding me about the "Persecuted Church" phenomenon, and for pointing out that such feelings are indeed at the roots of Christianity.

13. For a brief and excellent account of the dynamics of Colorado Springs' history, with a notable mention of the influx of family-minded evangelicals such as Focus, see the New York Times' bestseller, *Fast Food Nation: The Dark Side of the All-American Meal* by Eric Schlosser (Boston: Houghton Mifflin, 2001).

14. *Tolerance/Intolerance: Sexual Orientation Issues* (Colorado Springs: Pikes Peak Library District, 1993), videotape of panel.

15. Gallagher, "Colorado," 34.

16. Perry Miller, *The New England Mind: From Colony to Province* (Cambridge, MA: Belknap Press of Harvard University Press, 1953), 39.

17. On the rise and limits of this kind of "homoerotic" inclusion in the public sphere, see Eric Clarke, *Virtuous Vice: Homoeroticism and the Public Sphere* (Durham, NC: Duke University Press, 2000).

18. Judith Butler, *Excitable Speech: A Politics of the Performative* (New York: Routledge, 1997), 19.

19. Indeed, Westboro Baptist Church has picked up on the way people have called their version of queer bashing "hate speech" by featuring a weekly quotation from the Bible on its Web site called, "This Week's 'Hate' Speech."

20. Butler, *Excitable Speech,* 41.

21. For this type of work which I'm definitely *not* pursuing in this book, see, for select examples, Gary Comstock, *Gay Theology without Apology* (Cleveland: Pilgrim

Press, 1993); Robert Gross, *Jesus Acted Up: A Gay and Lesbian Manifesto* (San Francisco: Harper, 1993).

22. Raymond Williams, *Marxism and Literature* (Oxford and New York: Oxford University Press, 1977), 131.

23. Just a quick note. It is a great relief that stunning work about race and ethnicity has taken a hold of queer studies in the most productive ways. I'm thinking of projects such as Samuel Delany's *Times Square Red* (New York: NYU Press, 1999); José Muñoz's *Disidentifications: Queers of Color and the Performance of Politics* (Minneapolis: University of Minnesota Press, 1999); Mary Pat Brady's *Extinct Lands: Temporal Geographies, Discursive Spaces* (Durham, NC: Duke University Press, 2002); Robert Reid-Pharr's *Black, Gay Man* (New York: NYU Press, 2001); David Eng's *Racial Castration: Managing Masculinity in Asian America* (Durham, NC: Duke University Press, 2001); and Philip Brian Harper's *Are We Not Men? Masculine Anxiety and the Problem of African American Identity* (Oxford and New York: Oxford University Press, 1998), among other great studies. I'd like to imagine that my own work belongs, perhaps obliquely, to this new pantheon of dynamic critical race and queer work.

24. For an example of scholarship that attempts something like the transformation and critique of racial identities in the United States, see Walter Benn Michaels, *Our America: Nativism, Modernism, and Pluralism* (Durham, NC: Duke University Press, 1995).

25. Many thanks to José Muñoz for helping me understand this concept of minority feeling. His work, *Feeling Brown: Ethnicity, Affect, and Performance* (Durham, NC: Duke University Press, forthcoming), resonates with my questions.

26. Jakobsen and Pellegrini, *Love the Sin,* 13.

27. I thus depart wildly from Catharine A. MacKinnon's arguments in *Only Words* (Cambridge, MA: Harvard University, 1993).

Notes to Chapter 1

1. James Baldwin, *The Fire Next Time* (New York: Vintage, 1963), 16.

2. The National Association of Evangelicals, http://www.nae.net/about-mission .html, accessed 20 April 2003.

3. Kenneth Burke, *The Rhetoric of Religion: Studies in Logology* (Berkeley and Los Angeles: University of California Press, 1961), 25.

4. http://www.godhatesfags.com/main/purpose.html, accessed 8 June 2002.

5. Stanton L. Jones, "The Loving Opposition: Speaking the Truth in a Climate of Hate," *Christianity Today,* 19 July 1993, 19.

6. Ibid., 20.

7. Ibid.

8. Sacvan Bercovitch, *The American Jeremiad* (Madison: University of Wisconsin Press, 1978), 176.

9. Hannah Arendt tells us that sovereignty "resides in the resulting, limited independence from the incalculability of the future, and its limits are the same as those in the faculty itself of making and keeping promises." Such promises, such errands, attempt to control or "dispose" of the future, with attempts that produce a strong sensation of consensus: "The sovereignty of a body of people bound and kept together, not by an identical will which somehow magically inspires them all, but an agreed purpose for which alone the promises are valid and binding"; see *The Human Condition* (1958; Chicago: University of Chicago Press, 1998), 245.

10. I'm occluding Jewish and Mormon examples because they figure less crucially in the U.S. national religious rhetoric (not because they are unimportant, but because America's theocratic rhetorics tend to be more WASP and Catholic).

11. Family Research Council, http://www.frc.org/get.cfm?c=ABOUT_FRC, accessed 6 July 2004.

12. Kevin Tebedo's statements quoted in *Freedom Watch: The Citizens' Project Newsletter,* Colorado Springs, December–January 1993, 9. On file with author.

13. Thomas Frank, *What's the Matter with Kansas? How Conservatives Won the Heart of America* (New York: Metropolitan Books, 2004), 8.

14. Judith Butler describes: "Governmentality is broadly understood as a mode of power concerned with the maintenance and control of bodies and persons, the production of and regulation of persons and populations, and the circulation of goods insofar as they maintain and restrict the life of the population" (Butler, *Precarious Life: The Powers of Mourning and Violence* (New York: Verso, 2004), 52.

15. Numerous political theorists have argued this point. According to Susan Buck-Morss, "[T]here is no such thing as a merely legal legitimacy . . . [m]odern sovereignties also possess a supralegal or perhaps prelegal form of legitimacy, precisely the wild zone of arbitrary, violent power, and it lies at their very core"; see *Dream-world and Catastrophe: The Passing of the Mass Utopia in East and West* (Boston: MIT Press, 2000), 4.

16. Ibid., 8.

17. Giorgio Agamben, *Homo Sacer: Sovereign Power and Bare Life*, trans. Daniel Heller-Roazen (Stanford, CA: Stanford University Press, 1998), 8.

18. Ibid., 74.

19. See Emile Durkheim's *The Elementary Forms of Religious Life*, trans. Joseph Ward Swain (New York: Free Press, 1915), 366–392; Sigmund Freud, *Totem and Taboo: Some Points of Agreement between the Mental Lives of Savages and Neurotics*, trans. James Strachey (New York: Norton, 1950), 164–200; and René Girard's *Violence and the Sacred*, trans. Patrick Gregory (Baltimore, MD: Johns Hopkins University Press, 1979), especially his concept of the surrogate victim, 250–273.

20. Agamben, *Homo Sacer*, 82. Emphasis in the original.

21. Butler emphasizes this part of queer life in numerous places in her work, but see "Melancholy Gender/Refused Identification," in *The Psychic Life of Power* (Stanford, CA: Stanford University Press, 1997).

22. Indeed Agamben animalizes the forms of this sacred figure when he describes the sacred man as a werewolf in order to show off how those who are made sacred stop counting as human, as worthy of political life; Agamben, *Homo Sacer*, 105–111.

23. Ibid., 114–115.

24. Michael Warner, "Introduction," in *Fear of a Queer Planet: Queer Politics and Social Theory*, ed. Michael Warner (Minneapolis: University of Minnesota Press, 1993), xxv. For a more in-depth discussion of this model, see Steven Seidman's contribution to Warner's volume, "Identity and Politics in a 'Postmodern' Gay Culture," 105–142.

25. Beth Loffreda, *Losing Matt Shepard* (New York: Columbia University Press, 2000), 5.

26. This speech is endlessly available on the Web. My citations of the speech come from Matthew's mother's Web site, "Matthew's Place": www.matthewsplace.com/dennis2.htm.

27. Shirley Samuels, "Introduction," *The Culture of Sentiment: Race, Gender, and*

Sentimentality in 19th Century America, ed. Shirley Samuels (New York and London: Oxford University Press, 1992), 5.

28. For the kind of work that's been instrumental for many points of departure in my thinking, especially about the uses of subaltern forms of sentimentality, and especially her concept of the "unfinished business of sentimentality," see Lauren Berlant's work, especially, "Poor Eliza," *American Literature* 70:3 (September 1998), where she argues, "[I]n the United States a particular form of liberal sentimentality that promotes individual acts of identification based on collective group member-ships has been conventionally deployed to bind people to the nation through a universalist rhetoric of not citizenship per se but of the capacity for suffering and trauma at the citizen's core" (636). Berlant is rightly critical of sentimentality and worries over this kind of persistent marking of pain as the foundation of disen-franchised citizenship; I, however, am less convinced that this kind of pain is so literal and want to push the figurative dimensions of this pain further, as we shall see, as a strategic form of affiliation that does not necessarily truthfully describe the actual dynamics and protest of those suffering identities. Berlant, of course, helps us think deeply about the ways *Uncle Tom's Cabin* is adapted throughout the twentieth century, as I'm adapting it now to my argument; although we part in some ways on its usefulness, Berlant's analysis is extremely helpful.

29. GLAAD/Denver, "Civil Rights, Democracy, and Amendment 2," 1993.

30. ACLU pamphlet, 4.

31. Jakobsen and Pellegrini, *Love the Sin,* 93. They discuss the Halley article.

32. Janet E. Halley, " 'Like Race' Arguments," in *What's Left of Theory: New Work on the Politics of Literary Theory,* ed. Judith Butler, John Guillory, and Kendall Thomas (New York: Routledge, 2000), 66.

33. Ibid.

34. Miranda Joseph, "Analogy and Complicity: Women's Studies, Lesbian/Gay Studies, and Capitalism," in *Women's Studies on Its Own,* ed. Robyn Wiegman (Durham, NC: Duke University Press, 2002), 275.

35. Janet Jakobsen, "Queers Are Like Jews, Aren't They?" in *Queer Theory and the Jewish Question,* ed. Daniel Boyarin, Daniel Itzkovtiz, and Ann Pellegrini (New York: Columbia University Press, 2003), 71.

36. Ibid., 86.

37. Judith Butler, "Imitation and Gender Insubordination," in *The Lesbian and Gay*

Studies Reader, ed. Henry Abelove, Michele Aina Barale, and David Halpern (New York: Routledge, 1993), 309.

38. Gayatri Chakravorty Spivak, "More on Power/Knowledge," in *The Spivak Reader,* ed. Donna Landry and Gerald Maclean (New York: Routledge, 1996), 145–146. This whole difficult essay has been crucial in my thinking about the religious nominalism of queer sexuality, and my understandings of Foucault have been so helped by her challenging prose.

39. J. Hillis Miler, *The Ethics of Reading* (New York: Columbia University Press, 1987), 73.

40. Aristotle, *The Art of Rhetoric,* trans. with an intro H. C. Lawson-Tancred (London: Penguin, 1991), 216 (1404 a).

41. Hortense Spillers, *Black, White, and in Color: Essays on American Literature and Culture* (Chicago: University of Chicago Press, 2003), 203. For this point, also see Robyn Weigman's *American Anatomies: Theorizing Race and Gender* (Durham, NC: Duke University Press, 1995).

42. See Saidiya V. Hartman's very useful *Scenes of Subjection: Terror, Slavery, and Self-Making in Nineteenth-Century America* (New York: Oxford University Press, 1997).

43. Spillers, *Black, White, and in Color,* 458.

44. Ibid., 206.

45. Ibid., 443, emphasis in the original.

46. Spillers's stunning critique of African American intellectual work must be seriously dealt with by critics much wiser than I, and soon. See her "The Crisis of the Negro Intellectual: A Post Date," in *Black, White, and in Color,* 428–470.

47. Spillers, *Black, White, and in Color,* 4.

48. Hortense Spillers, "The Idea of Black Culture," talk delivered at Western Ontario University, 7 December 2002.

49. Spillers, *Black, White, and in Color,* 5.

50. In many ways, this strategy understands what Michel Foucault describes as the kinds of imaginative liberations "confession" and talk about sexuality are thought to offer when he outlines the dimensions of the "repressive hypothesis." See the primary text of sexuality studies: *History of Sexuality,* Vol. 1: *An Introduction,* trans. Robert Hurley (New York: Vintage, 1990), 3–49.

51. Lauren Berlant's work, again, is quite suggestive. In a different context, but with similar aims in mind, Berlant argues for moments when "the privileged

persons of national culture will respond to the sublimity of reason," and will actually use the testimony of those who have been injured by the national culture that privileges some and hurts others:

> I call these moments of Diva Citizenship. Diva Citizenship does not change the world. It is a moment of emergence that marks unrealized potentials for subaltern activity. Diva Citizenship occurs when a person stages a coup in a public sphere in which she does not have privilege. Flashing up and startling the public, she puts the dominant story into suspended animation; as though recording an estranging voice-over to a film we have all already seen, she renarrates the dominant history as one that the abjected people have once lived sotto voce, but no more; and she challenges her audience to identify with the enormity of the suffering she has narrated and the courage she has had to produce, calling on people to change the social and institutional practices of citizenship to which they currently consent. (Berlant, *The Queen of America Goes to Washington City: Essays on Sex and Citizenship* [Durham, NC: Duke University Press, 1997], 223)

This quotation has much to offer in an analysis of what must happen during sentimental protest moments by those who are disenfranchised so much so that they have no choice but to engage acts of political renarration. I would like to redirect some of the critical energy Berlant correctly argues for to assert that queer fundamentalists engage in acts of "Diva Citizenship," but in a different manner than Berlant describes: they do not speak as a voice-over story of suffering and courage that we've watched before but rather in voices that do not belong to them, with words that don't personalize their own particular experiences of suffering.

52. See Berlant, " '68, or Something," *Critical Inquiry,* Fall 1994.

53. Wendy Brown, *States of Injury: Power and Freedom in Late Modernity* (Princeton, NJ: Princeton University Press, 1995), 7.

54. Ibid., 75.

Notes to Chapter 2

1. See Dwight A. McBride, ed. *James Baldwin* (New York: New York University Press, 2000).

2. Henry Louis Gates, Jr., definitively explicates the tradition of "signifyin' " in

black letters in books such as *The Signifying Monkey* (New York: Oxford University Press, 1988).

3. Theophus H. Smith, *Conjuring Culture: Biblical Formations of Black Culture* (New York: Oxford University Press, 1994), 18.

4. Rene Hill, "Who Are We for Each Other? Sexism, Sexuality, and Womanist Theology," in *Black Theology: A Documentary History,* Vol. 2: *1980–1992,* ed. James H. Cone and Gayraud S. Wilmore (Maryknoll, NY: Orbis, 1993), 345–351. In this essay, she articulates the way homophobia persistently works in black theology, thereby undermining its healing and helpful spiritual/theological desires for lesbians, gays, bisexuals, and (implicitly) transgenders in black faith communities.

5. James Baldwin, *The Price of the Ticket: Collected Nonfiction, 1948–1985* (New York: St. Martin's Press, 1985), xviii.

6. Baldwin, *Go Tell It on the Mountain,* 193.

7. Ibid., 11.

8. Ibid., 19.

9. I will discuss John's queerness below.

10. Lauren Berlant and Michael Warner, "Sex in Public," *Critical Inquiry* 24:2 (Winter 1998): 558–564.

11. Ibid., 558.

12. Ibid.

13. See Biddy Martin's "Extraordinary Homosexuals and the Fear of Being Ordinary," *Differences* 6 (Summer–Fall 1994).

14. Lauren Berlant, "Intimacy: A Special Issue," *Critical Inquiry* 24:2 (Winter 1998): 285.

15. An interesting side note: in Louis Althusser's often quoted "Ideological State Appartuses," the Church functions as the supreme exemplar of an ideological apparatus, even after he has claimed that the Church has been replaced by the school as the most current and effective example of ideological interpellation.

16. See Michael Warner, *The Trouble with Normal Sex, Politics and the Ethics of Queer Life* (Cambridge, MA: Harvard University Press, 2000), 63.

17. Hartman is extraordinarily useful in outlining the historical lineage of the powerful pleasures involved in observing the slave body in spectacular and often oblique scenes of subjection in *Scenes of Subjection: Terror, Slavery, and Self-Making in Nineteenth-Century America* (New York: Oxford University Press, 1997).

18. Wendy Brown has been enormously useful in articulating many of these ideas. Also see Allen Feldman's *Formations of Violence: The Narrative of the Body and Political Terror in Northern Ireland* (Chicago: University of Chicago Press, 1991).

19. Michel Foucault, "Nietzsche, Genealogy, History," in *The Foucault Reader,* ed. Paul Rabinow, trans. Donald Bouchard and Sherry Simon (New York: Pantheon, 1984), 83.

20. Ibid., 83. Also see Wendy Brown, *States of Injury: Power and Freedom in Late Modernity* (Princeton, NJ: Princeton University Press, 1995); Berlant's "National Brands/National Bodies: Imitation of Life," in *Contemporary American Identities,* ed. Hortense J. Spillers (New York: Routledge, 1993).

21. Baldwin, *Go Tell It on the Mountain,* 200.

22. Mark Seltzer, "Wound Culture: Trauma in the Pathological Public Sphere," *October* 80 (Spring 1997): 24. When I mention the pathological public throughout the chapter, I am referring to the theories and readings Seltzer produces in this article as well as his seminar, "The Pathological Public Sphere," at the Society for the Humanities, Cornell University, Fall 1997, as well as his most recent book, *Serial Killers: Life and Death in America's Wound Culture* (New York: Routledge, 1998).

23. Eric J. Sundquist, *To Wake the Nations: Race in the Making of American Literature* (Cambridge, MA: Belknap Press of Harvard University Press, 1993), 458. Sundquist's work, especially on Du Bois, charts the way one part of religious experience, "Spirituals," inform an intellectual and cultural lineage that gives coherence to the kinds of double-vision Du Bois famously articulates in *The Souls of Black Folk.* Although he sidesteps the specific histories of African American religious experience, Sundquist explains the way Du Bois morphs religious experience into a figuration of black/slave history that provides Du Bois and others a formal structure for identifying with the very general themes of salvation, mourning, work, and endurance the spirituals announce. My argument about religious language's formal capabilities, however, differs from Sundquist's. I argue that religion helps evacuate official and traumatic versions of historical significance from the blackness of bodies in order to keep race an open abstraction that can only raise questions and suspend any final reading of the raced body.

24. See Carter G. Woodson, "The Negro Church, an All-Comprehending Institution," *Negro History Bulletin* 3:1 (October 1939): 1–3.; W. E. B. Du Bois, *The Souls of Black Folk* (1903; reprint, New York: Fawcett World Library, 1961), 142. Mechal

Sobel's *Trabelin' On: The Slave Journey to an Afro-Baptist Faith* (Princeton, NJ: Princeton University Press, 1979). Sobel argues:

> The black Baptist faith gave coherence to prewar slave society. It provided the possibility for meaningful lives with meaningful goals. It was a black creation, made in contact with the white Baptist faith and affecting that faith, but it remained the very special Sacred Cosmos of blacks, filled with spirit and joy and mourning and time past, all used to understand the present. Seeing themselves as the New Israel, waiting for God's redemption, black Baptists *knew* they would "emerge the conqueror." (xxiv)

Although this is an extremely useful and helpful intervention into understanding that religion is not always bad and oppressive, and although this is most certainly the case in some instances, this kind of specific lauding of the syncretic nature of the black Baptist faith and its influence on the historical importance of the black church for African American cultural projects sidesteps what hurts and hinders the articulation of African Americanness, which is a primary occupation of Baldwin's own writing. Hence, I am less willing to celebrate only the importance of the hybrid religious experience of African Americans when reading Baldwin, who is very critical of the way religion negatively codes the flesh of African Americans. For a longer version of my critique of this kind of reading, see my *Racial Blasphemies: Religious Irreverence and Race in American Literature* (New York: Routledge, 2005).

25. In an article by Michael Eric Dyson, "What's Derrida Got to Do with Jesus? Rhetoric, Black Religion, and Theory," in *One Nation under God? Religion and American Culture*, ed. Marjorie Garber and Rebecca L. Walkowitz (New York: Routledge, 1999), there is an initial attempt to focus on the religious rhetoric that is theoretically informed, and influenced by "cultural studies." His focus on the ways in which "speaking and writing can be viewed as a dominant shape of black intelligence; speaking and writing can be viewed as the crucial rhetorical surfaces on which black identity is inscribed," often lead us, however, to a very quick understanding of black identity and the surfaces that contain "speaking and writing" (76). Moreover, much like others before him, he focuses on religious rhetoric that yields more discussion about the historical significance of the black "oral" tradition, the political efficacy of black religious speech as an effective form of public-sphere speaking, and the ways in which African American experience can gain a logic and coherence through religious expression: "[W]ords can lend ontological credence to racial identity, and . . . religious language can house an existential weight, a self-regenerating energy, that can be levied against the denials of black being expressed in racist sentiment and practice" (84). At the heart of this analysis, the strictly literary qualities of religious language are often neglected in favor of social and historical explanation that can help articulate a program of resistance. Although I appreciate and often agree with this gesture, this brand of analysis tends not to adequately explore the ways in which the racial codes are often created by religious rhetoric. Thereby, the project of understanding the aesthetic relevance of religious rhetoric becomes complicated, especially if a literary project is not only directed toward giving "ontological credence" to an articulate shape of a "black being" that may or may not benefit from the aestheticization of blackness. In this chapter, however, we seek to explore the connections between religious rhetoric and the literary world where bodies are racialized through deliberate, formal techniques of language. A literary understanding of literature, moreover, need not imply a political evacuation. The concern with the language of any set of representations that appear in a literary text need not only be focused on a primarily mimetic idea of what literature is supposed to reflect. Furthermore, the need not to be "real," "natural," or "historical" seems important if race is to be named as the complicated abstraction it tends to be.

26. This statement refers to a now typical description about what "history" seems to mean for literary critics. See, for a prime example, Cary Nelson's *Repression and Recovery: Modern American Poetry and the Politics of Cultural Memory, 1910–1945* (Madison: University of Wisconsin Press, 1989), especially 1–19; see also Frederic Jameson's *The Political Unconscious: Narrative as Symbolic Act* (Ithaca, NY: Cornell University Press, 1981): "[O]nly a genuine philosophy of history is capable of respecting the specificity and radical difference of the social and political past while disclosing the solidarity of its polemics and passions, its forms, structures, experiences and struggles, with those of the present day" (18).

27. Baldwin was himself quite invested in assuring the primary importance of African American history—he lent his celebrity to a 1968 hearing on the establishment of a committee on "Negro history and culture," where he asserted, "My history is also yours" and maintained that the integration of the African American historical record in national curriculums was a key to the security of civil rights and successful integration; quote found in Howard N. Meyer, ed., *Integrating America's Heritage: A Congressional Hearing to Establish a National Commission on Negro History and Culture* (College Park, MD: McGrath Publishing, 1970), 42. In this instance, Baldwin follows a typical pattern of African American social reform that invested much in historical corrections. For instance, a 1939 NAACP pamphlet, "Anti-Negro Propaganda in School Textbooks," describes why African American history is so desperately needed: "They [the parents of African American children] are beginning to see, as never before, that these false theories [of a primarily white America and the inferiority of African Americans] that we hear so much about today, have been so deftly placed in our textbooks, that their subtle infiltration, not only in the minds of growing white youngsters but in the minds of Negroes themselves, has been an almost unconscious development"; see "Anti-Negro Propaganda in School Textbooks," pamphlet (New York: NAACP, 1939), 5–7. The correction of such omissions and stereotypes is often conceived as a revised historical knowledge that should become official curriculum, especially in public schools. Hence, Baldwin appeared before the special hearing to argue for the establishment of a national committee on African American history and culture.

28. Baldwin, 645–646.

29. The very influential Robert A. Bone, writing in 1956, offers an early reading that continues to take hold of most critics of this novel, forcing us to find exemplary African American historical tricks in the text. He, for example, writes, *"Go Tell It on the Mountain* is thus a novel of the Great Migration. It traces the process of secularization that occurred when the Negro left the land for the Northern ghettos. The theme, to be sure, is handled ironically. Baldwin's protagonist 'gets religion,' but he is too young, and too innocent to grasp the implications of his choice"; see Robert A. Bone, "James Baldwin," in *James Baldwin: A Collection of Critical Essays* (Englewood Cliffs, NJ: Prentice Hall, 1974), 33. For other versions of this argument, see Harris's introduction to *New Essays on Go Tell It on the Mountain* (Cambridge and New York: Cambridge University Press, 1996). The most glaring omission in Bone's argument is how all the characters, who migrate north, are not also migrating into secularization, but secularization's opposite: they all devote themselves to the hardness of the religious Word. Ironic or not, Baldwin perpetually leads his black characters back to church, back to the threshing floor where conversions occur, not merely to honor and repeat and reproduce a religious history, but also to give shape and words to what it means to be black in the United States. The bulk of *Go Tell It on the Mountain* tracks the sheer arduousness of what it takes to come to church, what it takes to belong to a place that would "swell with the Power" that the church "held, and like a planet rocking in space, the temple [John's church] rocked with the power of God" (15). Gabriel's, Elizabeth's, and Florence's stories of eventual evangelical acceptance, called "Prayers," are the interior sections of the text that are punctuated with severe injustices that cannot be avoided. All characters, moreover, have "sinned." And all of his characters really have no choice but to capitulate to the demands of the religious community.

30. Baldwin, "Everybody's Protest Novel," in *The Price of the Ticket*, 30.

31. Ibid., 30. Baldwin's frustration with the then dominant literary models of representing race, as his attack on Stowe and Wright suggests, is with a sense that the "realness" of African American characters had heretofore been achieved through an appeal to typicality, to an obvious articulation of recognition that cannot handle the otherwise messy qualities of "the human being." This forceful restriction of what blackness indicates resonates in John's own crisis. As a result, John's body, as he sees it, must come into a critical view that can help move beyond black typicality. For the most useful account of the way statistics and typicality have long informed the creation of American realist and naturalist modes (well before Wright's own racialized version of naturalist fiction), see Mark Seltzer's *Bodies and Machines* (New York: Routledge, 1992), especially chapter 3, "Statistical Persons," 91–118.

32. Although neither of the queers in this novel is explicitly African American, the final section of this chapter will demonstrate the ways queerness and blackness are intimately tied to one another in Baldwin's imaginary.

33. Baldwin, *Giovanni's Room* (1956; New York: Quality Paperback Book Club, 1993), 246–247.

34. Ibid., 247.

35. Ibid., 247–248.

36. Nancy Armstrong, "Why Daughters Die: The Racial Logic of American Sentimentalism," *Yale Journal of Criticism* 7:2 (1994): 18.

37. Berlant and Warner, "Sex in Public." They argue that the desire for social membership is often a frustrated practice that comes up too closely with the "couple

form" and "heterosexual marriage," an encounter that often produces disastrous results:

> People feel the price they must pay for social membership and a relation to the future is identification with the heterosexual life narrative; that they are individually responsible for the rages, instabilities, ambivalences, and failures they experience in their intimate lives, while the fractures of the contemporary United States shame and sabotage them everywhere. Heterosexuality involves so many practices that are not sex that a world in which the hegemonic cluster would not be dominant is, at this point, unimaginable. We are trying to bring that world into being. (557)

38. I am referring to the two most compelling accounts of the public sphere found in Berlant's *Queen of America* and Mark Seltzer's *Serial Killers*.

39. Thanks to my American Love class for this insight.

40. Baldwin, *Go Tell It on the Mountain*, 207.

41. Jonathan Culler, *Framing the Sign: Criticism and Its Institutions* (Normon and London: University of Oklahoma Press, 1988), 71.

42. See Emile Durkheim's *The Elementary Forms of the Religious Life* 1911 (New York: Free Press, 1965); all of Mircea Eliade's corpus, but especially *The Sacred and the Profane: The Nature of Religion* (New York: Harcourt Brace, 1959).

43. See two valuable volumes dedicated to Baldwin's work: Harris, ed., *New Essays on Go Tell It on the Mountain*; and *Critical Essays on James Baldwin*, ed. Fred L. Standley and Nancy V. Burt (Boston: G. K. Hall, 1988).

44. David Leeming, *Baldwin: A Biography* (New York: Henry Holt, 1994), 89.

45. Sondra A. O'Neale, "Fathers, Gods, and Religion: Perceptions of Christianity and Ethnic Faith in James Baldwin," in Standley and Burt, eds., *Critical Essays*, 141.

46. Hortense Spillers, "The Crisis of the Negro Intellectual," in *boundary 2* 21:3 (1994): 87.

47. Kenneth Burke, *The Rhetoric of Religion: Studies in Logology* (Boston: Beacon Press, 1961), 35.

48. Ibid., vi.

49. Ibid., 25–26.

50. See Derrida's, "La Structure, le signe, et le jeu dans le discours des sciences humaines," in *L'écriture et la différence* (Paris: Éditions de Seuil, 1967), 409–428.

51. Burke, *Rhetoric of Religion*, 27.

52. Baldwin, "Every Good-Bye Ain't Gone," in *The Price of the Ticket,* 644.

53. Baldwin, *Go Tell It on the Mountain,* 202.

54. Brown, *States of Injury,* 55.

55. Ibid., ix.

56. In this sense, Baldwin corroborates a religious theory of the body found in Elaine Scarry's inquiry into Western religious texts. Scarry writes: "The graphic image of the human body substitutes for the object of belief that cannot be represented." The hurt image of the human form, which, unlike "God," can be represented, is necessary because it assures the faithful of the belief's existence, the "realness" of God (and the religion's belief system organized under the image of God). In the Judeo-Christian texts, as Scarry points out, God's "realness" is both absent and present and thus needs some kind of formal structure in which the religious and the secular words can be made, destroyed, and remade; see Elaine Scarry, *The Body in Pain: The Making and Unmaking of the Word* (New York: Oxford University Press, 1984), 198. That is, when the realness of God and faith in God are in doubt, the corporeal human form will be narrated as a kind of suffering that serves as "evidence" of God's otherwise abstract, but still felt, ubiquitous power— a power that is everywhere and nowhere on every page of the Judeo-Christian scriptures, a power that is made manifest in words and bodies that believe in such words.

57. Baldwin, *Go Tell It on the Mountain,* 193–194.

58. Ibid., 194.

59. Ibid., 197.

60. The biblical phrase "seeing one's nakedness" may be an euphemism for "having sex with someone." There is debate as to whether this passage refers to seeing Noah's nakedness, or that of his absent wife. Nevertheless, the way it is transmitted to Baldwin and then his characters makes one see the nakedness as a homosexual action and sin. In his biography of James Baldwin, David Leeming writes, "Obsessed by guilt Jimmy [Baldwin] and John were fascinated by the story of Noah's son's sinful viewing of his father's genitals, and were turned to the rumors of sexuality in the church and the clear signs of it on the streets outside. . . . Both were saved by the direct help of young male 'saints' with whom they had fallen in love"; see Leeming, *James Baldwin* (New York: Henry Holt, 1994), 85. The specific

scriptural reference in Genesis is one where Ham incestuously takes advantage of his father's drunken stupor, brags to his brothers about it, and thus receives the curse for his son (Genesis 9.20–26). The annotation of the New Revised Standard Version argues that "the curse implies that Canaan's subjugation to Israel was the result of Canaanite sexual practices (Lev. 18.24–30)." The Leviticus reference is the passage after the infamous passage, "You shall not lie with a male as with a woman; it is an abomination (Lev. 18.22)," which makes such sexual transgressions enough of a crime to justify cultural alienation and forced exile. Whether the exile is a result of ritual impurity or homosexual offense is much debated. Nevertheless, John reads himself into the offense, and links it to his own "sinful" practices.

61. Lee Edelman, *Homographesis: Essays in Gay Literary and Cultural Theory* (New York and London: Routledge, 1994), 55.

62. Baldwin., *Go Tell It On the Mountain,* 144.

63. Ibid.

64. Even though much of John's conversion is textually represented as individualized, interior struggles, the "threshing floor" event is a public space replete with family, fellow saints, and a very publicly known Bible story detailing how queerness has inspired unequal race relations.

65. Baldwin, *Go Tell It on the Mountain,* 200–201.

66. Ibid., 219.

67. Ibid., 207.

68. Ibid.

69. Ibid., 194–195.

Notes to Chapter 3

1. Jean Toomer, *Cane* (1923; New York: Liveright, 1993), 83. Further citations will appear in the text.

2. Siobhan Somerville, *Queering the Color Line: Race and the Invention of Homosexuality in American Culture* (Durham, NC: Duke University Press, 2000).

3. Nominalism, moreover, is often related to the concept of "recognition," especially in queer politics. Although I disagree with her ideas about queer legibility and recognition, for an exploration and critique of the ways that minority "recognition" pervades contemporary politics, see Nancy Fraser's *Justice Interruptus: Critical Reflections on the "Postsocialist" Condition* (New York: Routledge, 1997), especially chapter 1, "From Redistribution to Recognition," 11–39.

4. Quoted in John D'Emilio, *Sexual Politics, Sexual Communities: The Making of the Homosexual Minority in the United States 1940–1970*, 2d ed. (Chicago: University of Chicago Press, 1998), 19.

5. See Appendix B, a list of sodomy laws in effect in the mid-twentieth-century United States, in Donald Webster Cory's *The Homosexual in America: A Subjective Approach* 1951 (New York: Castle Books, 1960), 280–292.

6. I'm referring to the "SILENCE=DEATH Project," started shortly before Act-Up in New York in response to the AIDS epidemic, drawing parallels between the late 1980s and Nazi Germany's extermination of homosexuals. The need to talk rather than be silent about the persecution and annihilation of gay people throughout history took hold among activists. The image that was generated, featuring the slogan with a pink triangle on a black background, is by now iconic.

7. The histories of pre-Stonewall gay and lesbian activism, charting and challenging the familiar narrative of the migration from individual acts to collective group identities, is impressive and growing. See, among other examples, John D'Emilio, *Sexual Politics, Sexual Communities* (Chicago: University of Chicago Press, 2d ed., 1998); Christopher Nealon, *Foundlings: Lesbian and Gay Historical Emotion before Stonewall* (Durham, NC: Duke University Press); George Chauncey, *Gay New York: Gender, Urban Culture, and the Making of the Gay Male World, 1890–1940* (New York: Basic Books, 1995); Jonathan Katz, *Gay American History: Lesbian and Gay Men in the U.S.A.* (New York: Plume, 1992), among many other titles.

8. D'Emilio, *Sexual Politics*, 64–65.

9. Will Roscoe, "Introduction," in Harry Hay, *Radically Gay: Gay Liberation in the Words of Its Founder* (Boston: Beacon Press, 1996), 44.

10. Michael Denning, *The Cultural Front: The Laboring of American Culture in the Twentieth Century* (London and New York: Verso, 1997), 4.

11. D'Emilio, *Sexual Politics*, 65.

12. D'Emilio in ibid., quoting papers and speeches from the Society's founders, especially the papers of Jim Kepner, 65. D'Emilio charts this history in more detail, although his discussion of the "ethnicity" of the debates is not as succinct as I state here; however, it is evident throughout the major claims of his book, as well as in the words of the founders themselves.

13. In Donald Cory's pseudonymically written *The Homosexual in America* (1951), the introductory chapter, "The Unrecognized Minority," a very familiar gesture toward all the beginnings of civil rights, frames his entire book: "In recent years the world has become extremely conscious of minority problems . . . the minority question has been studied exhaustively in recent years. Attention has been focused on the Jewish people in Germany and elsewhere in the world, the Hindus and Moslems in India and Pakistan, the Catholics in Ulster and the Protestants in Italy, the Negroes in America" (3–4). Religious minority difference in other parts of the world is made, perhaps carelessly, comparable to racial difference of "Negroes in America" for the reasons we've been discussing. The differences among citizens in the United States are so often cast as a race problem, with all the emotional impact this problem conjures in the minds of a nation that grudgingly and shamefully remembers slavery and segregation, reminding us that "white supremacy," as Cornel West asserts, "cuts through every tradition of resistance and critique" in the United States; see Cornel West on Heterosexism and Transformation: An Interview," in *Dangerous Liaisons: Blacks, Gays, and the Struggle for Equality,* ed. Eric Brandt (New York: New Press, 1999), 295. It makes sense that Cory, writing a few years before *Brown v. Board of Education,* would see "minority" in the United States as overwhelmingly a racial category.

14. Hay, *Radically Gay,* 79.

15. Denning, *Cultural Front,* 13.

16. Ibid., xv.

17. William Stott, *Documentary Expression and Thirties America* (New York City: Oxford University Press, 1973), xi.

18. Lionel Trilling, "The Promise of Realism," in *The Liberal Imagination* (New York: Doubleday, 1957), 29.

19. Rey Chow, "On Chineseness as a Theoretical Problem," in *Modern Chinese Literary and Cultural Studies in the Age of Theory,* ed. Rey Chow (Durham, NC: Duke University Press, 2000), 16.

20. Eve Kosofsky Sedgwick, *Tendencies* (Durham, NC: Duke University Press, 1993), 5.

21. Other literary examples of sexuality protest qua racial protest abound. We need think only of how Nella Larsen's 1929 novel, *Passing,* has sparked, largely due to Deborah McDowell's influential introduction, so much critical attention to the ways that racial passing works to conceal, yet still present, a queer subtext that is often too explosive. This is especially true in the context of the early twentieth century, and in the particular context of the precarious Harlem Renaissance, a literary and aesthetic movement that was deeply concerned with "appropriate subject matter." See my "Insolent Racing, Rough Narrative: The Harlem Renaissance's Impolite Queers," *Callaloo* 23:1 (Winter 2000): 328–351.

22. Jim Kepner, "Something Furtive," from *One,* quoted in his edited volume, *Rough News, Daring Views: 1950s' Pioneer Gay Press Journalism* (New York and London: Harrington Park Press, 1998), 45.

23. Ibid., 31.

24. Stephen Crane, "An Experiment in Misery," in *The Portable Stephen Crane,* ed. Joseph Katz (New York: Penguin, 1969), 154. The experiment is driven by a desire to understand, to "feel" another's experience, which is quite explicit in an introduction that was edited out after the sketch's first appearance in *New York Press,* April 22, 1894. Further citations will appear in the text.

25. Chauncey, *Gay New York,* 34.

26. Ibid.

27. Eve Kosofsky Sedgwick, *Between Men: English Literature and Male Homosocial Desire* (New York: Columbia University Press, 1985), 1–2.

28. Mark Seltzer, *Bodies and Machines* (New York: Routledge, 1992), 96.

29. Bill Brown, *The Material Unconscious: American Amusement, Stephen Crane, and the Economics of Play* (Cambridge, MA: Harvard University Press, 1996), 20.

30. Ralph Ellison, *Shadow and Act* (1953; New York: Vintage, 1972), 32.

31. For a fascinating discussion of value and African American race theory, see Lindon Barrett's *Blackness and Value: Seeing Double* (New York and London: Cambridge University Press, 1999).

32. Ellison, 32. *Shadow and Act.* Emphasis mine.

33. Ibid., 33.

34. Henry Louis Gates, Jr., *Figures in Black: Words, Signs, and the "Racial" Self* (New York and Oxford: Oxford University Press, 1987), 40.

35. Ellison, "Stephen Crane and the Mainstream of American Fiction," in *Shadow*

and Act, 62. In this piece, Ellison accounts for religion not just in thematic ways, but in the forms of religion that have had a tremendous impact on American literature, as on American nationality: "Surely if fundamentalist Christianity could get so authoritatively into national politics (especially in the Bible Belt), so ambiguously into our system of education (as in the Scopes trial issue), into our style of crime (through prohibition's spawn of bootleggers, gangsters, jellybeans and flappers) and so powerfully into jazz—it is about time we recognized its deeper relationship to the art of our twentieth-century literature. And not simply as subject matter, but as a major source of its technique, its form and rhetoric" (61–62).

36. New Revised Standard Version, 14.

37. Charles Madison, "Preface to the Dover Edition," in Jacob Riis, *How the Other Half Lives* (1900; New York: Dover, 1971), vii.

38. For an interesting, womanist theological account, see Emile M. Townes's study on Wells-Barnett, *Womanist Justice, Womanist Hope* (New York: Scholars Press–American Academy of Religion, 1993).

39. Madison, "Preface," v.

40. Riis, *How the Other Half Lives,* 5. Further citations will appear in the text.

41. Seltzer, *Bodies and Machines,* 96. Seltzer argues:

There are bodies-in-the-abstract that populate consumer and machine culture. But it is not merely that the privilege of relative disembodiment requires the more deeply embodied bodies (in consumer society: the female body, the racialized body, the working body) against which this privilege can be measured. Beyond that, it requires the more visibly embodied figures that, on one side, epitomize the tensions between the typical and the individual and between the aritfactual and the natural, and, on the other, are the figures through which these tensions can be at once recognized and displaced or disavowed. And, beyond that, it is just these tensions, epitomized by and displaced upon the overly explicit embodiments of physical capital, that fascinate and arouse interest in consumer culture: for instance, the erotic visibilities of the female body or the "raciness" of the racialized body. (64)

42. For a compelling account of the regulation of families and children since the eighteenth century, see Jacques Donzelot's classic, *The Policing of Families,* trans. Robert Hurley (1977; Baltimore: Johns Hopkins University Press, 1997).

43. Kenneth Warren, *Black and White Strangers: Race and American Literary Realism* (Chicago: University of Chicago Press, 1993), 72.

44. Tennessee Williams, *Suddenly Last Summer* (1958) in *Tennessee Williams: Four Plays* (New York: Signet, 1976), 26. Further citations will appear in the text.

45. See George Steiner, *After Babel: Aspects of Language and Translation* (London, Oxford, and New York: Oxford University Press, 1975); Jacques Derrida, "Des Tours de Babel," in *Difference in Translation,* trans. and ed. Joseph F. Graham (Ithaca and London: Cornell University Press, 1985), 165–205.

46. Derrida, "Des Tours de Babel," 165–166.

47. Ibid., 166.

48. For this publication history, see Brian Parker, "A Provisional Stemma for Drafts and Revisions of Tennessee Williams's *Suddenly Last Summer* (1958)," *Modern Drama* 41 (1998): 303–326.

49. For a discussion of cannibalism in Melville, and particularly in *Benito Cereno,* see Geoffrey Sanborn, *The Sign of the Cannibal: Melville and the Making of the Postcolonial Reader* (Durham, NC: Duke University Press, 1998).

50. Williams, "Desire and the Black Masseur," in *Tennessee Williams: Collected Stores,* intro. Gore Vidal (New York: New Directions Book, 1985), 205. Further citations will appear in the text.

51. Baldwin, "Everybody's Protest Novel," in *The Price of the Ticket* (New York: St. Martin's Press, 1985), 30–31.

52. James Baldwin, "The Devil Finds Work," in *The Price of the Ticket,* 561.

53. Baldwin, "Here Be Dragons," in *The Price of the Ticket,* 678.

54. Ibid., 689.

55. Ibid., 690.

Notes to Chapter 4

1. Lee Edelman, *No Future: Queer Theory and the Death Drive* (Durham, NC: Duke University Press, 2004), 24.

2. Michael W. Rosen, "Boycott Threats Will Only Harden Majority's Conviction," *Gazette Telegraph,* 20 December 1992, D5.

3. Janet E. Halley, " 'Like Race' Arguments," in *What's Left of Theory: New Work on the Politics of Literary Theory,* ed. Judith Butler, John Guillory, and Kendall Thomas

(New York: Routledge, 2000), 46. Halley continues: "[T]he central legal achievement of litigation waged on behalf of black civil rights movements was a historic succession of equal protection holdings: state-sponsored segregation was declared a violation of the Constitution, and the Court began to test its presumption (first announced in a case unsuccessfully challenging the Japanese-American internment) that other forms of race discrimination would be also found unconstitutional" (47).

4. Ibid., 47.

5. Although the emotionally loaded "special rights" campaign demonstrates an impatience with what the litigious successes of civil rights have brought to contemporary U.S. politics and culture—such as affirmative action, quotas, preferential treatments geared toward leveling an otherwise hierarchalized "playing field" in terms of employment, housing, education, institutional access, etc.—the right understands the explosive potential of being too obvious with such impatience and too open with an intolerance of civil rights. Overt racism, as the controversy over Trent Lott's 2002 remarks in support of Strom Thurmond's mid-twentieth-century segregationist presidency bid demonstrates, does not play well.

6. This argument runs throughout much of the discussion of the history of Amendment 2 and its court cases. This specific quotation comes from a helpful volume on the legal strategies of anti-Amendment 2 advocates by Lisa Keen and Suzanne B. Goldberg, *Strangers to the Law: Gay People on Trial* (Ann Arbor: University of Michigan Press, 1998), 40.

7. Mr. Justice Harlan's dissent, *Plessy v. Ferguson: A Brief History with Documents,* ed. Brook Thomas (Boston and New York: Bedford Books, 1997), 58.

8. 517 U.S. 620, 623 (1996).

9. 517 U.S. 620, 631 (1996).

10. 517 U.S. 620, 632 (1996).

11. 517 U.S. 620, 621 (1996).

12. The text of the amendment is widely available. This quotation comes from a pamphlet distributed by Colorado for Family Values, on file with the author.

13. Joseph Sobran, "The Truth about Shakespeare and the Gay Rights Agenda," *Gazette Telegraph,* 29 December 1992, A7.

14. Didi Herman's crucial study of the Christian right, *The Antigay Agenda: Orthodox Vision and the Christian Right* (Chicago: University of Chicago Press, 1997),

NOTES TO CHAPTER 4

particularly the chapter, "(Il)legitimate Minorities: The Construction of Rights-(Un)deserving Subjects," makes a more sophisticated, sensitive, and leftist argument of the concerns with minority status for gays and lesbians in roughly similar terms. Herman's work has been crucial for my study.

15. See all of Stephen Bransford, *Gay Politics v. Colorado and America: The Inside Story of Amendment 2* (Cascade, CO: Sardis Press, 1994), but especially 60–87.

16. Tony Marco, quoted in John Gallagher and Chris Bull, *Perfect Enemies: The Religious Right, the Gay Movement, and the Politics of the 1990s* (New York: Crown, 1996), 104.

17. "From the Mouth of McCartney," *Gazette Telegraph,* 14 February 1992.

18. Gallagher and Bull, *Perfect Enemies,* 108.

19. 517 U.S. 620, 644 (1996).

20. *Freedom Watch,* The Citizens Project Newsletter, vol. 2:3 (June–July 1993), 1. On file with the author.

21. Ibid., 1.

22. Waldo E. Martin, Jr., ed., *Brown v. Board of Education: A Brief History with Documents* (Boston: Bedford, 1998), 172–174.

23. Gallagher and Bull, *Perfect Enemies,* 5.

24. "Tenn. County Officials Seek to Ban Gays," www.foxnews.com/story/0,2933,114467,00.html, accessed 11 May 2004.

25. Gallagher and Bull, *Perfect Enemies,* 6.

26. See, for instance, Samuel Walker, *In Defense of American Liberties: A History of the ACLU* (New York: Oxford University Press, 1990).

27. I'm indebted to numerous histories of the Scopes trial, but for an especially concise and informative history, see Edward Caudill's introduction in *The Scopes Trial: A Photographic History,* intro. Edward Caudill, photo captions by Edward Larson, and afterword by Jesse Fox Mayshark (Knoxville: University of Tennessee Press, 2000), 1–20.

28. Frederick Mark Gedicks begins *The Rhetoric of Church and State* by stating what has become quite obvious in legal scholarship:

> Documenting the inconsistency of the Supreme Court's religion clause decisions is a virtual cliché in constitutional scholarship. The Court's decisions in this area have been described as "ad hoc," "eccentric," "misleading and distorting," "historically unjustified and textually incoherent," and—finally

—"riven by contradiction and bogged down in slogans and metaphors." (Frederick Mark Gedicks, *The Rhetoric of Church and State: A Critical Analysis of Religion Clause Jurisprudence* [Durham, NC: Duke University Press, 1995], 1) Gedicks uses this introduction to warn us that he, too, by even broaching the issue might get stranded in frustrating legal territory: because when the Court speaks about religion, it often says things with which the rest of the nation does not agree or understand:

> The contradictions and inconsistencies in the Court's religion clause doctrine are not just a challenge for academics. While the majority of Americans support the general principle of separation of church and state, most strongly disagree with the strictness and vigor with which the Supreme court has located and policed the boundary. The inability of most of the American populace to understand why the Constitution requires the doctrine that the Court has formulated has made its religion clause decisions among the most hotly disputed and widely disregarded in grassroots America. (Gedicks, *Rhetoric of Church and State,* 3)

29. But the history of public school making in the United States certainly has its religious roots. See Philip B. Kurland's descriptions of public schooling in "The Regent's Prayer Case," in *Church and State: The Supreme Court and the First Amendment,* ed. Philip B. Kurland (Chicago: University of Chicago Press, 1975).

30. The prayer: "Almighty God, we acknowledge our dependence upon Thee, and we beg Thy blessings upon us, our parents, our teachers, our country."

31. Donald L. Drakeman, *Church-State Constitutional Issues: Making Sense of the Establishment Clause* (Westport, CT: Greenwood, 1991), 16. Emphasis mine.

32. See *McCreary County v. ACLU of Kentucky,* 545 U.S. __ (2005), and *Van Orden v. Perry,* 545 U.S. __ (2005).

33. Lisa Duggan, "Queering the State," in *Social Text* 39 (Summer 1994): 9.

34. Jakobsen and Pellegrini, *Love the Sin: Sexual Regulation and the Limits of Tolerance* (New York: New York University Press, 2003), 97.

35. Ibid., 97.

36. Keen and Goldberg, *Strangers to the Law: Gay People on Trial* (Ann Arbor: University of Michigan Press, 1998), 37.

37. There may be many places to look for more material on this point. One legal scholar in particular, besides Halley, has been quite useful to me in understanding the trickiness of judicial scrutiny and the nation's minorities as the history of constitutional review changes throughout the 1930s, 1940s, and especially after *Brown v. Board of Education*: Robert Cover. See, for instance, "The Origins of Judicial Activism in the Protection of Minorities," in *Narrative, Violence, and the Law: The Essays of Robert Cover,* ed. Martha Minow, Michael Ryan, and Austin Sarat (Ann Arbor: University of Michigan Press, 1992): 49.

38. Ibid., 29.

39. Charles A. Miller, "Constitutional Law and the Rhetoric of Race," in *Law in American History,* ed. Donald Flemming and Bernard Bailyn (Boston: Little, Brown, 1971), 147.

40. Justice Harlan's dissent, 58.

41. Lauren Berlant, "The Subject of True Feeling: Pain, Privacy, and Politics," in *Feminist Consequences: Theory for the New Century,* ed. Elisabeth Bronfen and Misha Kavka (New York: Columbia University Press, 2001), 129.

42. Berlant, "The Subject," 128–129.

43. Ibid., 129.

44. Ibid.

45. Ibid.

46. Jakobsen and Pellegrini, *Love the Sin,* 17.

47. Berlant, "The Subject," 154.

48. This comment is a direct quotation I heard frequently in Colorado as I lived out the events of Amendment 2; in the first Colorado Springs Gay Pride parade the summer after Amendment 2's passage, one group of religious protestors' signs announced this phrase as I marched past them into the downtown's central park for a rally, and it has delighted me ever since.

49. Dana Seitler helped me understand this point of the Gay Agenda in personal conversations over the years.

50. My lawyer friend and queer activist Jeremy Patrick introduced me to this concept. I thank him for his keen analysis of this chapter's legal arguments.

51. Hortense Spillers, *Black, White, and in Color* (Chicago: University of Chicago Press, 2003), 203.

52. 517 U.S. 620, 635 (1996).

53. Keen and Goldberg, *Strangers to the Law.*

54. Shane Phelan, *Sexual Strangers: Gays, Lesbians, and the Dilemmas of Citizenship*

(Philadelphia: Temple University Press, 2001), 5. Phelan writes suggestively: "I believe that sexual minorities will remain strangers in the United States for a long time to come. This is not because the United States is a particularly Puritan country (although it is, in many ways)" (9).

55. Phelan's work is helpful here, especially in explaining why basic citizenship rights have been and continue to be such a concern:

> The phrase "second-class citizen" has been rhetorically effective both because it represents the duality of legal equality and daily marginalization and because it challenges the universalist ideals of liberal regimes. The belief that the United States is and should be a classless society makes the language of second-class citizenship a potent resource for argument; indeed the majority opinion in *Romer v. Evans* quoted Justice Harlan's famous statement that "the Constitution neither knows nor tolerates classes among citizens." (25)

56. Baldwin, *Go Tell It on the Mountain* (1952; New York: Modern Library, 1995), 15. Future citations will appear in the text.

57. James Baldwin, "The Harlem Ghetto," in *The Price of the Ticket: Collected Non-Fiction, 1948–1985* (New York: St. Martin's Press, 1985), 8.

58. "But 'protection' and 'rights' are not enough. A rights-based approach is too narrow to provide anything more than the type of liberal tolerance we criticized [earlier in the text]. . . . By moving the ground of debate away from a constricted focus on 'rights' to freedom, we hope to change a movement that, as it currently stands, is really only against something (discrimination) into one that is actively and embarrassedly for something (freedom)" (Jakobsen and Pellegrini, *Love the Sin,* 101). Again, their optimism and program are wonderful directives. Here, however, I'm wondering about their characterization of the narrowness of the rights-based debate, with the inevitable conclusion being one of mere tolerance. Perhaps there are effects and possibilities in an impoverished system of human articulation such as a rights-based system.

59. Cover, "Origins of Judicial Activism," 18–19.

60. Such an activity would require another book. For instance, in Brook Thomas's introduction to the volume on *Plessy v. Ferguson,* he is quick to point out the erosion of the distinction between "political" and "civil rights," which is an important distinction for the concerns outlined by Justice Harlan. Certainly this distinction would make a definition even harder to attempt. See Thomas's "Introduction," 12.

61. Berlant, "The Subject," 129.

62. Raymond Williams, *Marxism and Literature* (Oxford and New York: Oxford University Press, 1977), 131.

Notes to the Conclusion

1. James Baldwin, "Here Be Dragons," in *The Price of the Ticket: Collected Non-Fiction, 1948–1985* (New York: St. Martin's Press, 1985), 689.

2. For a recent study of the complicated and commodified transformation of evangelical messages and media, see Heather Hendershot, *Shaking the World for Jesus: Media and Conservative Evangelical Desire* (Chicago: University of Chicago Press, 2004). For greater insight into the conservative forces of the "intimate public sphere," see Lauren Berlant, *The Queen of America Goes to Washington City: Essays on Sex and Citizenship* (Durham, NC: Duke University Press, 1997).

3. "Mission: America," www.missionamerica.com/agenda1.htm, accessed 27 May 2003.

4. See John D'Emilio's optimistic but still very nuanced arguments about LGBTQ issues' move from margin to center of the American national consciousness in his collection of essays, *The World Turned: Essays on Gay History, Politics, and Culture* (Durham, NC: Duke University Press, 2002).

5. See Urvashi Vaid, *The Mainstreaming of Gay and Lesbian Liberation* (New York: Anchor/Doubleday, 1996); Andrew Sullivan, *An Argument about Homosexuality* (New York: Vintage, 1996); and Michael Warner, *The Trouble with Normal: Sex, Politics, and the Ethics of Queer Life* (Cambridge, MA: Harvard University Press, 2000).

6. Lisa Duggan, *The Twilight of Equality? Neoliberalism, Cultural Politics, and the Attack on Democracy* (Boston: Beacon Press, 2003), xx.

7. Ibid.

8. In addition to Duggan, there's more to read. Even if they might hate the language-based arguments I've made throughout this book, see Rosemary Hennessey, *Profit and Pleasure: Sexual Identities in Late Capitalism* (New York: Routledge, 2000); Alexandra Chain, *Selling Out: The Gay and Lesbian Movement Goes to the Market* (New York: Palgrave, 2001).

9. 386 U.S. 1, 11 (1967).

10. 539 U.S. 558, 562 (2003).

11. I will now work through the recent rise of Church sex scandals, and worry about the slips and slides between the associative landscape between pedophilia, incest, and homosexuality. Some works must be cited that mark more comprehensively (although in sometimes troubling ways) the connections. See Philip Jenkins, *Pedophiles and Priests: Anatomy of a Contemporary Crisis* (New York and London: Oxford University Press, 2001), and Mark Jordan, *The Silence of Sodom: Homosexuality in Modern Catholicism* (Chicago: University of Chicago Press, 2000).

12. David Sedaris, *Dress Your Family in Corduroy and Denim* (New York and Boston: Little, Brown, 2004), 212–213.

13. Gayle Rubin, "Thinking Sex: Notes for a Radical Theory of the Politics of Sexuality," in *The Lesbian and Gay Studies Reader,* ed. Henry Abelove et al. (New York: Routledge, 1993), 3–44.

14. Michael S. Rosenwald and Stephen Kurkjian, "Monthlong Plot to Kill Geoghan," www.boston.com/news/local/articles/2003/08/26/monthlong_plot_to_kill_geoghan/, accessed 10 October 2003.

15. "Sex Abuse Priest Killed in Prison," 25 August 2003, http://edition.cnn.com/2003/US/08/24/geoghan/, accessed 20 October 2003.

16. Although it is anecdotal, friends of mine had a conversation with a sociologist from a small, liberal arts college who works in queer, lesbian, and gay studies in which she took an almost intense glee from the news that the sexually abusive priest had received a particularly appropriate punishment. I was particularly struck by the manner in which the sociologist gave voice to so much other response I had been encountering as the murder was making its ways through the news cycle.

17. "Sex Abuse Priest Killed in Prison."

18. www.sfgate.com/cgi-bin/article.cgi?file=/news/archive/2003/04/22/national1737 EDT0668.DTL, accessed 24 October 2003.

19. Ibid.

20. See the iconic Gayle Rubin's "Thinking Sex: Notes for a Radical Theory of the Politics of Sexuality," in *The Lesbian and Gay Studies Reader,* ed. Abelove et al., 3–44.

21. Ellis Hanson is working on many of these connections and claims that discourses around pedophilia, incest, and "child love" quickly conjure up not so distant discourses around the homosexual. Some works that help him make this point and help us understand the hysteria around children are James Kincaid,

Child-Loving: The Erotic Child and Victorian Culture (New York: Routledge, 1992); Eve Kosofsky Sedgwick, "How to Bring Your Kids Up Gay," in *Tendencies* (Durham, NC: Duke University Press, 1993); Pat Califia, "The Age of Consent: The Great Kiddy-Porn Panic of '77," and "The Aftermath of the Great Kiddy-Porn Panic of '77," in *Public Sex* (Pittsburgh: Cleis Press, 1994), 39–70; Lela B. Costin, Howard Jacob Karger, and David Stoesz, *The Politics of Child Abuse in America* (New York: Oxford University Press, 1996); Elaine Showalter, *Hystories* (New York: Columbia University Press, 1997).

22. I'm particularly indebted to the debates by kinship theorists, especially dynamic feminist anthropologists. See, of course, Gayle Rubin, "The Traffic in Women: Notes on the 'Political Economy' of Sex," in *Toward an Anthropology of Women,* ed. Rayna R. Reiter (New York: Monthly Review Press, 1975). But also see *Reproducing the Future: Essays on Anthropology, Kinship, and the New Reproductive Technologies,* ed. Marilyn Strathern (New York: Routledge, 1992); *Gender and Kinship: Essays toward a Unified Analysis,* ed. Jane Fishburne Collier and Sylvia Junko Yanagisako (Stanford, CA: Stanford University Press, 1987).

23. Judith Butler, *Antigone's Claim: Kinship between Life and Death* (New York: Columbia University Press, 2000), 70–71.

24. Ibid., 71.

25. 539 U.S. 558, 606 (2003).

26. www.godhatesfags.com/main/index.html, accessed 10 January 2004.

27. Chauncey, quoted in Frank Rich, "And Now, Queer Eye for Straight Marriage," 10 August 2003. Final section 2, page 1, column 2.

28. Butler, *Antigone's Claim,* 73.

29. Alice Walker, *The Color Purple* (New York: Washington Square Press, 1982), 11. Further citations will appear in the text.

30. Spillers, *Black, White, and in Color.*

31. Ibid.

32. Ibid.

33. I'm inspired to recall Michael Moon's *Disseminating Whitman* (Cambridge, MA: Harvard University Press, 1991), and Michael Warner's work on Whitman in *Publics and Counterpublics* (Cambridge, MA: Zone Books, 2003).

34. Ann Cvetkovich, *An Archive of Feeling: Trauma, Sexuality, and Lesbian Public Cultures* (Durham, NC: Duke University Press, 2003), 101. Her discussion of Allison and the novel's connection to a collection of concerns of lesbianism, trauma, and sexual violence is deeply helpful.

35. Dorothy Allison, *Bastard Out of Carolina* (New York: Plume, 1992), 135. Further citations will appear in the text. Chris Nealon makes a brief reference to *Bastard* when he calls the text an example of contemporary literary founding narratives that "depict hardscrabble southern U.S. childhoods whose economic misery and family violence breed a passionate prepolitical sense of there being an 'elsewhere' less murderous and more welcoming, of certain secret forms of difference left unnamed: queer readers of these stories are left to fill in what are, for their young protagonists, still blanks"; see *Foundlings: Lesbian and Gay Historical Emotion before Stonewall* (Durham, NC: Duke University Press, 2001), 179.

36. Judith Butler's "Critically Queer," in *Bodies That Matter* (New York: Routledge, 1993).

37. Hortense J. Spillers, *Black, White, and In Color: Essays on American Literature and Culture* (Chicago: University of Chicago Press, 2003), 254.

38. Butler, *Antigone's Claim,* 81.

39. Slavoj Žižek writes, "In short, what melancholy obfuscates is the fact that the object is lacking from the beginning, that its emergence coincides with its lack, that this object is *nothing but* the positivization of a void/lack, a purely anamorphic entity which does not exist 'in itself' "; see *Did Somebody Say Totalitarianism?* (New York: Verso, 2001), 143.

40. Butler, *Antigone's Claim,* 82.

41. Ibid., 78.

42. Ibid., 82. I'm also reminded here of Sharon Holland's work on representations of race and death, *Raising the Dead: Death and "Black" Subjectivity in Twentieth-Century Literature and Culture* (Durham, NC: Duke University Press, 2000).

43. Quoted in Jane Lapman, "Gay Marriage: Clergy Gear for Amendment Battle," *The Christian Science Monitor,* on-line edition: www.csmonitor.com/2004/0109/p13s01-lire.html?livingNav, accessed 9 February 2004.

44. Text of majority opinion of question presented by the Massachusetts Senate, found on www.boston.com/news/specials/gay_marriage/sjc_020404/, accessed 5 February 2004.

45. Tony Kushner, *Angels in America, Part Two: Perestroika* (New York: Theatre Communications Group, 1992), 95.

46. Ibid., 146.

47. Ibid.

48. Ibid., 95.

49. Ibid.

50. Lee Edelman, *No Future: Queer Theory and the Death Drive* (Durham, NC: Duke University, 2004), 3.

51. Ibid., 77.

Index

Abington Township v. Schempp, 127

Abortion, 158

Adoption, 9

Advocate, 5

African Americans: authors and incest narratives, 165–66; and blackness, 47–50, 171; and Christian rhetoric, 16; and ethnicity, 83; race theory, 204n31; and racism, 44; and religion, 195n24; religion and history in the work of Baldwin, 58–60, 196–97n27; and signifying, 140; and social reform, 97–98; and "special rights," 41; typicality and representation, 198n31; in work of Ellison, 92–93. *See also* Blackness; Race

Agamben, Giorgio, 33–36, 67, 153, 176, 189n22

AIDS, 181, 202n6

Allison, Dorothy, 20, 172–178, 214–15n34, 215n35

Althusser, Louis, 193n15

Amendment 2 (Colorado), 4–6, 12, 18, 29, 40, 120, 140–41, 147, 210n48; and analogy between queerness and race, 19, 114, 116–19; and authority, 29; campaign, 119–23; and language of religious right, 18; legal challenges to, 130–31; responses to passage of, 115–17, 130, 186n10; and sentimentality, 137; and "special rights," 41–42; and "suspect classes," 117–19, 131, 207n6; text of amendment, 120. See also *Romer v. Evans*

American Civil Liberties Union (ACLU), 126, 208n26

American Civil Liberties Union (ACLU) (Colorado), 4, 41

Americans with Disabilities Act, 41

Analogy, 44, 140. *See also* Queer(ness), analogy with race

Andrews, George, 127

Angels in America (Kushner), 180–84

Antigone, 178

Anti-slavery, 40–41, 96–97; and literature of protest, 84; and sentimentality, 41

Appelby, Scott, 155–56

Arendt, Hannah, 33, 176, 188n9

Aristotle, 46

Armstrong, Nancy, 63, 198n36

Aspen, Colorado, 119

Baldwin, James, 16, 114, 146, 199n43; and analogy between sexuality and race, 93, 111; use of blackness and Christian rhetoric, 53–54, 58–61; and civil rights, 143; "Every Good-bye Ain't Gone," 59, 69; *Giovanni's Room*, 61–62, 198n32; *Go Tell It on the Mountain*, 17, 54–60, 64, 71–78, 82, 87, 93, 113, 142–45, 168, 197n29, 199n43, 201n60, 201n64; "Here Be Dragons," 111–12; and "identity politics," 143; on masculinity and violence, 112; and race protest, 110–11; on religion and the body, 200n56; religion and history in work of, 58–60, 196–97n27; and religious violence, 54; representation of

Baldwin, James (*continued*)
African Americans, 198n31; story of
Noah and Ham, 72–73, 96, 200n56; on
Stowe, 60, 111, 198n31; use of religious
rhetoric, 64–65, 70, 197n29
Bankruptcy laws, 31
Baptists, 195n24
Barrett, Lindon, 204n31
Bastard Out of Carolina (Allison), 172–78,
214–15n34, 215n35
Beloved (Morrison), 63
Bercovitch, Sacvan, 7, 25–26
Berlant, Lauren, 55, 63, 135–37, 145–46,
190n28, 191n51, 194n20, 198n37,
199n38, 212n2
Bible, 22–24, 53. *See also* Leviticus; Reve-
lations, Book of
Blackness, 47–50; Ellison's uses of, 92–93;
in *Go Tell It on the Mountain*, 87; and
language of opposition, 171, 178, 182,
184, 194n23; and minoritization, 50;
and queerness in story of Noah, Ham,
and Canaan, 72–73; in *Suddenly Last
Summer*, 103, 106. *See also* African
Americans; Queer(ness); Race
Bone, Robert A., 197n29
"Born that way" argument. *See* Homosex-
ual(ity), biological determinism and
immutability
Boulder, Colorado 119
Brady, Mary Pat, 187n23
Bransford, Stephen, 122
Brown, Bill, 91–92
Brown, Wendy, 51–52, 57, 71, 194n18,
194n20
Brown v. Board of Education, 124–26, 179,
203n13, 210n37
Buck-Morss, Susan, 32, 188n15
Bull, Chris, 125

Burke, Kenneth, 22, 48, 65–69, 84
Burt, Nancy V., 199n43
Bush, George H. W., 29
Bush, George W., 8, 180
Butler, Judith, 9, 20, 32, 45, 159, 164,
176, 178, 188n14, 189n21
Byrd, James, Jr., 40

Cable, George Washington, 99
Califia, Pat, 214n21
Cane (Toomer), 18, 79–81, 113
Cannibalism, 103–9, 206n49
Carlyle, Thomas, 88
Catachresis, 45–46
Catholic Church, and sex scandals, 19,
153–60, 213n11
Catholicism, 27, 188n10
Caudill, Edward, 208n27
Chain, Alexandra, 212n8
Chauncey, George, 89, 132, 164,
202n7
Children. *See* Family
Chow, Rey, 86
Christian Coalition, 4
Christian fundamentalism. *See* Funda-
mentalism
Christianity: and Americanness, 14;
claims of persecution, 5, 186n12; and
education, 124–27; queerness and con-
version, 74–75. *See also* Christian rheto-
ric; Christian right; Disestablishment;
Fundamentalism
Christian rhetoric: and African Americans, 16; and American nationality, 27,
205n35, 212n2; and analogy between
race and queerness, 13; and authority,
22; in *Cane*, 79–81; as cover story for
sexuality, 111; and security, 22, 26; and
sovereignty, 15, 52, 130; in *Suddenly*

Last Summer, 106–7; in work of Baldwin, 16, 56

Christian right, 10, 41; and anxieties about race, 116–17; and conservatives in United States, 185n5; and disestablishment, 128; and same-sex marriage, 153; weakened by accusations of hate, 149. *See also* Fundamentalism

Chronotope, 92

Church. *See* Baptists; Catholic Church; Christianity; Christian rhetoric

Citizenship: African Americans and, 19, 133; Berlant on models of, 135–36; church-state separation, civil rights and, 126; and demands for social change, 137; "diva citizenship," 192n51; and education, 125; queers and, 19, 141–42, 148, 210–11n54, 211n55; second-class, 42, 211n55; and sentimentality, 135; suspended, 176. *See also* Nationality

Citizens Project, 124

Civil rights: and Amendment 2, 116–19; Baldwin on, 143; and church-state separation, 129; "Cultural Front" and, 83–84; as "figures" of pain, 145; limits of discourse based on, 211n58; and minority politics, 146; queers and, 9, 30–31, 40–41, 114, 118, 122–23, 130, 186n10; race and, 47, 118, 126, 130, 179, 207n5; and rhetoric of representation, 146; and sentimentality, 41, 146; versus political rights, 211–12n60; and vulnerability to majority will, 145

Civil Rights Act (1964), 40–41, 122

Civil Rights Act (1968), 40

Civil rights movement, 40, 83, 130, 207n3

Clarke, Eric, 186n17

Cobb, Michael, 195n24, 204n21

Colorado, 4–6, 18, 29, 41, 114–24, 130, 138, 186n10

Colorado for Family Values (CFV), 4–5, 29, 41, 115, 120, 123

Colorado Springs, Colorado, 4–5, 29, 115, 119, 186n13, 210n48

Colorado State University, 1–2

Color Purple, The (Walker), 165–71

Comstock, Gary, 186n21

Concerned Women for America, 4

Constitution. *See* United States Constitution

Cory, Donald, 84, 202n5, 203n13

Costin, Lela B., 214n21

"Counterintimacies," 55

"Counterpublics," 55

Cover, Robert, 145, 209–10n37

Cowley, Malcolm, 84

Crane, Stephen, 18, 89–95, 113, 114, 204n24

Culler, Jonathan, 64

"Cultural Front," 84–85

Cvetkovich, Ann, 172, 214–15n34

Daughters of Bilitis, 82

Dayton, Tennessee, 125

Defense of Marriage Act, 6

DeGeneres, Ellen, 151

Delany, Samuel, 187n23

D'Emilio, John, 84, 151, 202n7, 212n4

Denning, Michael, 83–84

Denver, 119

Derrida, Jacques, 67, 102, 199n50

"Desire and the Black Masseur" (Williams), 103–6

"Devil Finds Work, The" (Baldwin), 111

Disability rights movement, 41

Disestablishment, 124–30, 209n28, 209n31
Documentary, 85
Donzelot, Jacques, 205n42
Dos Passos, John, 84
Drakeman, Donald L., 209n31
Dred Scott case, 133
Druce, Joseph, 155–56
Du Bois, W. E .B., 97, 194n23, 194n24
Duggan, Lisa, 128, 146, 151
Durkheim, Emile, 34, 189n19, 199n42
Dyson, Michael Eric, 195n25

Eagle Forum, 4
Edelman, Lee, 73, 114, 182
Education, 124–27, 209n29
Eliade, Mircea, 199n42
Ellender, Allen J., 127
Ellison, Ralph, 49, 92–94, 107, 205n35
"Encantadas, The" (Melville), 102
Eng, David, 187n23
Engel v. Vitale, 126–27
Entitlement, 22, 68
Equal Protection Clause. *See* Fourteenth Amendment
"Ethnic harassment bill" (Colorado), 119
Everson v. Board of Education, 126, 130
"Every Good-bye Ain't Gone" (Baldwin), 59, 69
Excitable Speech (Butler), 9
"Experiment in Misery, An" (Crane), 89–95, 106, 113, 204n24

Family: concerns over children, 124–25, 158–59, 163; "family values," 129; and nation, 163; perceived threat to heterosexual family, 9, 32, 156–59, 161; queer families, 159; regulation of, 205n42
Family Research Council, 28, 153

Federal Marriage Amendment, 153
Feminism: and literature of protest, 85
Fictitiousness, 17, 21, 171
Figurativeness, 114, 146
First Amendment, 128. *See also* United States Constitution
Focus on the Family, 3–5
Fort Collins, Colorado, 1
Foucault, Michel, 33, 57, 191n38, 191n50
Fourteenth Amendment, 15, 19, 42, 116, 118, 130, 135. *See also* United States Constitution
Frank, Thomas, 30–31
Fraser, Nancy, 202n3
Freud, Sigmund, 34, 189n19
Fundamentalism, 125, 185n5, 205n35. *See also* Christian right; Religion

Gallagher, John, 125
Gates, Henry Louis Jr., 93, 192n2
Gay. *See* Homosexual(ity); Lesbian/gay rights movement; Queer(ness)
Gay Agenda, The (film), 138
Gay and Lesbian Alliance Against Defamation (GLAAD) (Denver), 40–41
Gay Politics v. Colorado and America (Bransford), 122
Gay rights movement. *See* Lesbian/gay rights movement
Gazette Telegraph (Colorado Springs), 115, 121
Gedicks, Frederick Mark, 208n28
Geoghan, John, 20, 155–56, 213n16
Giovanni's Room (Baldwin), 61–62
Girard, René, 34, 189n19
"godhatesfags.com" (Web site), 2, 23–24, 163
Goldberg, Suzanne, 131, 207n6

Gospel music, 173–75
Go Tell It on the Mountain (Baldwin), 17, 54–60, 64, 71–78, 82, 87, 93, 113, 142–45, 168, 197n29, 199n43, 201n60, 201n64
Governmentality, 188n14
Graham, Billy, 127
Great migration, 85, 197n29
Green, Richard, 132
Griswold v. Connecticut, 158
Gross, Robert, 187n21

Hall, Radclyffe, 88
Halley, Janet, 16, 43, 116, 146, 206–7n3
Harlan, John M., 118, 133–34, 211n55, 211n60
Harlem Renaissance, 88, 204n21
Harper, Philip Brian, 187n23
Harris, Trudier, 199n43
Hartman, Saidiya V., 191n42, 193n17
Hate speech. *See* Religion, and hate speech
Hawaii, 6
Hawthorne, Nathaniel, 92
Hay, Harry, 84
Hendershot, Heather, 212n2
Hennessey, Rosemary, 212n8
"Here Be Dragons" (Baldwin), 111–12
Herman, Didi, 207–8n14
Heteronormativity, 128, 198n37
Heterosexual(ity): and traditional values, 37; and the "normal," 55. *See also* Heteronormativity
Hill, Rene, 193n4
Hobbes, Thomas, 33
Holland, Sharon, 215n42
Homoerotics, 92, 186n17
Homophobia: in black theology, 193n4; and racism, 73, 116. *See also* Christian rhetoric; Christian right; Homosexual(ity); Queer(ness); Religion
Homo sacer, 33–36, 67, 148, 162, 189n22
Homosexual(ity), 42, 157; biological determinism and immutability, 43, 121, 132; civil rights and affirmative action, 122; conflation with pedophilia and incest, 153–64, 180, 213n11, 213n21; as "defective," 140; and "disease," 121; and ethnicity, 122, 202–3n12; "gay agenda," 119–20, 150, 161; and "survival value," 121. *See also* Marriage, same-sex; Queer(ness)
Homosexual in America, The (Cory), 84, 202n5, 203n13
"Homosocial," 89
Howells, William Dean, 99
How the Other Half Lives (Riis), 95–98
Hughes, Langston, 84
Human Rights Ordinance (Colorado Springs), 119
"Hyperembodied bodies," 96, 205n41

Illinois ex rel. McCollum v. Board of Education, 126
Incest, 19–20, 153–78, 213n11, 213n21
Industrialization, 85, 89
Invisible Man (Ellison), 49
"It": concept of God in *The Color Purple*, 168–71; queerness as ambiguous "it" in *Go Tell It on the Mountain*, 72–73

Jakobsen, Janet R., 14, 43–45, 128–29, 136, 145, 146, 185n6, 211n58
James, Henry, 99
Jenkins, Philip, 213n11
Jeremiad, 7–8, 16, 63, 123, 129, 141; and American national identity, 25–26, 30, 47, 57, 129, 141, 182; and authority,

Jeremiad (*continued*)
27, 30; and citizenship, 138;
"deformed," 80; and politics of differ-
ence, 10; and sovereignty, 34, 50; as
structure of feeling, 11
Jones, Stanton, 24–25
Jordan, Mark, 213n11
Joseph, Miranda, 44
Judaism, 27, 188n10
"Judicial activism," 145
Judicial review, 130–34, 140, 145,
209–10n37

Karger, Howard Jacob, 214n21
Katz, Jonathan, 202n7
Keen, Lisa, 131, 207n6
Kennedy, Anthony, 118–19, 134, 140–41
Kincaid, James, 213–14n21
Kinsey, Alfred, 82
Kinship systems, alternative, 159-60,
214n22
Kintz, Linda, 185n5
Krugman, Paul, 31–32
Kurland, Philip B., 209n29
Kushner, Tony, 180–84

Laramie Project, The (film), 185n1
Larsen, Nella, 204n21
Lawrence v. Texas, 151, 153, 157, 161
Leeming, David, 64, 200n60
Lesbian, gay, bisexual, transgender, queer
(LGBTQ). *See* Queer(ness)
Lesbian(ism): and incest in *Bastard Out of
Carolina*, 172–78; in *The Color Purple*,
169–71
Lesbian/gay rights movement, 41, 83,
202n7. *See also* Civil rights, queers and;
Queer(ness)
Leviticus, 26, 201n60

"Like race" analogy. *See* Queer(ness), anal-
ogy with race; Race
"'Like Race' Arguments" (Halley),
206–7n3
Loffreda, Beth, 185n1
Logology, 65–66
Lott, Trent, 207n5
*Love the Sin: Sexual Regulation and the Lim-
its of Religious Tolerance* (Jakobsen and
Pellegrini), 185n6, 211n58
Loving v. Virginia, 152, 164
L Word, The (TV show), 151

MacKinnon, Catharine A., 187n27
Marco, Tony, 208n16
Marriage: as fundamental right, 152;
rights and the family, 9; same-sex, 4, 8,
28, 145, 148, 151–53, 160; same-sex
compared to interracial, 164
Martin, Biddy, 193n13
Marty, Martin, 125
Massachusetts Supreme Court, 179
Mattachine Society, 82–86, 88,
202–3n12
Matthew Shepard Story, the (film), 185n1
McBride, Dwight A., 192n1
McCarthy, Joseph, 82
McCartney, Bill, 123
McCreary County v. ACLU of Kentucky,
209n32
McDowell, Deborah, 204n21
McKinney, Aaron, 40
Melancholy, 177, 215n39
Melville, Herman, 102–3, 206n49
Michaels, Walter Benn, 187n24
Miller, Charles, 133
Miller, J. Hillis, 46
Miller, Perry, 7
Minorities, and emotion, 136

Minoritization. *See* Blackness; Queer(ness); Race
Mission: America, 149–50
Mobile, Alabama, 128
Moon, Michael, 214n33
Moore, Roy, 128
Mormonism, 27, 188n10
Morrison, Toni, 63, 92
Muñoz, José Esteban, 187n23, 187n25

National Association for the Advancement of Colored People (NAACP), 126
National Association of Evangelicals, 22
Nationality: and neoliberalism, 151; religious morality, queers and, 21; rhetoric of in United States, 46, 205n35; and security, 28; and sentimentality, 190n28. *See also* Citizenship
National Legal Foundation, 4
Naturalism, 85, 89–90, 92
Nealon, Christopher, 202n7, 215n35
Negation, politics of, 182, 184
Nelson, Cary, 196n26
Neoliberalism, and the left, 151–52
New York City, 89, 95, 202n6
New York City Board of Regents, 127
9/11, 33
Ninth Circuit Court of Appeals, 128
Nominalism, 201–2n3
Nondiscrimination policies, 119
Nussbaum, Martha, 132

O'Neale, Sondra A., 64–65
One Magazine, 88
Oregon, 6
Orlando (Woolf), 88

Parker, Brian, 206n48
Parkhurst, Charles H., 96

Passing (Larsen), 204n21
Pathological public, 58, 63–64, 72, 147, 194n22
Patterson, Orlando, 164
Perfect Enemies (Gallagher and Bull), 125
Public. *See* Pathological public
Pedophilia, 19–20, 153–64, 213n11, 213n21
Pellegrini, Ann, 14, 43, 128–29, 136, 145, 146, 185n6, 211n58
Perkins, Will, 120, 186n10
Phelan, Shane, 141–42, 210–11n54, 211n55
Phelps, Fred, 1–3
Pike, James A., 127
Plessy v. Ferguson, 12, 118–19, 133, 211n60
Popular Front, 83–85
Privacy, right to, 157–58
Proposition 9 (Oregon), 6
Protestantism, 27, 188n10
Puritans, 7

Queer(ness): activism and same-sex marriage, 151; and AIDS activism, 202n6; analogy with race, 12–13, 15, 18–21, 37, 42–52, 86, 88, 92–93, 99, 116–17, 123, 132, 134, 140, 149, 153, 162, 179, 183; and blackness in *Go Tell It on the Mountain*, 87; blackness, opposition and, 49–50, 171; centering of queer issues in U.S., 212n4; and citizenship, 141–42; expressed by religious rhetoric of race, 76–78, 99, 101, 144; in late nineteenth century New York, 89; and limits of tolerance, 161; minority status, 50, 121, 148, 163, 207–8n14; nominalism and recognition, 81, 201–2n3; politics and literature, 88; politics and

Queer(ness) (*continued*)
racial/ethnic models, 37, 83–84,
202–3n12, 203n13, 204n21; pre-
Stonewall activism, 82–86, 202n7;
queer as *homo sacer*, 34–36, 162, 180;
"queer relations," 99, 106; queers'
"aberrant future," 180; queers as
enemies and scapegoats, 30, 35, 123;
queers' use of language of religious
hatred, 70; race and ethnicity in queer
studies, 187n23; racialization and
minority status, 42, 150, 204n21; and
sentimentality, 138; and "special
rights," 41, 149; as "suspect class," 131;
as terrorists, 31–32. *See also* Christian
rhetoric; Civil rights; Heterosexual(ity);
Homophobia; Homosexual(ity); Race;
Religion
Queer Eye for the Straight Guy (TV show),
151

Race: analogy with queerness, 12–13, 15,
18–21, 37, 42–52, 86, 88, 92–93, 99,
116–17, 123, 132, 134, 140, 149, 153,
162, 179, 183, 204n21; as "cover" story
for queerness, 87, 111; and "darkness,"
142; as fundamental category for queer
politics, 130; as fundamental category
of difference in U.S., 19, 45, 133; "mantle of respectability" of race discourse,
116–17; and minoritization, 50,
203n13; and "passing," 204; race and
ethnicity in queer studies, 187n23; religious rhetoric of race used to express
queerness, 37, 76–78, 99, 101,
195–6n25; and sentimentality, 39–40,
56, 106, 134; transformation of
racial identities, 187n23; and violence,
40. *See also* African Americans; Black-

ness; Queer(ness); Race relations;
Racism
Race relations, 99, 106, 109, 164
Racism: in *Bastard Out of Carolina*, 175;
and homophobia, 73, 116; and
immutability, 43; and segregation,
207n3
Realism, 59, 85–86, 89–90, 92, 99,
147
Realpolitik, 147
Recognition, politics of, 81, 201–2n3
Red Badge of Courage, The (Crane), 94
Reid-Pharr, Robert, 187n23
Religion: and civil rights, 127; and
education, 126, 209n29; and hate
speech, 9–11, 13, 17, 46, 50, 52, 163,
175, 183, 186n19; and language of
queer desire, 62; religious hatred,
147–48, 150; rhetoric of, 27, 30, 46, 55,
65–68, 173, 181, 183, 195–6n25,
200n56; rhetoric and entitlement, 23;
rhetoric and identity positions, 110,
195–96n25; rhetoric and queer expres-
sion, 63, 144, 161–62, 183; and
sovereignty, 56, 70; and violence, 38.
See also Christianity; Christian rhetoric;
Disestablishment
Religious Coalition for Freedom, 179
Representation, politics of, 81, 139,
201–2n3
Republicanism, 181
Republican Party, 3, 28–29, 31
Revelations, Book of, 177
Rhetoric, 46; rhetorical strategies of
queers, 21, 139, 179; and queer litera-
ture, 17. *See also* Christian rhetoric
Riis, Jacob, 95–98
Robertson, Pat, 4
Romance, 91, 99

Romer v. Evans, 12, 118–19, 123, 134, 140, 211n55. *See also* Amendment 2 (Colorado)

Rooney, John, 127

Roscoe, Will, 83–84

Rosen, Michael W., 115–16

Rubin, Gayle, 155, 159, 214n22

Sacrifice, 34–37, 148

Samuels, Shirley, 39

Santorum, Rick, 20, 156–60, 162

Scalia, Antonin, 123, 134, 153, 161

Scarry, Elaine, 200n56

Schempp. See *Abington Township v. Schempp*

Schlosser, Eric, 186n13

Schmitt, Carl, 33

Schroeder, Pat, 123

Scopes, John, 125

Scopes trial, 125–26, 129, 205n35, 208n27

Sedaris, David, 20, 153–55

Sedgwick, Eve Kosofsky, 87, 89, 214n21

Seidman, Steven, 189n24

Seltzer, Mark, 57–58, 90, 96, 194n22, 198n31, 199n38, 205n41

Sentimentality, 18; anti-slavery, civil rights and, 41; and arguments for equality, 39–40; and hatred, 179; and national identity, 190n28; and queer self-articulation, 138; and queerness in the work of Williams, 100–101; race, protest and, 56, 98–99, 133, 182, 184

September 11, 33

"Sex in Public" (Berlant and Warner), 55, 198n37

Sexual orientation, 81, 119, 131–32, 134, 146. *See also* Heterosexual(ity); Homosexual(ity); Queer(ness)

Shadow and Act (Ellison), 107

"Shadowy realm," 176–78

Sheldon, Lou, 4

Shepard, Dennis, 37–40

Shepard, Matthew, 1–2, 6, 37–40

Showalter, Elaine, 214n21

SILENCE=DEATH Project, 202n6

"Sissy Boy" Syndrome and the Development of Homosexuality, The (Green), 132

Slavery, 47, 98, 118, 133. *See also* Anti-slavery

Slavery and Social Death (Patterson), 164

Smith, Theophus, 53

Sobel, Mechal, 194–95n24

Sobran, Joseph, 121

"Social death," 164, 176

Social negation, 147

Social reform, 95–98

Social Security, 31

Sodomy, 81, 128, 153, 202n5

Somerville, Siobhan, 79

Souls of Black Folk, The (Du Bois), 194n23

Sovereignty, 188n9; and authority, 24, 56; and the collective, 33; and the family, 29, 129; and hatred of queers, 159; and minority complaint, 81; as power over life and death, 32, 34–35; religion and language of, 14–15, 28, 30, 70, 129–30, 137, 183; United States and, 32, 180, 182; and "war zones," 32, 34, 188n15

"Special rights," 41, 149, 207n5

Spellman, Francis Joseph, 127

Spillers, Hortense, 47–49, 92, 140, 165–66, 175, 191n46

Spivak, Gayatri, 45–46, 191n38

Standley, Fred L., 199n43

Steiner, George, 101

Stewart, Jon, 31

Stoesz, David, 214n21

Stott, William, 85

Stowe, Harriet Beecher, 39, 99

Strangers to the Law: Gay People on Trial, 141, 207n6

Structures of feeling, 11, 147, 162

Subaltern, 135–36, 148

Suddenly Last Summer (Williams), 18, 100–103, 106–10, 113, 206n48

Sullivan, Andrew, 151

Summit Ministries, 4

Sundquist, Eric, 58, 194n23

Supreme Court. *See* United States Supreme Court

Tebedo, Kevin, 5, 29

Terrorism, 31. *See also* September 11; War on Terror

Thirteenth Amendment, 118. *See also* United States Constitution

Thomas, Brook, 211n60

Thurmond, Strom, 207n5

Toomer, Jean, 18, 79–81, 93, 113, 114

"Tours de Babel, Des" (Derrida), 102

Tower of Babel, 94–95, 101–2

Townes, Emile M., 205n38

Traditional Values Coalition, 4

Trilling, Lionel, 85

Twilight of Equality?, The (Duggan), 151

Uncle Tom's Cabin (Stowe), 39, 98–99, 111, 190n28

United States: and Christian rhetoric, 52; as classless society, 211n55; conservative regimes, 182; and rhetoric of nationality, 46, 205n35; and sovereignty, 32, 128, 180, 182; traditional values, 127–28. *See also* African Ameri-cans; Christianity; Christian right; Civil rights; Citizenship; Disestablishment; Fundamentalism; Nationality; United States Constitution; United States Supreme Court

United States Constitution, 126, 133, 158, 209n28, 211n55. *See also* First Amendment; Fourteenth Amendment, Thirteenth Amendment

United States Supreme Court, 4, 12, 126, 157; and religion clause decisions, 208–9n28

United States v. Carolene Products Co., 145

University of Colorado, 123

Urbanization, 85, 89

Vaid, Urvashi, 151

Van Orden v. Perry, 209n32

Vermont, 6

Walker, Alice, 20, 165–71

Walker, Samuel, 208n26

Warner, Michael, 37, 55, 63, 151, 198n37, 214n33

War on Terror, 30

Warren, Kenneth, 98–99

"War zones," 32, 34, 188n15

Well of Loneliness, The (Hall), 88

Wells-Barnett, Ida B., 96, 205n38

West, Cornel, 203n13

Westboro Baptist Church, 1–4, 23, 186n19

Whipple, Dianne, 185n4

White, Alfred T., 96

Whiteness, 110

Whitman, Walt, 88, 214n33

Wilde, Oscar, 88

Will & Grace (TV show), 151

Williams, Raymond, 11
Williams, Tennessee, 18, 100–110, 113, 114, 206n48
Wilson, Edmund, 84
Women's movement, 41, 83
Women's suffrage, 40

Woodson, Carter G., 194n24
Woolf, Virginia, 88
Wright, Richard, 111
Wyoming, 5, 38

Žižek, Slavoj, 215n39

ABOUT THE AUTHOR

Michael Cobb is Assistant Professor of English, University of Toronto.